DATE DUE

MAR 02 2016		
MAR 22 2018		
APR 30 2018		
		PRINTED IN U.S.A.

Why Muslim Integration Fails in
Christian-Heritage Societies

Why Muslim Integration Fails in Christian-Heritage Societies

Claire L. Adida
David D. Laitin
Marie-Anne Valfort

 Harvard University Press

Cambridge, Massachusetts
London, England   2016

Library of Congress Cataloging-in-Publication Data
Adida, Claire L., 1979–
Why Muslim integration fails in Christian-heritage societies / Claire L.
Adida, David D. Laitin, and Marie-Anne Valfort.
    pages cm
  Includes bibliographical references and index.
  ISBN 978-0-674-50492-9 (alk. paper)
1. Muslims—France—Public opinion.   2. Islamophobia—France.
3. France—Emigration and immigration.   4. Immigrants—France—
Social conditions.   5. France—Ethnic relations.   I. Laitin,
David D.   II. Valfort, Marie-Anne, 1978–   III. Title.
    DC34.5.M87A35 2016
    305.6'970944—dc23

                                                        2015014163

To Antonin, Ethan, Gabi, Ida,

Julia, Louise, and Mina—the seven children

and grandchildren from our three families

born while we were producing this book—in

the hope that they grow up in a world

where all barriers to achievement due to

discrimination have been lifted.

Contents

Figures and Tables

Tables

Preface

THE ORIGINS OF THIS BOOK go back to the co-participation of Gilles Kepel and David Laitin in the Giorgio Cini Foundation's "I Dialoghi di San Giorgio" in September 2006 on the topic of martyrdoms. In the interstices of this erudite colloquium, Kepel and Laitin discussed the threats to Europe coming from radicalized Islam. Kepel is a renowned expert on the Islamic world and author of a major text on Islam in France. He served as a consultant to President Jacques Chirac's Stasi Commission, which addressed the French response to the *affaire* concerning the legality of students wearing the foulard, a symbol of religious identity, in their schools. Kepel then organized with department chair Astrid von Busekist at Sciences-Po of Paris, where they both taught, to invite Laitin to deliver a course to graduate students in the fall of 2007 in his comparative politics specialization. Laitin agreed and, inspired by his conversations with Kepel, made it his agenda to determine whether he could advance his research on the cultural foundation of political behavior through a study of Muslim integration into Europe. He consulted with colleagues as well as with a set of excellent students and postdocs in Kepel's program on the Arab and Muslim world at Sciences-Po.

While teaching in Paris, Laitin narrowed his concerns to a specific question. He wondered whether Muslims faced higher barriers to socioeconomic integration into France than they would if everything about them were the same but they weren't Muslim. While living in Europe, he observed the vitriol hurled across the English Channel in which French intellectuals decried the accommodations to Muslim culture in what they called "Londonstan"; meanwhile, British intellectuals decried French insouciance to the cultural practices of its Muslim migrants. Both of these orientations were based on biased inferences without any systematic data.

Upon reflection on this question, Laitin saw an opportunity to deploy modern social science techniques to address a question that remained a subject of speculation and polemic in Europe. This required him to isolate a migrant population of Christians and Muslims living in France that were alike in all other respects save religion. He relied on his earlier specialty as an Africanist to identify two small ethnic groups in Senegal—the Serers and the Joolas—who met these criteria. He spent his final weeks at Sciences-Po exploring the feasibility of this effort and, upon returning to his home institution at Stanford, wrote a National Science Foundation (NSF) application to conduct such a study. He relied heavily on an informal collaboration with Claire Adida, his then PhD student (now an assistant professor at UCSD), who is French by nationality and an Africanist by specialty. She had worked with a state-of-the-art field experimental group in Uganda and taught Laitin the intricacies of writing game protocols, as well as inventing the speed-chatting protocol that proved crucial to the research design. Laitin was awarded an NSF grant (SES-0819635) for a project entitled "Muslim Integration into EU Societies: Comparative Perspectives" and prepared himself to spend the 2008–2009 academic year in France to conduct this research.

In the course of receiving feedback for his NSF proposal, Laitin conducted seminars at several institutions—in particular the University of California (Irvine) and Columbia University. In the audience at Columbia was Marie-Anne Valfort, then a PhD student in economics ready to begin her teaching career and now an associate professor of economics at the Paris School of Economics—Paris I Panthéon Sorbonne University. She was intrigued by the proposal, and upon Laitin's arrival in Paris, she invited him to give a lecture to her students at the Sorbonne. Shortly thereafter, Valfort and Laitin agreed to collaborate on the NSF-supported project, and they began working together to design the game protocols that constituted the core methodological innovation of this project. Valfort brought high technical skills to the project as well as a firm grounding in experimental game theory.

In the meantime, Laitin worked with a team including Vincent Tiberj and Yann Algan at Sciences-Po to design a survey instrument to obtain information for a high number of matched second- and third-generation Muslim and Christian Serers and Joolas in France about their families and their integration experiences in France; both Tiberj and Algan gave their time and expertise to fashion a survey appropriate for the research design and consistent with the realities of France. Laitin worked closely with Daniel Sabbagh and Eric Cédiey to design the correspondence test. For the survey, he worked with Sabine Mélèze and Frédérique Rougier from the French marketing firm Conseils-Sondages-Analyses (CSA), both of whom went far beyond their contract obligations and turned every stone to find eligible Serers and Joolas living in France to meet the study's goals for the sample and to ensure the quality of the data.

Adida joined Valfort and Laitin for the implementation of the experimental games conducted in Paris's Nineteenth Arrondissement. This involved a month of frenetic organizational efforts. At its termination, at the end of March 2009, the team of Adida, Laitin, and Valfort (calling themselves ALV) agreed that all future publications based on any of the research program would be jointly authored, indicating equal effort and intellectual input by the three collaborators. Indeed, in the course of writing the technical papers in peer-reviewed journals, Valfort and Adida played the principal roles in specifying the theoretical models, devising the econometric tests, and serving as corresponding authors. The outline for this book was developed first as a graduate course that Valfort offered at the Sorbonne. Laitin combined these materials and was responsible for the initial draft of this book.

The experimental protocols would not have gotten off the ground without a devoted group of graduate students who lived the project for several months, giving an incredible amount of their time. Their leader, Jacinto Cuvi Escobar, was indefatigable. And Mathieu Couttenier, Karine Marazyan, Etienne Smith, Josselin Thuilliez, and Severine Toussaert were not only assiduous but constantly added value to the project through their suggestions on the protocols. Natan Sachs and Jessica Gottlieb, Stanford graduate students at the time of field research, helped with experimental design and data analysis. Ben

Adida provided expert service for the computerized game protocols for the team's 2010 experiments at well below market rates. Etienne Smith and Mahnaz Shirali did the complementary ethnographic work with care and insight.

The experiments conducted in 2009, as readers of this book will know, were insufficient to nail down several relationships that ALV believed were determinative of the observed outcomes. Thanks to a generous grant from the French-American Foundation, Laitin was able to reassemble the ALV team in France in 2010 to implement a follow-up set of games.

In the course of writing the technical papers that preceded the publication of this book, ALV incurred many intellectual debts. They include Yann Algan, Ilf Bencheikh, Lisa Blaydes, John Bowen, Samuel Bowles, Jennifer Burney, Pierre Cahuc, Gary Cox, Rafaela Dancygier, Henry Farrell, James Fearon, Harvey Feigenbaum, James Fowler, Guy Grossman, Jens Hainmueller, Seth Hill, Macartan Humphreys, Amaney Jamal, Peter Katzenstein, Adria Lawrence, Neil Malhotra, Rahsaan Maxwell, Craig McIntosh, Susan Olzak, Daniel Posner, Roland Rathelot, Molly Roberts, Daniel Sabbagh, Sebastian Saiegh, Raul Sanchez de la Sierra, Simone Schüller, Jasjeet Sekhon, Patrick Simon, Paul Sniderman, David Stasavage, Sidney Tarrow, Mark Tessler, Jean-Robert Tyran, James Vreeland, Jonathan Wand, and André Zylberberg.

The team also acknowledges the welcome we got at many institutions where we presented earlier versions of this research. At different stages we presented updates and papers from this project at the American Political Science Association, Bocconi University (Milan), Columbia University, the Council of European Studies (held in Boston), Georgetown University, George Washington University, Harvard University, the High Authority for Antidiscrimination and Equality, Institut National d'Etudes Démographiques, Institut National de la Statistique et des Études Économiques, the Institute for the Study of Labor, the Library of Congress (at which Laitin received a Kluge Fellowship allowing him to use the resources at the library to further this project), the London School of Economics and Political Science, the Midwest Political Science Association, New York University, Paris School of Economics, Princeton University, Sciences-Po (Paris), SOS Racisme, Stanford in Washington (which hosted Laitin and Valfort for a month of joint data analysis), the University of California (Berkeley), the University of California (Los Angeles), the University of Maryland, the University of Minnesota, the Toulouse School of Economics, the University of Wisconsin, and the Working Group on African Political Economy. The penultimate manuscript was presented to the comparative politics workshop at Stanford University and prompted final revisions.

Finally, the ALV team relied on the willingness of other scholars to share their data and thus their time, and the following did so generously: Claudine Attias-Donfut, Chris Beauchemin, Rémi Gallou, Susan Holmes, Amaney Jamal, and Alain Rozenkier.

Findings presented in this book were established in, and passed muster among methodological experts in, *Proceedings of the National Academy of Sciences; Economics and Politics;* the *Journal of Population Economics; Economic Inquiry;* and the *Annals of Economics and Statistics.* They are all cited in the text and references; we thank these journals for providing an engaging forum for developing our ideas and permission to reproduce figures and tables originally published in their articles, for which they have copyright. Here we thank the many peer reviewers who compelled us to report as precisely as possible on what our data taught us, no more, no less. Readers of this book should feel confident that the broad summary descriptions of our technical models have been properly vetted by the scientific community.

The ALV team thanks all of these scholars and organizations for their support, though of course we take full responsibility for what is written herein.

Why Muslim Integration Fails in
Christian-Heritage Societies

PART I

Introduction

THE PURPOSE of Part I is to situate our study in the larger debate about Muslim immigration in Christian-heritage societies. Chapter 1 documents the reality of "Islamophobia," that is, the fear of Muslims in these societies. The chapter outlines the negative implications of Islamophobia—especially in Europe—for security, economic growth, and political solidarity. We point out that research has yet to pinpoint the mechanisms driving Islamophobia and the degree to which its thrust is against Muslims or more generally against the wave of foreign migrants in the past generation.

In Chapter 2, we introduce our research design that enables us to isolate a Muslim effect in France. Relying on that research design, we demonstrate that the French, despite a century of resolute secularism, condition their behavior on the religion of the people with whom they interact. Moreover, and here relying on an experiment, we demonstrate that Muslim households, in comparison with matched Christian households, suffer from this discrimination in terms of income. Part I therefore sets the stage for analysis as to why this discrimination exists and what might be done to ameliorate it.

1

The Challenge of Muslim Migrants into Christian-Heritage Societies

If all the Arabs . . . of Algeria were considered French, how could they be prevented from settling in France? My village would no longer be called Colombey-les-Deux-Eglises but Colombey-les-Deux-Mosquées.

—Charles de Gaulle[1]

CAN MUSLIM IMMIGRANTS integrate into the Christian-heritage societies of the West?[2] In view of recent international events, many citizens of the host societies would answer with a resounding no.

Although tensions involving Muslim immigrants in Europe's Christian-heritage societies had been brewing throughout the 1980s, the fatwa issued by Iranian revolutionaries in 1989 against Salman Rushdie for his supposedly anti-Islamic novel marked a clear violent turn in what came to be known as "political Islam."[3] Several failed attempts at terrorist attacks by Islamicist groups on European targets followed. But successful ones occurred, too: bombings in Paris and Lyon in 1995–1996; the 2001 al-Qa'ida attacks in the United States; the 2002 terrorist acts in Bali in which Australians suffered the bulk of the casualties; the Islamicist-inspired bombings in Spain

(2004) and London (2005); the murder of Theo van Gogh in the Netherlands in 2004 for his depiction of Muslim sexuality; the unceasing violence against Kurt Westergaard for his unflattering portrayal of the Muslim prophet in a Danish cartoon published in 2006; the brutal attacks on soldiers in Britain and France by Islamist militants in 2013; the evidence of Muslim citizens from Christian-heritage societies joining jihadist militias in Syria and Iraq in 2014 with some anxious to deploy their newly developed murderous skills upon their return to Europe; and the hideous murders in the editorial offices of *Charlie Hebdo* and in the Hyper Casher supermarket in Paris perpetrated by self-proclaimed jihadists in the name of Islam in 2015. These events all have contributed to portray Muslims as posing a threat to Christian-heritage societies.

It is no wonder, then, that a spate of books depict a clash of civilizations, with images of the Crusades permanently setting a boundary between the worlds of Christian and Islamic cultures. Even the most secular European elites—as exemplified by the epigraph from President de Gaulle—see their society as fundamentally Christian. The clash today is portrayed as that between Muslim immigrants and their host populations (Caldwell 2009). Such accounts justify the Islamophobia of ordinary citizens in Christian-heritage societies by presenting it as a rational response to a clear and present danger.[4] In this context, Islamophobia would simply be the host populations' legitimate answer to a real Muslim threat.[5]

Survey-based evidence confirms that Muslims are widely perceived as a menace by host populations in Christian-heritage societies. In France, 43% of individuals interviewed in 2012 in a survey sponsored by the newspaper *Le Figaro* agreed with the statement that the Muslim community in France is "a menace to the identity of France." Only 17% thought of this community as "a factor that culturally enriches our country" (the remaining 40% could not decide between these two options) (Institut français d'opinion publique [IFOP] 2012). In Germany, the Religion Monitor[6] found that 51% of those interviewed in 2013 believed that Islam poses a threat to their way of life.[7] Even young Europeans, who are supposed to be more tolerant than their parents toward immigrants (see Ford 2012a, 2012b), express anti-Muslim sentiment. Of the 1,000 18- to 24-year-olds interviewed in Britain by BBC Radio 1 Newsbeat in June 2013, 27%

said they do not trust Muslims (this proportion is only 16% concerning Hindus or Sikhs, 15% concerning Jews, 13% concerning Buddhists, and 12% concerning Christians).[8] The justification of such distrust by one of the respondents is revealing: "When you hear about terrorism, more often than not it is Muslims that have carried it out. I just feel they're all out to do that, they're all the same" (Kotecha 2013).

This book puts the assumptions driving Islamophobia to test. Evidence to date leaves two questions unanswered: First, is the host population in Christian-heritage societies really Islamophobe? Many experimental studies have shown that Muslim immigrants from Muslim-majority countries—that is, those with greater than 50% of the population and here listed in Table 1.1—are discriminated against relative to natives on an everyday basis. But it is not clear whether such discrimination is due to religion per se (Islamophobia) or to confounding factors, such as region of origin (xenophobia). Caldwell's (2009) widely acclaimed book provides a good example of this confound. He illustrates his claims of a Muslim challenge to France with an incident involving a Congolese immigrant. While traveling by train in France without a ticket, this immigrant was stopped by the police, shouted for help, and found solace among a crowd chanting "Nique la France" (Fuck France). Yet the incident in no way illustrates a Muslim effect. Not only was the Congolese man, whose name is Angelo Hoekelet, not likely a Muslim; the incensed crowd was also not necessarily Muslim (Laitin 2010). Identifying whether religion is, in and of itself, a special source of discrimination against Muslim immigrants from Muslim-majority countries carries important implications for how we frame the issue and seek solutions. And yet, research to date has assumed, rather than shown, that religion is the source.

Second, if Islamophobia is confirmed, is it indeed a rational response to a real threat? Or is Islamophobia at least partly nonrational, meaning that the rooted populations in Christian-heritage societies discriminate against Muslims even when they do not expect any particular hostility from the Muslim immigrants with whom they interact?

Answering this question is vital for devising policy prescriptions. Islamophobia is likely to be self-perpetuating, whereby both

Table 1.1   Share of the Muslim population in Muslim-majority countries

Country	Share of the Muslim population (%)	Country	Share of the Muslim population (%)
Asia-Pacific		Lebanon	59.7
Afghanistan	99.8	Libya	96.6
Azerbaijan	98.4	Morocco	99.9
Bangladesh	90.4	Oman	87.7
Brunei	51.9	Palestinian territories	97.5
Indonesia	88.1	Qatar	77.5
Iran	99.7	Saudi Arabia	97.1
Kazakhstan	56.4	Sudan	71.4
Kyrgyzstan	88.8	Syria	92.8
Malaysia	61.4	Tunisia	99.8
Maldives	98.4	United Arab Emirates	76.0
Pakistan	96.4	Western Sahara	99.6
Tajikistan	99.0	Yemen	99.0
Turkey	98.6		
Turkmenistan	93.3	**Sub-Saharan Africa**	
Uzbekistan	96.5		
		Burkina Faso	58.9
Europe		Chad	55.7
Albania	82.1	Comoros	98.3
		Djibouti	97.0
Middle East/ North Africa		Gambia	95.3
		Guinea	84.2
Algeria	98.2	Mali	92.4
Bahrain	81.2	Mauritania	99.2
Egypt	94.7	Niger	98.3
Iraq	98.9	Senegal	95.9
Jordan	98.8	Sierra Leone	71.5
Kuwait	86.4	Somalia	98.6

Notes: This table displays the share of the Muslim population in the forty-seven Muslim-majority countries (i.e., countries where more than 50% of the population is Muslim), as reported by the Pew Research Center Forum on Religion and Public Life (2011) for the year 2010.

Muslim immigrants and the host population are encouraged in their hostility toward the other group. To break it, one must identify all the mechanisms that sustain it. Otherwise, we are doomed to draw policy recommendations that will surely fail. For instance, identifying only the rational component of Islamophobia puts all the blame of Muslims' integration failure on Muslims themselves. In this context, policy prescriptions will aim exclusively to influence

Muslim behaviors that are problematic for integration into their host societies. However, if the host population reveals an unprovoked distaste for Muslims in their midst, then such an approach cannot break the self-perpetuating discrimination that Islamophobia generates.

Significant Discrimination against Muslim Immigrants from Muslim-Majority Countries

Discrimination refers to treating individuals unequally for illegitimate reasons. Many experimental studies have shown that Muslim immigrants from Muslim-majority countries are discriminated against relative to natives in Christian-heritage societies. This means that Muslim immigrants are treated less favorably than natives even in situations where immigrants and natives are equal with respect to relevant characteristics.

Take the example of labor market participation. Consider two groups of job applicants: one composed of natives, the other of Muslim immigrants. Imagine these applicants are endowed with similar résumés, meaning that the productive characteristics observed on these résumés (education, work experience, etc.) are equal. A recruiter discriminates against Muslim applicants if he or she is systematically more likely to offer a job interview to natives than to Muslim immigrants, in spite of the fact that these applicants' observable indicators of productivity—the sole characteristic that should motivate the recruiter—are equal. Gary Becker (1957) defines such labor market discrimination as the unequal treatment of individuals who are equally productive.

Evidence of hiring discrimination against Muslim immigrants relies on correspondence tests.[9] These tests consist of sending fictitious résumés of applicants endowed with the same productive characteristics in response to real job openings. Researchers typically signal the origin or religious tradition of the applicant by manipulating the first and last name on the résumé. They then measure differences in callback rates between résumés that signal the applicant was native and résumés that signal the applicant was a Muslim originating from a Muslim-majority country. If these differences are statistically significant, meaning that they are large and systematic enough to ensure they were not uncovered by chance, then discrimination is at work.

Findings provided by these correspondence tests are disturbing. Amadieu (2004), Cédiey and Foroni (2007), and Cédiey, Foroni, and Garner (2008), testing the French labor market, showed that callbacks received by applicants with Muslim North African–sounding names were much lower than those received by applicants with Christian French–sounding names. Similarly, Duguet et al. (2010) computed that for every hundred positive responses a fictive native French candidate receives, the matched fictive Muslim North African candidate receives only twenty-five. Muslim North African applicants have also been found to be discriminated against in Belgium (Nayer and Smeesters 1998), the Netherlands (Bovenkerk, Gras, and Ramsoedh 1995; Blommaert, Coenders, and van Tubergen 2013), and Spain (Actis et al. 1996). In Sweden, Carlsson and Rooth (2007), Carlsson (2010), and Rooth (2010) identified substantial discrimination against applicants with Muslim Middle Eastern–sounding names (relative to applicants with Christian Swedish–sounding names). Goldberg and Mourinho (1996) as well as Kaas and Manger (2012) showed that applicants with Muslim Turkish–sounding names are discriminated against in the German labor market (relative to applicants with Christian German–sounding names). But discrimination against Muslim immigrants is not confined to Western European countries. For instance, Booth, Leigh, and Varganova (2012) showed that applicants with Muslim Middle Eastern names are discriminated against in Australia relative to applicants with Christian Anglo-Saxon names.

Further experiments have shown that Muslim immigrants are not discriminated against in the labor market only. All other things equal, they are also less likely to be called back by landlords in Sweden's rental housing market (Ahmed, Andersson, and Hammarstedt 2010) or to be admitted into night clubs.[10]

Little Is Known about the Source of Such Discrimination

There is little doubt that Muslim immigrants are discriminated against relative to natives in Christian-heritage societies. Yet the above studies do not demonstrate whether such discrimination is due to their religion or to their region of origin. Save for Albania, Muslim-majority countries are located outside of Christian-heritage regions. Individuals originating from Muslim-majority countries may therefore activate a particularly intense xenophobic feeling among the host populations in these regions. Consider the correspondence test conducted by Duguet et al. (2010) in the French labor market. The name "Yassine Mokraoui" sends to the recruiter two pieces of information: the applicant's region of origin (North Africa) and the applicant's religious tradition (Islam). Therefore, differences in callback rates between Yassine Mokraoui and Clément Meunier (the native) cannot be attributed to differences in religion only. They may also reflect that these applicants differ with respect to geographic origin. If we want to be able to devise appropriate policy responses to discrimination against Muslim immigrants, we first need a method for isolating the religious signal from other confounds.

If it is indeed the case that Muslim immigrants are discriminated against because of their religion—something our research will demonstrate—we must then ask why such discrimination occurs. Addressing this question is critical for eradicating Islamophobia and the social, economic, and political challenge it poses.

The challenge posed by Islamophobia is clear. It is likely to generate a vicious circle whereby both Muslim immigrants and their host population are encouraged in their hostility toward each other. The perpetuation of this vicious circle—thereby sustaining discrimination—is especially worrisome. Muslims are expected to constitute a growing share of the population in Christian-heritage societies through continued migration and higher-than-average fertility rates (Pew Research Center Forum on Religion and Public Life 2011). Consistent with a worsening of the situation, the 2014 report of the National Consultative Commission for the Rights of Man (CNCDH) underlined that among racist acts directed at religious minorities, those that were Islamophobe were the only ones growing for three consecutive years. The CNCDH underlines that "It is worrisome, because this increase refers more to acts . . . than to threats."[11]

Islamophobia is also a challenge to Western countries' economic performance. Not being able to integrate Muslims successfully in the labor market amounts to renouncing a full-fledged workforce diversity that has been proven to boost firms' productivity (see Hoogendoorn and van Praag 2012). Moreover, hiring discrimination against Muslims leads to the constitution of Muslim ghettoes on the peripheries of Western cities in which skyrocketing unemployment rates feed crime and violence and further undermine social cohesion.

Finally, Islamophobia poses a political challenge. Nationalist parties throughout Europe have raised the specter of Islam in language not dissimilar to the way extremist parties in the 1930s scared compatriots about the Jewish threat. This rhetoric has been disseminated into mainstream politics. For instance, in October 2012, one month before being elected president of the Union for a Popular Movement, the leading center-right political party in France, Jean-François Copé publicly proclaimed: "There are areas where I can understand the frustration of some of our compatriots, fathers or mothers returning from work in the evening and learning that their son, while heading home from school, was stripped of his chocolate croissant by thugs who explain to him that one does not eat during Ramadan."[12] By filtering into the mainstream of Western political discourse, the prejudicial portrayal of fanatical Muslims tyrannically ruling their communities is likely to exacerbate relations between Muslim immigrants and rooted populations.

What is the source of discrimination against Muslims qua Muslims? Research in social science points to two candidates. Anti-Muslim discrimination can first be based on negative stereotypes,[13] that is, on negative beliefs about average productive characteristics among Muslims. Assume that a recruiter correctly believes that unobserved productive characteristics (that is, those that are typically absent from a résumé, such as the ability to work in teams) are lower on average among Muslims than among Christians. This belief will lead the recruiter to rationally favor Christian applicants even if Muslim and Christian applicants are endowed with the exact same résumés.

Yet even if this unequal treatment were rational (that is, based on beliefs that are correct), discrimination would not be legitimate. The law recognizes that even if Muslims and Christians indeed differ in terms of average unobserved productive characteristics, any indi-

vidual Muslim applicant may have above average unobserved productive characteristics, and any individual Christian applicant may
be below average in this regard. Social groups are never completely
homogeneous, that is, composed of individuals whose characteristics are exactly equal to the group's average characteristics. Exceptions always exist, and indeed the stereotype may represent a highly
visible minority. In other words, even statistically correct stereotypes
should not permit discrimination. But if the recruiter does discriminate on the basis of average group performance, discrimination in
this case is called "statistical," a term specified by Ned Phelps (1972)
and further analyzed by Kenneth Arrow (1973).[14] Statistical discrimination occurs when the recruiter relies on a statistic (what he or she
believes is the average unobserved productivity among different social groups) to make a decision.

   Anti-Muslim discrimination can also be based on prejudice, that
is, on a negative feeling toward non-coethnics (that is, those who do
not share the same ethnicity or any one of the cultural traits that
are associated with ethnicity) even when no particular threat is expected from this outgroup.[15] Prejudice against Muslims obviously
leads recruiters to discriminate against them in a nonrational manner.
In this case, discrimination is "taste-based." This term was formu-
lated by Gary Becker (1957) to portray the situation where the taste
or distaste of the recruiter toward various social groups accounts for
his or her hiring decision.

   One may reasonably ask from whence does this distaste come?
Although Becker has been the source defining this mechanism, he
(and his fellow Nobel prize–winning coauthor George Stigler) admitted that there is "no accounting for taste" (Stigler and Becker
1977). We think we can do better, based on what we present in
Chapter 7 on the sources of nonrational Islamophobia. There we see
that a small level of cultural distance between a minority and a
dominant majority could lead the latter to fear the implications of
growing numbers of that minority for the dominant culture. Historians have observed this in seventeenth-century England with a
genuine fear of a growing Catholic threat to the dominant Anglican culture that was radically exaggerated with conspiracy theories as to what Catholics would do once they captured the throne.

A fabrication known as the "popish plot" to kill Charles II scared and outraged the Anglican majority (Pincus 2009). Mass hysteria was finally contained with the Act of Settlement (1701), which excluded Catholics from the throne. In our time, Americans have exaggerated fears of becoming a bilingual country when rates of assimilation by the descendants of Mexican migrants are hardly different from those of nineteenth-century immigrant groups from Europe.[16] The exaggerated fears of conspiracies that cultural minorities will unalterably undermine social cohesion, consistent with Becker's sparse model, can be considered a source of nonrational discrimination.

Is anti-Muslim discrimination taste-based or statistical? In the labor market, for instance, do recruiters discriminate against Muslims because Muslims' average characteristics are indeed problematic for their firm's productivity? Or is anti-Muslim discrimination also taste-based, such that recruiters would discriminate against Muslims even if they knew their productive characteristics are on average similar to those of Christians? Disentangling the rational and the nonrational components of Islamophobia is essential in devising policy prescriptions seeking to maintain social cohesion in Christian-heritage societies.

What Can Be Done?

Integration of immigrant populations is typically thought of as inclusion of these immigrants in a host society, such that they have a full range of mobility options open to them. That is, integration is successful to the extent that there are no structural constraints in the society preventing members of these immigrant groups from competing in the labor market (or other markets, such as housing or marriage) equally with members of the host society. As we discuss later (in Chapter 8), this need not involve dropping connections with their host society, or even becoming culturally indistinguishable from the modal citizen of the host society. We ask here what the conditions are for successful integration and whether those conditions have been met for Muslim immigrant groups.

Up until now, scholars and policy makers have debated over two orientations toward immigrant minorities on how best to integrate them into their societies—assimilationist and multiculturalist. Assimilationist approaches champion a model in which integration is best achieved through compulsory assimilation policies (Goodman 2010; Ireland 1994; Koopmans 2013; Lahav 1997). From this perspective, immigrants need to be compelled to adhere to the common set of values and norms idealized by the predominant culture of the native majority. To do so, again from the perspective of the native majority, guarantees the moral order and coherence of their society. The premise of this model is rooted in the idea of cultural incompatibility that recalls Samuel Huntington's (1997) "clash of civilizations" and later applied to recent failures in American assimilation (Huntington 2004). Based on this perspective, and claiming that new immigrant groups are not assimilable, many newly appearing political parties throughout Europe have been running on popular anti-immigrant platforms.

The main contrasting framework to the assimilationist approach are theories of multiculturalism that reject the notion of cultural incompatibility and argue for a cultural pluralism based on the coexistence of different cultures and values (Bloemraad 2011; Parekh 2002; Taylor 1994; Wright and Bloemraad 2012). According to the multicultural approach, forcing immigrants to assimilate is impossible or even counterproductive and more likely to reinforce preexisting cultural identities (Fouka 2014). Instead, the successful integration of immigrants is best realized if governments celebrate the cultural diversity that is entailed by recent immigration and acknowledge the cultures of minority groups as having equal value to the mainstream culture.

Public remarks by Prime Minister David Cameron of the United Kingdom and German Chancellor Angela Merkel have signaled a death warrant for multicultural experiments, for in the assessment of Merkel, they have "utterly failed" (Kymlicka 2012, 15). But despite this vibrant and long-standing debate both in academic publications and in public pronouncements, there have been no compelling tests that examine the validity of the contradictory predictions from the different approaches. This book will provide a preliminary test comparing these approaches for the integration of Muslim immigrants in Europe and the United States.

Our Argument in Brief

Our research confirms that Muslims qua Muslims are discriminated against. Moreover, it establishes that both Muslim immigrants and the host population in France bear joint responsibility for the failure of Muslims not only in France but in other Christian-heritage societies as well. From our experiments and surveys described in subsequent chapters, we show that the host population discriminates against Muslims even when it does not expect any particular hostility from them. At the same time, Muslims behave in ways that feed rational Islamophobia. As this book shows, this shared responsibility constitutes the basis for what we call a discriminatory equilibrium in which both Muslim immigrants and rooted French act negatively toward each other, and this is mutually reinforcing. Public policy, we argue, must take into account this self-reinforcing process, which at best sustains discrimination and at times even exacerbates it. Further, we report tentative evidence that state policy oriented toward assimilation has better returns for integration than do policies that emphasize multiculturalism. But an assimilationist policy orientation by itself is not sufficient to undermine the discriminatory equilibrium that we have identified. We insist that a set of measures, involving sacrifices by members and institutions of both the host and immigrant societies, at the micro, meso, and macro levels, needs to be adopted for an equilibrium shift. We view these policy recommendations, informed by our research, as promoting fair-minded and vibrant host societies that are enriched by religious diversity.

2

Anti-Muslim Discrimination
in the French Labor Market
and Its Consequences

T HIS BOOK ADDRESSES two questions. The first is whether
Muslim immigrants from Muslim-majority countries are indeed
discriminated against because of their religion. And if there is religious discrimination, the second asks why the host population
in Christian-heritage countries discriminates. In this chapter, we
foreshadow the details of our research strategy implemented in
France (which will be fully described in Chapters 3–5) in order to
address systematically the first question, for if there is no discrimination against Muslims qua Muslims, the question of mechanisms
becomes irrelevant.

We find that there is very much a problem to be solved.[1] Our
results show that while rooted French citizens are resolutely secular,[2] they condition their behavior on religion in the context of
diversity. Furthermore, French employers, also conditioning their
employment choices on religion, systematically discriminate against
Muslim applicants. Finally, we show that this discrimination has consequences likely to generate resentment among Muslims: Muslim
immigrant families in France are poorer than a matched set of Christian immigrant families.

To reach these conclusions, we needed to isolate the religious factor from other sources of discrimination so that we could reckon the magnitude of this discrimination. The fundamental challenge we faced was to isolate a set of Muslims and Christians who are alike in every respect save for their religion and to examine whether one of the two matched groups faces higher barriers to success in their adopted country. As we will elaborate, this challenge in isolating a religious effect was not trivial. Basically, we needed to conduct a careful experiment in a well-controlled field site.

We chose France. As we elaborate in the Appendix, our choice was in large part based on the size and prominence of the Muslim population in France and the degree to which its presence was magnifying as a public concern. Although we hoped social science could bring light to social and political questions that generate so much heat, we could not make any claim that a focus on France would allow us to infer principles that could be generalized beyond France's borders.

But once that choice was made, we could get scientific leverage (allowing for more general conclusions) if we found a population within France that, if studied carefully, could help us determine whether Muslim migrants, being Muslim, faced added barriers to successful integration. Our strategy was to isolate a set of matched Christians and Muslims from the Serer- and Joola-speaking communities of Senegal who migrated to France in the 1970s.

Who Is Being Compared to Whom?

The question of Muslim integration in France (as emphasized in our discussion in the Appendix of France as a field site) is typically posed as a question about Algerians specifically and Maghrebis (Tunisians and Moroccans as well as Algerians) more generally. The vast literature on Islam in France naturally focuses on the fate of Algerian immigrants and their descendants and conflates the Maghrebi and Muslim populations in France, as if they were one and the same (Leveau, Wenden, and Kepel 1988, 9–25). Our purpose was precisely to avoid this confound. In our attempt to identify religious discrimination, to whom should we compare Muslim immigrants to France who mainly arrived in the 1970s, just before the decline in factory labor? Can we compare them to the Poles who immigrated in the nineteenth century or to the Portuguese who came to France in the golden age of post–World War II industrial growth? These are different eras, with different opportunities. These are also different countries of origin, with different experiences likely to influence migrants' adaptation to the host country. What about comparing Muslim Algerian immigrants to those of European extraction (the *pieds noirs*) who settled in coastal Algeria? Here, the differences in success in France could be attributed to religion or to the many social networks the pieds noirs could exploit in easing their transition to metropolitan France. Furthermore, even if the networks were equal, would we know if the key factor of difference were race, religion, or culture? Finally, what about comparing Algerian Arab Christians with Algerian Arab Muslims to isolate the difference in success in France that is due to religion? This would surely be an improvement, but Algerian Arab Christians are not only miniscule in numbers, they are also not a natural comparison group. Indeed, the social and political context in which Arab Algerians converted to Christianity or Islam is such that Christian converts and Muslim converts were, from the start, very different groups of people. Therefore, our comparison would be between two different types: an average Algerian (who is Muslim) and an atypical one. This is called, in the language of statistics, a bias due to an omitted variable—the factors that led Algerians to convert to Christianity are likely to be those that allowed their children to perform better as immigrants. Not religion but those (largely unobservable) inherited characteristics would be driving the difference. In sum, for lack of a comparison population, we cannot measure the barriers to successful immigration into France posed by Islam by even the most careful observation of the largest Muslim group in France.

France is not unique in posing a problem to researchers of measuring the barriers to Muslim integration. Much of the commentary about Muslims or about Islam in Christian-heritage societies fails to separate out a "Muslim factor" from other factors correlated with religion. In Germany, there is no natural comparison for its largest Muslim population, those with historical connections to Turkey. In the United Kingdom similarly, it would be difficult to isolate a

Muslim factor for Pakistanis or Bangladeshis. The question to be answered is whether Muslims face barriers to their progress in Christian-heritage societies that would be lower if everything about them were the same but they were Christians. The challenge is to find a population equal in all social, economic, and cultural respects who migrated to Christian-heritage societies for similar reasons at a similar time with similar skills, yet was divided by religion, Muslim and Christian. If we found such a group, it would solve what social scientists call the "identification" problem—being able to attribute the fate of Muslims immigrants in France today to their religion.

To address this identification problem, we took advantage of a natural experiment.[3] In the nineteenth century, a wave of jihadists, relying on trade opportunities and conquest, traveled across the African savannah from the north and east. Their imperial advances were constrained south of the savannah where tsetse flies were threats to their horses. At more or less the same period, now coming from the south, Christian missionaries and European imperial states teamed up to create conditions for legitimate (that is, not slave) trade and Christian conversion. There was thus a zone, somewhat south of the savannah, where indigenous populations met evangelical Christians at the same time as jihadist Muslims.[4]

For future migrants to France, this zone is centered in southwestern Senegal and is populated by two linguistic communities, the Serers and the Joolas. While around 90% of Senegalese are from the Muslim tradition, about a third of the Serer and Joola families have Christian family roots. Previous research, as we shall demonstrate in Chapter 3, reveals that in these areas families that became Christian were no different from those that became Muslim. Therefore, there is no relevant variable predicting the type of person who became Muslim or Christian. If, additionally, we assure readers (as we attempt in Chapter 3) that becoming a Christian in a future colony ruled by Catholics did not give them undue advantages for future success, then we gain confidence that we can identify the effect of the group's religion on its socioeconomic fate once it is settled in the host country. Any differences between Muslims and Christians over a few generations in France could be explained only by their religious affiliations rather than by factors that might have determined which affiliation to adopt in the country of origin or by the socioeconomic consequences of this affiliation in the country of origin.

To summarize: our first research question is whether Muslims face higher barriers to success in the Christian heritage societies of the industrialized West than if everything about them were the same but they were Christian. In this section, we introduced our identification strategy, a micro-study of carefully matched Christian and Muslim immigrants in France—to answer this question in a causal manner. The data can now speak—and show the depth of the problem that remains to be solved.[5]

Establishing That There Is a Problem to Be Solved

The Voting Game

Common interpretations of the Muslim challenge to Christian-heritage societies today (and France in particular) portray a profound conflict between a religious fundamentalist immigrant population and highly secularized autochthonous populations. Indeed, the notion of a secular France was supposedly enshrined with the promulgation of laws in the early twentieth century that promoted *laïcité*, usually glossed as "secularism." The diminished role of the church because of *laïc* laws was not only a modern or urban phenomenon. It was observed as well in the rural region of the Vaucluse, where an American scholar spending his sabbatical there in the 1950s reported that religion was a matter of practical conformism, not something that evoked a deep sense of loyalty to the church (Wylie 1957). Our research offers a rather different interpretation—namely, that the French (even in the most cosmopolitan of districts) condition their behavior, whether or not they are aware of it, on the religious heritage of others. To put it a bit more crudely, laïcité does not imply the irrelevance of religion in public life; rather, it enjoins the French not to talk openly about religion in public settings.[6]

To support this claim—and to seek out a congeries of mechanisms that might be at play—we designed a set of experimental protocols in the diverse Nineteenth District of Paris. In this district, we recruited randomly from the population living in or passing through the district. We paired these recruits with a set of Serer and Joola Christians and Muslims in eight groups of ten (and thus eighty players).[7] At the beginning of the game session, players could observe each other's looks, their manners, their dress, and their first names, which they were asked to write on a label and paste on their chest.[8] No other information about fellow players was known. None wore any clothes or jewelry revealing religious affiliation, with the exception of one non-Senegalese player, who wore a headscarf signaling a Muslim identity. In an attempt to understand the salience of various social cues in France, we relied on a speed chatting game that mimics everyday interactions between strangers and then tested which social dimensions—gender, age, ethnicity, religion, socioeconomic class—were relevant when it comes to deciding with whom to associate. In this speed chatting game, each recruit met five others (as in a "speed dating" framework), and all were invited to "get to know" each other. Subsequent to these chat sessions, each player was asked to vote for a team leader (among the five he or she chatted with) who would be given a thirty-euro prize to divide between him- or herself and the five other members of his or her "electorate." More details on this procedure will follow. But we jump ahead of ourselves in order to learn about how our subjects chose their leaders in a decision with monetary stakes and whether religion played a role. If it did, we will have experimental evidence that despite the professed insouciance of the French to each other's religion—as demanded in the notion of laïcité—they condition their behavior on each other's (assumed) religion.

Here we separate out two types of determinants of electoral victory in our voting game: the characteristics of candidates and the social distance between candidate and voter. From this information, we calculate the factors that are most predictive of the choice for a team leader. We run a set of statistical analyses with a range of robustness tests to assure ourselves that our findings hold up to rigorous challenge.

Two results stand up to these tests and stand out for explaining French understanding of religion.[9] First, no sociodemographic characteristic is robustly significant in predicting any particular candidate's success. In other words, a candidate's gender, age, income, education level, race, and religion have no bearing on his or her likelihood of being elected as a team leader. In fact, we explain very little of the variation in voting choice—a mere 3%—with just those variables.

Second, once we add the social distance variables, one unambiguous result reveals itself: the religious distance between the voter and the candidate is the only variable that significantly correlates with the voter's decision to vote for the candidate; the higher this distance, the lower the probability that the voter votes for the candidate. These results are driven in part by the subsample of voters with long intergenerational ties to France, meaning that the tendency in France to associate with individuals of the same religion is not imported by individuals of recent immigrant background. To give a sense of the magnitude of the effect, we find that the predicted probability of voting for a candidate is approximately 17% when voter and candidate do not share a religious identity and 30%—a 76% increase—when they do.

Our analysis so far reveals that, in the context of our voting game, rooted French players recruited within the Nineteenth District of Paris (along with our Serer and Joola subjects, who were from other districts), who did not know each other prior to our experimental intervention, conditioned their leader choice on the religion of the available candidates. Pitting gender, age, race, education, family income, and religion against one another, we find that, more than any other factor, the rooted French voters condition their electoral choice on the religion they share or do not share with each candidate.

After the speed chats (and before the electoral choice), we posed a set of eight questions to each participant about each of the players she or he had just met in the speed chatting game. The results of this quiz allow us to measure the kind of information that strangers exchanged about one another during the speed chatting game as well as the kind of information strangers did not bring up explicitly but were able to infer by simply guessing. Our results of this speed chatting quiz indicate that religion was not discussed during the speed chat (and we know this by reviewing the notes they took after meeting each partner); however, participants correctly guessed whether their partner shared their religion 80% of the time. In sum, religious membership was not a relevant concern in getting to know one another, but it was implicitly taken into account.

Despite the fact that religion is an unspoken value, religious homophily, or the preference of individuals to associate with coreligionists, prevails in France. What are the consequences of religious homophily for a Christian-heritage society in which a significant minority hails from a different religious heritage? In the next section, we show that job recruiters similarly condition their choices on the religion of applicants, with deleterious implications for those who are assumed to be religiously different.

The Correspondence Test

To determine whether human resources (HR) recruiters for French firms condition their choice on religion, we implemented a correspondence test.[10] As described in Chapter 1, the standard protocol is to send out to employers fictional résumés that are comparable in terms of productive characteristics, while changing in one respect (race, gender, social class) a quality of the applicant that is irrelevant for assessment of productivity. The dimension we sought to vary and make evident in a perusal of the résumé is the religious affiliation of the applicant. We accomplished this without confounding religion and country of origin as previous correspondence tests have.

Our protocol demanded three comparable résumés.[11] Two of them were from women with an obvious Senegalese surname (Diouf) but one with a well-known Muslim first name (Khadija) and the other with a well-known Catholic first name (Marie). The third résumé was from a woman with a typical French name (Aurélie Ménard). Our résumés thus created three types of candidates: a French citizen with no obvious immigrant background (Aurélie Ménard); a Muslim French citizen of Senegalese origin (Khadija Diouf); and a Christian French citizen of Senegalese origin (Marie Diouf). In addition to differences in the first names, we introduced two signals of religious identity related to the work and volunteer experiences of our fictitious candidates. One of Khadija's past positions was with Secours Islamique (Islamic Relief), and one of Marie's was with Secours Catholique (Catholic Relief). Also, Khadija did voluntary work for the Scouts Musulmans de France, whereas Marie did the same for the comparable Catholic organization, Scouts et Guides de France. Aurélie, different from both Marie and Khadija, was associated only with a secular association and was employed only in a secular firm.

The remaining qualifications and backgrounds were identical for all three applicants: all were single, were twenty-four years old, and had two years of postsecondary education. They also held three years of experience on the job market in the accounting sector, the type of position our fictional applicants sought to fill. We deliberately chose occupations that entailed interaction with clients or company partners, such that recruiters would be paying greater attention to the expected reactions of these potential clients to their employees. A nongovernmental organization, ISM-CORUM,[12] collected job announcements nationwide for accountants published on the Pôle Emploi (the French national employment agency) Web site during the spring of 2009. For each pair of job announcements matched by region, sector, company size, and position, ISM-CORUM administrators randomly sent the Aurélie/Khadija candidate pair to one and the Aurélie/Marie candidate pair to the other. Aurélie Ménard was used solely as the "reference" candidate: her résumé allowed us to avoid sending Marie and Khadija's applications for the same position. Because these applications were identical in both form and content (except for the religious identity signals), sending both résumés would have inevitably awakened suspicion among recruiters that their choices were being put under an experimental microscope. Our analysis of the experimental results entails what social scientists call a difference-in-difference design: we compare callback rates to Khadija and Aurélie on the one hand and those to Marie and Aurélie on the other. We then compare the difference between those two differences, evaluating how much more Khadija's employment opportunities deviate from Aurélie's than do Marie's.

The results are startling (see Figure 2.1). We first observe that the reference candidate, Aurélie Ménard, received the same positive response rate from employers who received Marie's résumé and from employers who received Khadija's résumé (27% and 25%

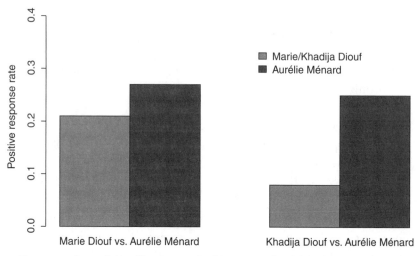

Figure 2.1. Interview callback rates for Marie Diouf and Khadija Diouf. From Claire L. Adida, David D. Laitin, and Marie-Anne Valfort, "Identifying Barriers to Muslim Integration in France," *Proceedings of the National Academy of Sciences* 107, no. 52 (2010), Figure 2A, p. 22388.

respectively, with no statistically significant difference between the two). This indicates that the companies receiving Marie's résumé were, on average, similar to those receiving Khadija's résumé. This is much expected given that the Aurélie/Khadija and Aurélie/Marie pairs were randomly sent to recruiters. But this confirmation lends greater confidence to our comparison of Marie's and Khadija's positive response rates. And it reveals a striking difference. Although Marie Diouf received a positive response rate of 21%, Khadija Diouf received a positive response rate of only 8%. This thirteen-percentage point difference is statistically significant and indicates that for every hundred positive responses received by Marie Diouf, Khadija Diouf received only thirty-eight positive responses, or 2.5 times fewer.

Note how well Marie Diouf performed relative to Aurélie Ménard. When matched up against one another, Aurélie Ménard received a response rate of 27% while Marie Diouf received a response rate of 21%, a difference that does not reach statistical significance. In other words, the religious similarity between Aurélie (who HR personnel in France, by default, would assume to be from a Christian tradition) and Marie (whom we signaled as Christian through her first name and her work for and participation in Catholic organizations) overcame the traditional race-based discrimination that other ré-sumé experiments have found. According to these, the French candidate with no recent immigration background is favored over the French candidate from a sub-Saharan African background (Foroni 2008). Our result, though differing from past experiments, is very much in line with the conclusions that we derived from the voting game: once we separate out race from religion, the French candidate with no recent immigration background is not systematically favored over the Christian French candidate from a sub-Saharan African background; but both are systematically favored over the Muslim French candidate from a sub-Saharan African background.

When the directors of ISM-CORUM began examining the early results in which Marie had received a much higher rate of positive responses than Khadija, they worried that perhaps the HR employees of these firms did not recognize "Diouf" as an African name and were therefore treating Marie as neither African nor Muslim. They were also concerned that Marie was perhaps perceived as a rooted French candidate having married a Senegalese. Finally, they worried that recruiters were treating Khadija as a North African rather than as a sub-Saharan African. We therefore changed our protocol mid-course (after 214 applications had been sent) and included a photo-graph (the same face, without any religious symbols, of a young Senegalese woman) for Marie and Khadija for the next sixty-one applications. The results with and without the photographs were not statistically different from each other. Furthermore, these results held up in an analysis neutralizing the effect of differences in loca-tion, employment sector, company size, occupation, contract type, as well as whether the résumé included a photograph. This experiment thus provides a clear indication that in at least one sector (accounting) of the French labor market and holding the candidate's race constant (both Marie and Khadija were black Africans), there is significant religious discrimination against Muslims.

Survey Results on Relative Income

We have so far established that French citizens, despite their ideology of laïcité, condition their choices for a team leader on whether the person shares a religious heritage. We also know that HR personnel similarly condition their choices on job candidates' religious heritage. The final question for this chapter is whether the discrimination experienced by Muslim players in experimental games and as candidates in the French labor market corresponds to an economic disadvantage on the part of Muslim immigrants relative to their Christian counterparts.[13]

To answer this question, we rely on a survey of 511 second- and third-generation Serer and Joola Christians and Muslims living in France in 2009 (whom we call Senegalese Muslims [SMs] and Senegalese Christians [SXs], respectively).[14] From the identification strategy we described earlier, we know that first-generation migrants in SM and SX families arrived with similar socioeconomic status in France. However, given the discrimination SM individuals face in the French labor market, one can suspect the emergence of an income gap between both communities. Do we indeed observe that second- and third-generation migrants are poorer in SM than in SX families? To address this question, we compare the reported current monthly household income of the respondent depending on whether he or she is Muslim or Christian. With this procedure, we can be confident that any differences found between the two groups are the result of some aspect of their religious upbringing or practice, as no other factors differed across these groups upon arrival to France.

Our results show that the mean net household income for our SX respondents is 1,900 euros per month; meanwhile, the mean net household income for our SM respondents is 1,500 euros per month. In an analysis that neutralizes the effect of potential other differences between SM and SX households,[15] we find that this difference in income is statistically significant. On average, Muslim households make 400 euros less than Christian households each month, the equivalent of 13% of the average net monthly household income for France in 2009 (the year of the survey).[16] Figure 2.2 nicely illustrates the effect of household religion for each income category: it indicates that Muslim households are significantly more likely to fall into lower income categories, whereas Christian households are significantly more likely to fall into higher income categories. In sum, there is a

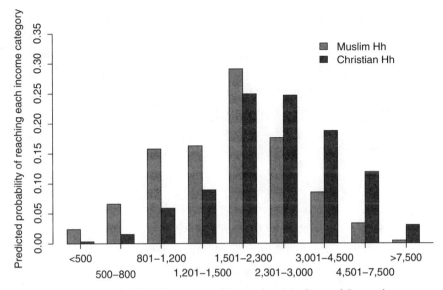

Figure 2.2. Household (Hh) income of Senegalese Muslim and Senegalese Christian survey respondents. From Claire L. Adida, David D. Laitin, and Marie-Anne Valfort, "Identifying Barriers to Muslim Integration in France," *Proceedings of the National Academy of Sciences* 107, no. 52 (2010), Figure 3, p. 22389.

significant negative Muslim effect on present-day household income. We can therefore infer that the anti-Muslim job discrimination revealed in this chapter has broad implications for Muslims' economic success in France.

Conclusion

In the early twentieth century (with this history summarized in the Appendix), France under radical republican governments laid out a doctrine of laïcité working assiduously to secularize French society. Yet, as the data in this chapter show, France is also a society in which citizens are keenly concerned with the religious heritage of their interlocutors, and they condition their behavior on that concern. On the national job market, HR personnel rely on signals about the religious heritage of applicants and systematically discriminate against those—in this case Muslims—who are from a different religious heritage from that of the majority. The implications of this discrimination are rather telling, as we learn from our survey that Muslim families are significantly less endowed with income than matched Christians. These results beg for further scrutiny, to learn the sources of religious discrimination as a first step in ameliorating a situation that violates France's republican ideals.

PART II

Research Strategy

PART I OF THIS BOOK introduced the difficulty in identifying a Muslim challenge to immigrant integration into Christian-heritage societies. It proposed a solution: the study of a group of Senegalese immigrants from two ethnolinguistic communities who immigrated to France at the same time and for the same economic reasons, and who are split among Muslims and Christians. Then, relying on this identification strategy, we demonstrated that Muslims indeed face greater discrimination in the French labor market, with important consequences for socioeconomic integration.

In Part II, we delve into our research strategy. The chapters that follow, aimed perhaps at the more social-scientific reader, provide a sense of the inferential challenges we faced in identifying a causal effect of religion on immigrant integration. It elaborates on our proposed solution—the study of Senegalese Christian and Muslim immigrants from the Joola and Serer communities—explaining why and how it works as a solution. Finally, it expands on the methods we used to obtain a sample of subjects and to measure discrimination and the mechanisms that underlie it.

3

Solving the Problem of
Causal Identification

Our research seeks to know whether the religion of Muslim and Christian immigrants to France who stem from the same country of origin influences their chances of integration in France. This, of course, involves analysis of the differential likelihood of successful integration given a migrant's religion. But one should take care in making any claim of causality when data analysis merely correlates a factor that is taken as causal (the religion of the migrant) and its supposed effect (such as labor market success in France). We all should be suspicious of anyone giving a causal interpretation to correlations of this sort for two reasons. For one, it may be the case that some third factor, often unmeasurable, is correlated with both the religious tradition of the individual and that individual's ability to integrate. As an illustration, it may be the case that the French colonial authorities gave special help to Christians that was denied to Muslims, and it was colonial support rather than religion that explains subsequent integration success in France. Inability to include this third factor in a statistical analysis leads to what social scientists call an "omitted variable bias." Second, it may be the case that the most successful Muslim immigrants from Senegal hide their religious identities in order to succeed in France while the most successful Christian immigrants from Senegal are more visible. In this case, interviewers would likely "miss" the rich set of Muslims while observing the rich set of Christians. If this were the case, the correlation between income and religion would be a false one, due to a biased selection of subjects. The omitted variable bias and the selection bias present what social scientists call an "identification problem," that is, the problem of properly identifying the causal factor that drives the outcome of interest. In the next chapter, we address our solution to possible selection bias issues. In this chapter, we show how our research procedures addressed the challenge of omitted variable bias.

We already foreshadowed our solution to this identification problem in Chapter 2, arguing that Serer and Joola migrants, both Christian and Muslim, came to France with similar prospects for success, with the only difference between them being their religion. If over one or two generations, the Christians were outperforming the Muslims, we stipulated, it could only be due to their religious difference. We promised a fuller defense of that stipulation, and this chapter as well as subsequent chapters of Part II will provide it.

Conditions for Establishing a Religious Effect

To impute for a Christian and Muslim immigrant population any differences in integration in France to their different religious affiliations, five conditions must be fulfilled. First, of course, this population must be composed of people from both Muslim and Christian traditions. Second, they must be from the same country of origin and the same ethnic group. Third, and now we get to the more difficult conditions, the original religious conversion in the country of origin must not be correlated with the economic and social success of the migrants' ancestors. In other words, we should not be able to impute the eventual differences in success between the Muslims and Christians to any factors connected with the original conversions. Fourth, after conversion but before immigration to France, there must not have been an economic advantage for one religious group that was not accorded to the other. Both Conditions 3 and 4 work to guarantee that the differences found in France between Muslims and Christians were not linked to differences in economic success already present in Senegal. Finally, the conditions facing both groups of immigrants upon arrival in France would have to have been the same, both in terms of the timing of immigration and the purposes that motivated the migrants to move to France. The Serer and Joola migrants, we seek to demonstrate, meet these five conditions.

Conditions 1 and 2: Muslims and Christians from the Same Country and Ethnic Groups

The first and second conditions, on isolating Muslims and Christians from the same background, are easily demonstrated. Both Serers and Joolas historically occupied zones in Senegal's west, as shown in Figure 3.1. The Serers are the third largest ethnic community in Senegal (after the Wolofs and the Peuls) and represent about 15% of the Senegalese population. The Joolas are the fourth largest ethnic group and represent some 4% of the Senegalese population. They live mostly in the Lower Casamance region just south of the Gambia.

Of importance for our first condition, both Serers and Joolas contain a nonnegligible proportion of Catholics, far more than the average of 5% for all groups in Senegal. In Senegal, according to the census of 2002, 9.32% of the Serers were Christian and 90.44% were Muslim. Among the Joolas, 20.17% were Christian and 75.61% were Muslim.[1] While there is no way of knowing the proportions of Muslims and Christians of Joola or Serer immigrant background in France (for reasons discussed in the Appendix), we were able in our survey of these two groups to achieve a sample of about 25% Catholic, with the remaining 75% Muslim.[2] Although they are a minority, the Catholics from these ethnic communities are sufficiently numerous that we can compare their life trajectories with those of their Muslim homologues.

Focusing on Muslims and Christians from the same country and ethnic groups is a substantial step toward limiting the omitted variable bias (further limitation is provided by Conditions 3–5). It guarantees that differences in integration in France between Serer and Joola Christians and Muslims (whom we continue to identify as SX and SM, respectively, as in Chapter 2) are not attributable to differences in countries of origin or even differences in subnational cultures.

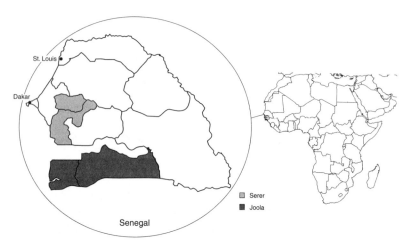

Figure 3.1. Senegalese origins of our Senegalese Muslim and Senegalese Christian populations.

Condition 3: Success in Senegal Does Not Predict Conversion to One or the Other Religion

Historical and ethnographic records suggest that, before conversion, the SM and SX populations did not differ on characteristics that would determine social mobility of their descendants in France. If they did, it could well be that differential success of present-day Senegalese immigrants who differ as to religion can be explained by their ancestors' levels of ambition (an omitted variable). But this is unlikely to be the case. In those parts of western Senegal populated by the Joola and Serer communities, both Muslim jihadists and Christian missionaries arrived at the same historical juncture in the mid-nineteenth century. Yet conversion to the world religions was slow in these Joola and Serer communities largely until the 1950s, when the economic returns to conversion became more attractive (Asante 2009; Cannot-Brown 2009). At that time, conversion to Islam or Christianity became associated with religious networks allowing individuals to better market their crops and access credit (Gastellu 1981). The crops targeted by each religion were different: while Muslim jihadists encouraged the development of the groundnut trade, Christian missionaries helped in the development of commerce in palm oils and wines, an enterprise that was scorned by the Muslims (Linares 1992). But the crops targeted by each religion presented similar economic returns. This evidence increases our confidence that Christian and Muslim original converts did not differ in terms of economic and social ambitions.

Ethnographic studies lend further support to our claim that the third condition has been met, namely, that the Muslims did not recruit from a different pool of Serers and Joolas than did the Christians. These ethnographies show that because of the strength of their traditional religion, both Serers and Joolas long resisted conversion to world religions. For the Serers, Asante (2009, 606–607) emphasizes the societal importance of a supreme deity in the traditional religion and points out that they were one of the very few Sahelian groups to successfully reject Islam when it was first presented to them as part of a jihad. Catholic missionaries were not better treated. A similar pattern occurred among Joolas. Cannot-Brown (2009, 354–355) reports that the Joolas were monotheist as well, with belief in Ata Emil (Person of the Sky) as creator god. The ethnographic works of Coly (2002, 2:47–49, 3:49–50) show how hard it was for the world religions to get local Joolas to extract themselves from traditional practices, and when they did, they mixed the world religions with their own rituals. As late as the mid-1960s, Linares (1992) observed no fasting during Ramadan and rare fulfillment of any of the pillars of Islam. Although the traditional age grade structure was crumbling, she wrote that Islamicization "as a clearcut moral charter, capable of guiding the political and economic decisions of community members, has yet to be completed" (84). More recently, in an ethnography of a Joola village with nearly all Muslim converts, M. Lambert (2002) reported continued adhesion to the animist religion, with almost no penetration of what might be called the high Islam of the courts in the northern emirates. In sum, because both Muslims and Christians in southwestern Senegal similarly resisted the two world religions and used them mostly for trade advantages, we can reasonably infer that there was no omitted variable (such as ambition or elective affinity with one of the world religions) that explains who became Christian and who became Muslim.

Condition 4: No Pro-Christian Support from
French Colonial Authorities

Although the characteristics of the original converts were equivalent
at the moment of conversion, it is still possible that those characteristics diverged before their descendants migrated to France. French
colonial authorities might indeed have given freedom and opportunity to Catholic converts, making them better able to integrate into
France. Our identification strategy is not, however, compromised
by colonial backing of Christian converts to the disadvantage of
Muslims.[3] Indeed, in contrast to the whole Mediterranean region of
Algeria, and largely due to climate, Senegal never became a destination for hundreds of thousands of settlers. There was no project of
"Sénégal français" comparable to that of "Algérie française." Not
having settlers to carry the principal administrative load, Senegal
required a greater accommodation of Islam to help the colonial
power rule than was the case in Algeria. As a result, it was Islam,
rather than Christianity, that the French colonial authority favored
in Senegal.

Muslims in colonial Senegal, to the chagrin of European missionaries, were advantaged by colonial administrators. As far back as
1792 in the commune of Saint-Louis (the commercial port on the
northern coast of today's Senegal), 12,000 Africans, most of them
Muslims, were granted full rights of French citizenship. As the colony
grew with the establishment of three more communes (which were
legally part of France) and the conquest of the interior, the exigen-
cies of governing required the French to come to terms with Islam.[4]
Colonial policies developed from the mid-nineteenth century
through the period preceding independence accommodated (and
even relied on) Islam. Of primary importance, there was the need to
educate intermediaries who would collect taxes, provide forced labor
(the corvée), recruit soldiers, and deal with local conflicts and appeals
through reference to Islamic texts. When Louis Faidherbe became
governor of Senegal in 1854, he established an educational infrastructure in Senegal with a school for the sons of chiefs and lay
schools for Muslims to equalize the two Catholic primary schools
run by missionaries. A key training ground for future officials, this

School for the Sons of Chiefs in Saint-Louis in 1906 took the name of a "Franco-Muslim Médersa" (relying on the Arabic word for "school"), with one-third of the training in Islamic law.

At this time, radical republicanism had reached its ascendancy in metropolitan France. Thus, part of the motivation (for the obvious slap in the face of Christian-supplied education in Saint-Louis) was from "a French *laïc* inclination to annoy the (Catholic) priests." Emile Combes, a leader of the radical republicans and once prime minister, "apparently carried his secularist revivalism far enough to propose the establishment of Islam as an official state religion in France's colonies. Catholic missionaries in West Africa throughout the colonial period complained of the pro-Islamic preferences of senior administrators" (Cruise O'Brien 1975, 89–90). Ultimately, Senegal's three elite gymnasiums became centers in French West Africa for secondary education that were secular (that is, without missionary influence) and state run: the Lycée Faidherbe, the Lycée Van Vollenhoven, and the École Normale William Ponty.

Also supporting the accommodation with Islam in Senegal, French administrators referred to African civilization as having little value, while they respected Islam highly. In the biting words of Cruise O'Brien (1975, 92–93), "Islam [was seen and propagated by these scholars] as a step up the ladder to civilization (French) from the depths of pagan barbarism."

Finally, there were economic reasons for the French administration to accommodate (and even support) Islam. As international demand for groundnuts was expanding, the Muslim clerics who organized the cultivation of this crop and provided credit to its cultivators became invaluable middlemen in that trade.

In sum, French administration in Senegal did not favor Catholic converts. Still, because of the missionaries, the Catholics could well have had an education advantage. Catholic primary schools provided a well-structured curriculum. They possibly offered better opportunities for secondary education than did the madrasas that served the Muslim population. If that were the case, a gap between the converts to Catholicism and converts to Islam could have opened subsequent to their conversion. To address this concern, we rely on our survey of 511 second- and third-generation Joola and Serer immigrants to France that we conducted in 2009.[5] In this survey, we asked about the education and professional levels of their family's first migrant to France, either parent or grandparent. We found that the Christian and Muslim first migrants to France from Serer and Joola roots did not have, at their moment of emigration from Senegal, significantly different levels of education or levels of professional competence. More precisely, both Christians and Muslims arrived in France similarly endowed with basic education. Moreover, both were equally likely to have been involved in nonfarm activities before migration. These data give us assurance that differential educational opportunity for Christian and Muslim converts in Senegal (plausibly an omitted variable) would not substantially bias our results.

Condition 5: Similar Timing and Purpose for Migrating

Finally, the conditions upon arrival in France of the two religious groups from Senegal were quite similar. As confirmed by our 2009 survey, the majority of both groups arrived in the decade of the 1970s, a period of repeated droughts in their home country that forced many to leave home. Neither group arrived with a political agenda; they came for work. At that very moment, France offered them opportunities for blue-collar employment in the rapidly expanding industrial suburbs surrounding France's great cities.

Moreover, the first Senegalese Catholic and Muslim immigrants to France (those who arrived before the 1970s) settled at similar times. This ensures that the better integration of subsequent Catholic migrants cannot be accounted for by the fact that the first migrants in Catholic families arrived earlier than the first migrants in Muslim families. Catholic migrants from Senegal did not benefit from greater "network effects," that is, access to a broader and better-integrated network of fully settled coreligionists. Thus, this final potential omitted variable (timing of immigration) does not bias our analysis.

Some Limits

To be sure, the world rarely offers perfect identification strategies outside an experimental laboratory. For our study, one can note two limits to our comparison. First, the Senegalese Catholics (those who are SX) were a minority in Senegal while the Senegalese Muslims (correspondingly, those who are SM) were a majority. Perhaps those who are SX, as a minority in their home country, had developed a capacity for adaptation to the dominant culture better than their SM homologues, who never needed to adapt to a dominant (religious) culture before emigration. A sixth criterion for perfect identification would therefore be that the country of origin should have equal proportions of both groups, such that neither had a minority perspective.

Only two countries in the world (with immigrant communities in Europe) have populations that meet this criterion: Bosnia-Herzegovina and Lebanon. But choosing either of these countries would not solve nearly as well the five criteria we originally proposed. The immigration waves from Bosnia have been quite recent, mostly during the wars after the collapse of Yugoslavia, and it would be impossible to compare intergenerational trajectories as we are able to do with our Senegalese populations. Besides, violating the fourth criterion, the Bosniaks (the Muslims from Bosnia) suffered much more from the war than did the Christians, and this surely would have an effect on their success in their adopted countries. Lebanon presents equally daunting inferential problems. First, it does not fulfill the fifth condition. Lebanese Christian immigrants who were the first to migrate to the West did so in an earlier era than did the first Lebanese Muslim immigrants. This situation enabled subsequent Lebanese Christian migrants to take advantage of (Christian) Maronite networks to integrate into their new societies, an opportunity that was not as easily available for their Muslim counterparts. Second, the bulk of the Lebanese emigration occurred during the Lebanese Civil War (1975–1990). As in the case of Bosnia-Herzegovina, this puts the fourth condition at risk. Researchers aiming to analyze the integration patterns of Muslim and Christian Lebanese immigrants in the West have no means to ensure that these populations were similarly exposed to the war intensity before migrating. Simply taking into account the number of years people are exposed to the war is not enough to capture the intensity with which war affected them. Yet, exposure to war intensity in one's home country is likely to greatly influence one's ability to integrate in a host country.

Researchers then would face an omitted variable bias, with no compelling way to overcome it.

In any case, we think it improbable that the results we presented in Chapter 2 showing relative economic success of the SX respondents were driven by the fact that the ancestors of our SX respondents were minorities in Senegal. Indeed, as we report in Chapter 9, the Christian émigrés from prewar Bosnia-Herzegovina were less susceptible to feelings of discrimination in their host countries than their Muslim counterparts even though they were not a minority in their home republic, either in Yugoslavia or in Bosnia-Herzegovina.

A second possible limit to our identification strategy is that our population of Muslims from sub-Saharan Africa is not spontaneously associated with the "collective imagination" of Islamness in France. The everyday French notions of Islam are indeed intimately connected with images of the Middle East or North Africa, not with images of sub-Saharan Africa. However, concentrating on these clearly Islamic populations would have yielded an identification failure. Save for Lebanese immigrants, the countries in the Middle East and North Africa do not contain populations of comparable Christians to permit a comparison with Muslim counterparts. We contend, however, that any bias from focusing on Muslims from sub-Saharan Africa should lead us to underestimate the actual intensity of religious discrimination in France given that the French do not spontaneously associate Muslims from sub-Saharan Africa with Islam.

Conclusion

We conclude from this chapter that there is no better population than the Serers and Joolas that would permit us to isolate the religious factor in accounting for immigration success in France. Yet we need to take one more step to ensure proper identification—we need to assure ourselves that our sample of SMs and SXs (and the French with whom they interact) is representative of the SM, SX, and native French populations in France. How to address this concern of selection bias is our principal task in Chapter 4.

4

Procuring a Sample

W E HAVE NOW been introduced to the immigrant population of interest in France: the Senegalese Muslims (SMs) and
Senegalese Christians (SXs). These groups are matched by race,
language, culture, premigration experience, and timing or purpose
of migration. They therefore allow us to investigate why there are
added barriers for Muslim immigrants, qua Muslims, in integrating
in France. To tease out the mechanisms of anti-Muslim discrimination, we need to observe how SMs and SXs interact with members
of the host population, that is, with French citizens with no recent
immigrant background. In the following, we define these rooted
French as those who report that all four of their grandparents were
born within the French hexagon. We abbreviate this category,
calling them FFF—standing for French born, French parents, French
grandparents.

But how do we obtain representative samples of the SMs, the SXs,
and the FFFs? Obviously, we cannot observe all SMs, SXs, and FFFs
living in France. We are constrained to sample some of them instead.
However, while doing so, we must ensure that our sample is representative of the population about whom we want to generalize. Put
differently, we must again guard against what statisticians call a
"selection bias" in our sampling procedure; or, if this selection bias
occurs, we must properly adjust for it. This chapter reports on the
procedures we followed to guard against such bias. It therefore com-
plements Chapter 3 (where we addressed issues of omitted variable

bias) in resolving the "identification" issue that allows us to attribute causal force to religious difference in accounting for integration success into France.

But let us first clear away a possible misconception about our term FFF. When we report that "the French" discriminate based on religion in the labor market, to what group in the population are we referring? We do not subscribe to the view, popularized by the political right in the Third Republic, that there is a "true France" rooted in eternal values of the peasantry. This notion, up through General de Gaulle's use of it to discredit those who had collaborated with the Nazis during the Vichy regime, was both a political tool and, according to Lebovics (1992, xiii, 9–11, and later chapters), a powerful myth that infused the French language, state-sponsored art, and colonial strategy. It was a myth that hid the fact that the French economy had industrialized and French society had experienced waves of immigration for centuries.

Rejecting this rather essentialist view of French culture, our strategy was to sample a population of French subjects who are well rooted in French culture and specified as those who report that all four of their grandparents were born within the French hexagon. In other words, we chose our French population not by cultural values, political ideologies, or historical memories but, rather, by being raised in a family with long exposure to French society. We relied on these FFF subjects, because without recent migratory history, they were less likely than French citizens of more recent migratory experience to have had extended social contacts with recent immigrant communities such as the SXs or SMs.

Even with a well-specified criterion for who is a member of each group, selection biases remain a concern. Assume SMs in France show, on average, lower integration skills than do SXs. But imagine that we inadvertently sample those among SXs with the lower integration skills and those among SMs with the higher integration skills, such that SMs end up showing integration skills that are higher than those of SXs. In addition, imagine that we sample those among FFFs who are the least open to diversity, while believing we are dealing with the typical French. These selection biases would lead us to wrongly conclude that SMs are discriminated against in France only because the host population is inherently and nonrationally Islamophobe.

In this chapter, to alleviate worries over selection bias, we present the sampling procedure in the four stages of our research seeking to unravel the causes of Muslims' barriers to integration in France: the experimental games of 2009, the survey of 2009, the ethnographic interviews of 2009, and the experimental games of 2010. For each of these stages, we discuss whether the sampling procedure is conducive to selection bias and, if so, what cautions we have taken enabling us to generalize our results.

Experimental Games of 2009

In order to understand the source of the discriminatory behavior we have highlighted in Chapter 2, we conducted a set of experimental games to compare everyday interactions between FFFs and SXs with those between FFFs and SMs. The goal was to further determine whether differences in the comportment of the FFFs exist when they interact with SMs as opposed to SXs and, if they do, whether they do so on the basis of reasoned beliefs. We therefore sought to test whether anti-Muslim discrimination is only "statistical" (that is, rational) or whether it is also "taste-based" (that is, nonrational).

Eight sessions of experimental games were conducted over two weekends in March 2009. As we shall explain, we sought a culturally diverse setting to situate our games; a language school in the Nineteenth District of Paris, where we rented rooms, fit our bill. Each session comprised ten players.[1] Of the eighty players, twenty-seven were from the Serer and Joola communities (nearly all of them first-generation migrants into France): eleven were SX (ten of whom were first generation), and sixteen were SM (fifteen of whom were first generation). These Senegalese "target" players were recruited through the good offices of local ethnographers from the Paris region and of a Senegalese night watchman (who was neither Serer nor Joola) who was well connected to several Serer and Joola networks. The other players (and, most important, the FFFs) were recruited through a random protocol on the streets of the Nineteenth District.

In administering our random protocol, we went through several steps. First, we mapped all of the twenty-two Metro stations in the district. Second, we used census data to determine the population density within a short walking distance from each station. Third, we assigned a weight to each Metro station based on this population density, with the higher-density stations getting proportionally more cards in our random draw. Fourth, each recruitment team drew a Metro station for each recruitment day and placed itself at this station. Fifth, the recruitment team drew a random number from a bag with one slip of paper for each number from one to ten. This number would inform them how many passersby at the station they should let pass before they solicited the participation of the next passerby. For example, a recruitment team that randomly drew the number three was to solicit participation from every third passerby. This random method yielded a pool of fifty-three players. Among them, twenty-nine were of European origin, with Christian or Jewish religious roots. Of these twenty-nine players, twenty-one met the criteria for FFF—that is, having all four grandparents born within France's hexagon. The characteristics of the twenty-four remaining players were as follows: six were of sub-Saharan African and Christian origins; six were of sub-Saharan African and Muslim origins; and twelve were of North African and Muslim origins.[2]

Recruiting FFFs

The choice of the Nineteenth District was not random. We targeted it for two reasons. First, we needed to ensure that the presence of several individuals of African origin in a group of ten players would be considered as normal by FFFs. Otherwise, FFF behavior in our games might not have reflected their everyday behavior. Conducting our experiments in the Nineteenth District allowed us to reach this objective. The Nineteenth District (along with its Eighteenth and Twentieth District neighbors) is indeed one of the most ethnically and religiously diverse neighborhoods in Paris (hence in France). From the 1999 census, we know that only 63.5% of the inhabitants of this district were born in France (compared with 82.4% for all of Paris). Given the placement of our experiment, it was perfectly usual for FFFs living in this district to see themselves surrounded by people who were culturally different from them.

The second reason we chose the Nineteenth District is related to the first: we wanted to recruit among FFFs those who would be the most open to cultural diversity. Therefore, any degree of noncooperation with Muslims would be the lower bound for all of France. In other words, by choosing the rooted French players least likely to be unnerved by interaction with ethnically and religiously different individuals, we were setting ourselves up to identify the minimum level of distaste and/or distrust. Had we recruited instead in an ethnically homogeneous district, critics might have argued that we found discrimination because we were focusing on those French who were likely to be more prejudiced. This selection bias would have induced greater skepticism among critics on the validity of our findings.

Although, as we claimed above, the recruitment of our players was random, there is still possibility for a selection bias among FFFs. About one-third of those whom we approached at the Metro stations (through our random procedure) refused our invitation to participate "in games to determine how individuals from Île-de-France [the region that encompasses Paris and its suburbs] behave about money," as it was explained in the script our recruitment teams followed. These refusals, we feared, were not random. We may therefore face a selection bias in the type of FFFs who agreed to participate in our study. As a consequence, we must ask ourselves to what extent the FFFs whom we recruited were different from the average FFFs living in the Nineteenth District and more generally from a representative sample of FFFs in France.

A bit of reflection on the district and on the sample suggests that we were more likely to get acceptances from FFFs who were on average more tolerant of diversity. Why is that? As part of our recruitment protocol, we told potential recruits that they would be interacting with typical folk from Île-de-France, one of the most diverse departments in all of France. Those living there surely know this fact, and those who would prefer not to interact with typical folk from their district were more likely to turn our offer down. Therefore, if there is bias in our results, it would be to reveal far less discrimination than there exists more generally in France.

Public opinion data give support for our intuition in this regard. In Chapter 1, we referred to a survey sponsored by the newspaper *Le Figaro* in 2012 in which respondents were asked whether the Muslim community in France was "a menace to the identity of France" or rather "a factor that culturally enriches our country." The respondents' position on a left–right scale of political preferences constitutes the best predictor of their answer.[3] The more the respondent sees him- or herself on the political left, the more likely he or she is to report viewing Muslims as culturally enriching France. We rely on this correlation to infer attitudes toward cultural diversity among the FFFs we were able to recruit.

Our sample pool was more on the left than the average French district and therefore, we can infer, more open to diversity. To demonstrate this, we refer to data from the European Social Survey (ESS) of 2009, using a subsample of only those respondents with two parents born in metropolitan France. This is not quite as demanding as our criterion for FFFs (whose parents and grandparents were born in metropolitan France), but it is reasonably close and is the only option, as the 2009 ESS did not collect data on respondents' grandparents. From an examination of this sample, we find that our FFF players from the Nineteenth District of Paris are on average more politically left than a representative sample in France. We can thus conclude that, if anything, the FFFs in our experiments conducted in 2009 were (holding their gender, age, education, and income constant) on average more accepting of diversity than the average rooted French citizen. Any finding of intolerance toward Muslims in our experiments is surely a lower bound estimate for France at large.

Recruiting SMs and SXs

We know that first-generation Senegalese Muslim and Senegalese Christian immigrants from the Serer- and Joola-speaking communities left Senegal in roughly similar socioeconomic circumstances. But we need to assure ourselves that this is more or less the same for our experimental subjects who, on average, were living in France for less than ten years. The answer, as depicted on Table 4.1, is largely yes in terms of gender (balanced for both groups), age (the mean for

Table 4.1 Balance test for the 2009 Senegalese Muslim (SM) and Senegalese Christian (SX) players

Variable	SM (a)	SX (b)	Difference (b) – (a)
Female	0.50 ($n=16$)	0.55 ($n=11$)	+0.05 ($p=.83$)
Age	33.19 ($n=16$)	31.45 ($n=11$)	−1.74 ($p=.59$)
Education	7.33 ($n=15$)	7.63 ($n=8$)	+0.30 ($p=.83$)
Household income	3.79 ($n=14$)	4.00 ($n=9$)	+0.21 ($p=.85$)
Religiosity	2.60 ($n=15$)	4.90 ($n=10$)	+2.30 ($p=.00$)
Knows players from previous game sessions	0.43 ($n=16$)	0.36 ($n=11$)	−0.07 ($p=.71$)

Table source: Claire L. Adida, David D. Laitin, and Marie-Anne Valfort, "Muslims in France: Identifying a Discriminatory Equilibrium," *Journal of Population Economics* 27, no. 4 (2014), Table 5, p. 1054. Copyright © 2014 Springer-Verlag Berlin Heidelberg.

Notes: The table reports arithmetic means for the subsamples of SM and SX players and two-tailed t tests assuming unequal variances. *Female* is a binary variable coded as "1" if the participant is female and "0" otherwise. *Age* is equal to the age of the participant. *Education* is an ordinal variable ranging from "1" (less than primary school completed) to "10" (higher than college degree completed). *Household income* is an ordinal variable ranging from "1" (less than 500 euros a month) to "11" (more than 7,500 euros a month). *Religiosity* is an ordinal variable ranging from "1" (never attends religious services) to "7" (attends religious services several times a week). *Knows players from previous game sessions* is a binary variable coded as "1" if the participant knows players who participated in previous game sessions and "0" otherwise. SM = Senegalese Muslim; SX = Senegalese Christian.

both groups is in the young thirties), education (the mean for both groups is having some secondary education), and income (both groups' mean income is in the range of 1,200–1,700 euros per month). There is, however, one major exception. Our data reveal that SX and SM participants in the games are not representative of the set of first-generation immigrants from Serer and Joola backgrounds in terms of religiosity. This is a crucial concern for us since our FFF players were making inferences about SM and SX religion during the games. Therefore, different levels of religiosity by SX and SM players would presumably mean different ability for FFFs to guess or learn the religion of their SM and SX counterparts. We know from a broader study that Muslims are more religious than are comparable Christians in their countries of origin and also upon arrival to destination countries (Fish 2011). Such differences were confirmed in our 2009 survey when we analyzed the first migrants' level of piety.[4] However, perhaps because of Qur'anic injunctions against gambling, and because our invitation to participate suggested the possibility of earning money through the playing of games, the SM players who agreed to our terms had levels of piety that were less than those of our SX players, who were not similarly exposed to injunctions against gaming. When asked about the frequency with which they attended religious services, our SM players on average reported somewhere between once or twice to several times per year. Meanwhile, and this difference is statistically significant, our SX players reported on average between two and three times per month. What this implies, to the extent that personal religiosity is reflected in one's presentation of self, is that the FFFs would have more difficulty in associating the SM players with Islam than the SX players with Catholicism. Thus, as with FFFs being more open to diversity (than the typical rooted French person), the SMs being less pious than the SXs would be a bias against finding FFF discrimination against SMs in our experiments. Our results will again be an underestimation of the degree of religious discrimination in France. Similarly, this bias would also underestimate any differences in behavior toward the FFFs by Muslims as compared with matched Christians. In both directions, then, this difference in religiosity works against finding differences in cooperative behavior between Muslims and rooted French as compared with matched Christians and rooted French.[5]

There is a final worry about the comparability of our SM and SX players. Given that SXs are culturally closer to the host population (since they share the same religious tradition) than are SMs, it is presumably easier for them, at least in the first years that follow their arrival in France, to interact with rooted French. But if this is the case, then SMs on average would be more reluctant to participate in experiments conducted by researchers from well-known research universities in France and the United States. This suggests that our recruitment pool would again be weighted in favor of those SMs who are more open to Christian-heritage cultures than the average SM immigrant. If so, this selection bias again would lead us to underestimate actual differences in cooperation toward FFFs of SMs and SXs at large.

Let us recapitulate our discussion of biases in the selection of our players. First, the FFFs who agreed to participate in our games are likely to be more open to Muslims than a representative sample of FFFs in France. They are also less susceptible to associating our SM players to Islam than they would be for players from the Maghreb or Middle East, and especially so because our sample of SMs is less pious than the typical SM in France. All discrimination that we detected in our experiments is in all probability an underestimate of the discrimination that the majority of Muslims likely face in France. Second, the SMs and the SXs who participated in our experimental games were comparable on key characteristics. And the difference in religiosity suggests that our data could catch only an underestimation of any behavioral differences between SM and SX immigrants to France that could feed discrimination by FFFs. In sum, given the sampling issues that we have encountered, our results should be more optimistic about Muslim integration into France than they would be if we had a perfectly matched sample of first-generation SM and SX immigrants as well as the most representative FFFs in the country playing our games.

Survey of 2009

Simultaneous to the experimental games, we conducted a survey of second- and third-generation Serers and Joolas residing in France. The fundamental purpose of this survey was to trace over one or two generations the degree to which Muslims integrate in France as compared with matched Christians. This intergenerational perspective allowed us, as discussed in Chapter 2, to demonstrate a rather long-term advantage of SX households as compared with SM households in family income. Here we provide more details about the sample of respondents.

Overall, 511 respondents living in France but with ethnic heritages going back to the Joola and Serer communities in Senegal were interviewed by the French survey firm Conseils-Sondages-Analyses (CSA). Of these 511, 332 were interviewed by telephone (with North African interviewers phoning from Casablanca). The telephone interviews relied strictly on mobile phone connections, which were much more effective in reaching our target sample than landlines would have been. Many immigrants rely principally on mobiles for their telephonic communications, and of course people who work long hours are difficult to reach at home. To find SX and SM interviewees who met our criteria was a challenge, and given their miniscule presence in France, calling random numbers would have been vastly inefficient. We therefore provided our survey firm with a list of about fifty family names typical for Serers and Joolas, and they relied on proprietary Internet sources to connect phone numbers with family names. They then called from an initial list of about 6,000 names people who were likely to meet our criteria for inclusion. Respondents were first asked a few screening questions assuring our surveyors that they did have Serer or Joola roots, with at least one grandparent a native speaker of Serer or Joola; that they were born in France; and that they were themselves adults. If they met these criteria and if they agreed to be further interviewed, the survey began.

The remaining 179 interviewees were contacted by a method known as "chain-referral sampling." In this approach, surveyors travel to neighborhoods known to have significant populations of immigrant families from Africa and ask around for possible subjects who meet the research criteria. Once someone is found, after the interview, following a protocol developed by Heckathorn (1997, 2002), the interviewer asks for the names of several people who the interviewee knows might also meet our criteria. With three names, the interviewer randomly sorts them and goes down the list until someone meets the criteria and is willing to be interviewed. These interviews had the same set of questions as those on the phone but were conducted face to face by trained ethnographers, all of them of sub-Saharan African descent.

Selection bias is not absent from the 2009 survey. First, due to legal constraints in the collection of data by French statistical bureaus (see

Appendix for details), we remain ignorant of the demographics of the entire Serer and Joola populations in France. Thus, we could not assure ourselves of a representative sample of these two groups living in France. Second, respondents were those who agreed to answer our survey. This suggests that our recruitment pool is again weighted in favor of those SMs who are more open to an association with French and American institutes and universities whose sponsorship was declared in the survey introduction than the average SM immigrant might have been. Put more emphatically, any difference in integration or in norms conducive to integration between SM and SX respondents should be considered as a lower bound of the difference we would have found with a perfectly representative sample of SMs and SXs in France.

Ethnographic Interviews of 2009

The survey instrument, largely because it permits statistical comparisons, has many advantages. But the long list of questions and the impersonal tone of surveys can blind one to the actual realities of integration into a foreign society. This is why we employed an ethnographic element to our research program. We collaborated with two experienced field researchers, Etienne Smith and Mahnaz Shirali. Smith had conducted extensive field research for his dissertation in Senegal and was a fluent speaker of Wolof, the lingua franca of Senegal (spoken by 43% of the grandparents of our Serer and Joola respondents in the survey and, outside of French, the language our respondents relied on most to speak with their parents). Shirali is an expert in the sociology of religion and has written extensively on Muslim youths in France. Both Smith and Shirali were given the charge of extensively interviewing twenty Serer or Joola families living in France (ten from each religious tradition), meeting members from several generations, and learning about their family histories and the special problems they faced in integrating into France. (Their final reports covered twenty-two Christian and nineteen Muslim families.) The families were not to know that the research concern centered on their religion, but they did know that the research team was studying Serer and Joola incorporation into France.

In no way can we consider the forty families who were extensively interviewed "representative" of any population. Yet we tried to ensure that our ethnographers were not interviewing informants from a single network, one that could have been particularly unrepresentative of each of the four subgroups (for example, Serer Muslims) we were investigating. To ensure that Smith and Shirali had a broader range of the four subgroups of interest, they were instructed to choose two zones each for half of their interviews from the following list: the Eighteenth or Nineteenth Districts of Paris; the northern suburbs of Paris; Lyon; and Marseille. And for each of their two zones, they were asked to implement the chain-referral method (Heckathorn 1997, 2002) described earlier.

Experimental Games of 2010

Analysis of our 2009 experimental games left several questions unanswered about the motivations of our FFF players in regard to interactions with SMs and SXs. In 2010, we therefore organized a new protocol to better assess how FFF players were responding to their SX and SM counterparts. We could not contact those FFFs who played in 2009 because we were required to destroy all records of their real names and addresses to meet the privacy requirements of the institutional review board that is responsible for ethical practices in research. We therefore needed to recruit a new set of FFFs who were likely to be similar to our 2009 sample in most respects.

To administer the new protocol, we set up shop in the Eighteenth District (neighboring the district where we conducted the games in 2009) in an office mostly dedicated as a call center for surveys. Again with the help of the survey firm CSA, we recruited by phone fifty participants of varying age, gender, and neighborhood in the Nineteenth district. We relied on quotas to obtain as representative a sample as possible without relying on randomization. Eligibility demanded that the player have four grandparents all born within the French hexagon. The demographic profiles of the FFFs in 2009 and 2010 were virtually identical in terms of gender, age, income, education, religiosity, and political preferences. This is hardly surprising as our recruitment methods were similar in 2009 and 2010.

In recruiting this new sample of FFFs, we explained as we did for our 2009 recruits that the objective of these games was for us "to study the behavior of those living in Île-de-France in games that allowed for the winning of money."

Conclusion

In our quest to understand the sources of anti-Muslim discrimination, we needed to obtain a sample of our target group (SMs and SXs) as well as a sample of the host population (FFFs). As shown by this chapter, there hardly exist perfectly representative samples that would allow us to generalize our findings without reservation. Our sampling procedure is no exception. Like many others, it suffers from a selection bias. But the biases we encountered, if anything, lead us to underestimate the actual discrimination faced by Muslims in France. Our results should therefore be more optimistic about Muslim integration into France than they would be if we had a perfectly representative sample of SMs, SXs, and FFFs playing our games. In the next chapter, we detail the content of the research protocols (experimental games, survey, and related ethnographies) that helped us sort out the sources of anti-Muslim discrimination.

5

Research Protocols

THIS IS THE THIRD and final chapter delving into the specifics of our research design that seeks to understand the sources of religious discrimination in France. We first needed to identify a religious effect, and we did this by limiting our sample to a matched group of Muslims (SMs) and Christians (SXs) as shown in Chapter 3, with special attention to omitted variable bias. We then needed to assure ourselves that our sample of SMs and SXs was matched as closely as possible and that our rooted French host population (the FFFs) was representative of its coethnics in France, in order to keep selection biases under control. Doing so enables us to confidently generalize our findings beyond the few folk who participated in our study, as explained in Chapter 4. We now need to lay out the content of our protocols allowing us to infer the mechanisms driving anti-Muslim discrimination in France.

Survey of 2009

The 2009 survey comprised ninety-six questions and took about forty-five minutes to complete. There were four sets of questions: those that determined (1) whether the respondents met our research criteria, in terms of Serer/Joola background, age, and how many generations their family had been living in France; (2) the religious heritage and practice of the respondent's family; (3) the respondent's family history, including date of arrival in France of the first family migrant to France, the last job that migrant held in Senegal, the degree to which family members had married out of the ethnic and religious communities of the first migrant, and then the levels of education and job status of that migrant's descendants in France; and (4) the levels of economic, cultural, political, and social integration into French society as well as the degree of connections maintained with relatives still living in their home country. After the end of the interview, surveyors rated the respondent's facility in French.

Ethnographic Interviews of 2009

Our ethnographers, Etienne Smith and Mahnaz Shirali, visited each of the forty families they contacted several times, meeting with family members of different generations and even different households. In these interviews, the ethnographers collected information on each family's social and economic conditions upon leaving Senegal. This involved going back to the first migrants to France and the situation of later generations as they faced the challenges of integrating into the economic and social world of the host country. The ethnographers wrote biographies of each member of the wider family across generations, highlighting education, jobs and income, housing, difficulties in dealing with French authorities, associations to which they belong, and marriages. These biographies were to include information on their political views in France and in Senegal; the degree of religious belief and practice of family members across generations; examples of return migration and the reasons for it; descriptions of each interview milieu in which they conducted their interviews, including observations about family relations, pictures on the walls, the role of women in the household, and everyday practices that are similar to or different from norms in French households; and information about the culture, religion, and national origin of each household's closest neighbors and the degree to which respondents reported social interaction with each of their neighbors. The qualitative vignettes of the interviews served as illustrative materials helping to provide real-life examples of the patterns uncovered in the 2009 survey.

Experimental Games of 2009

Our experiments focused on the nature of the interactions between SMs and FFFs as compared with the interactions between SXs and FFFs. Laying out the protocols for these experiments (for those of both 2009 and 2010) is the principal task for this and the two following sections. It will serve as a reference for readers as we analyze our results in Part III. Readers may find it easier to skim these protocols now but refer back to them when we report on our results.

When we recruited our players for the 2009 experimental games in the Nineteenth District of Paris, we provided them with information as to when they could register. Registration constitutes the first phase of our experimental protocol. In this phase, we collected demographic data that we later used for the composition of the player sets in the game phase that would take place approximately two weeks later.

For the actual game phase, the subjects played a series of experimental games. As already outlined, we supervised eight sessions of games of ten players each that were held in a private language school we rented in the Nineteenth District in Paris, over the course of two weekends. Three of the sessions were all male; three of the sessions were all female; and two of the sessions were mixed gender.

We have already (in Chapter 2, in our discussion of the voting game) described the setting of our games when our subjects arrived for check-in. After this check-in was completed, players were brought to an open room with the other players, given magazines to read, and monitored in a way that discouraged any conversation or interaction.

Each session comprised five experimental games, all of which were designed to examine how SMs and FFFs interact with one another (relative to SXs and FFFs): (1) a simultaneous trust game; (2) a speed chatting game; (3) a voting game; (4) a dictator game; and (5) a strategic dictator game. We now describe how each of these games worked.

The Simultaneous Trust Game

The 2009 simultaneous trust game was the first game participants played in our experimental setup. In this game, subjects sat quietly in a waiting room (and were supervised such that they could not communicate with one another) and were called to a table in an adjoining room in pairs. For each pair, one player was assigned the role of "sender" and the other "receiver." The pairs were created to ensure that all FFFs in a session played the simultaneous trust game twice with each Senegalese player in that session, once for each role.

In the game setup, the sender was allotted three euros in his or her account[1] and could send any amount {0, 1, 2, 3} to the receiver by marking this amount on a sheet that the receiver would never see. As part of the instructions, senders and receivers learned that whatever the sender sent to the receiver, the amount in the receiver's account would be tripled. If the sender sent one euro to the receiver, the receiver would actually receive three euros; if the sender chose two euros, the receiver would receive six euros; if the sender sent three euros, the receiver would receive nine euros. Simultaneously (and without ever knowing how much actually was sent by this sender), the receiver offered a fraction {0, ⅓, ⅔, 1} of the amount received to be sent back to the sender.[2] For example, if the receiver chose ⅓ while the sender sent one euro, the sender would end up with two euros from the initial allocation plus one-third of three euros from the transaction, for a total of three euros; the receiver, for his or her part, would end up with three euros from the sender minus one euro returned to the sender, for a total of two euros. After each play, the senders and the receivers returned to the waiting room, not knowing the decisions of their partners in the interaction, if they would be called again, or in what role.

Experimental economists commonly consider the amount sent by the sender in the trust game as a sign of trust, hence the name given to this game. Indeed, if senders trust receivers, that is, if they believe that the receiver will be generous enough to send back a strictly positive share of the amount he or she receives (in this case, any option but zero), then the sender should send the totality of his or her initial endowment (three euros) to the receiver. By doing so, senders are assured to end the interaction with receivers with at least the same amount in their account as when they started: the sender gets three euros if the receiver sends back one-third (the receiver's lowest strictly positive option), six euros if the receiver sends back two-thirds, and nine euros if the receiver sends back the totality. However, if senders do not trust receivers, that is, if they believe that the receiver will not send back anything to them, then senders should keep the three euros for themselves. We presented the sender's strategy to our players in these terms, thereby making obvious that their moves as senders should reflect the players' trust toward the receiver.

As for the amount sent back by the receiver in the simultaneous trust game, it is most plausibly interpreted either as a signal of pure altruism or as a signal of belief-based reciprocal altruism or both. Pure altruism refers to the receiver's willingness to be generous to the sender irrespective of what the sender does. Belief-based reciprocal altruism describes the receiver's willingness to be generous to the sender because the receiver believes the sender is being kind to him or her, that is, the sender is sending a strictly positive amount to the receiver.

The simultaneous trust game offers the advantage of capturing the two common types of discrimination, taste-based and statistical discrimination, described in Chapter 1. Differences in pure altruism by the receiver should reveal taste-based discrimination reflecting the "special disutility" (Becker 1957) that a player attaches to contact with another player. By contrast, differences in trust on the side of the sender and differences in belief-based reciprocal altruism on the side of the receiver should reveal statistical discrimination, coming from the negative belief that a player holds about the desire of another player to be kind to him or her (Arrow 1973).

The Speed Chatting Game

For this game, which followed the 2009 simultaneous trust game, our ten players were placed into two teams of five. Each player on a team was instructed that he or she would have a few minutes to meet (and, we emphasized, "to get to know") each member of the other team, thereby "speed chatting" with five other players, sequentially, as in a speed dating situation. The original idea behind the speed chatting game was to see if, by sharing a religious culture, the FFFs and SXs would be able to "read" each other more successfully than the FFFs and SMs, in the sense of being able to make correct inferences about each other from a limited set of signals. The easier it is to communicate, we conjectured, the more productive would be any interchange, and this could be a contributing source to overcoming discrimination. Habyarimana et al. (2009) refer to this as the "technology" mechanism, in the sense that a common religion provides a technology for successful communication. We test for this "technology" mechanism in Chapter 6.

In our speed chatting protocol, after chatting with each partner, players were given a minute to jot down notes on a piece of paper. After five of these "getting to know you" sessions, each player received a sheet of paper with the picture of each person he or she had just met and a series of eight personal questions about them: their age, their religion, their job, whether they had obtained their *baccalauréat* (the French high school diploma), the country in which they were born, the district in which they live, whether they are married, and their favorite hobby. Players were allowed to consult their notes. For each question, subjects provided their answer (or selected "don't know") and indicated whether they learned this information from their chat or simply guessed the answer. For each correct answer, whether it was learned or guessed correctly, subjects earned one euro. Finally, players were asked to report any additional information they had learned about their interlocutor, as well as whether they believed they could be friends with or feel comfortable recommending this interlocutor to an employer. Figure 5.1 illustrates a sample sheet for the speed chatting game.[3]

Interactions between players in the 2009 simultaneous trust game were "in the cold," and players could make inferences about each other—for example, their trustworthiness—based only on their first names, looks, manners, and cultural expectations. However, interactions after the speed chatting game, which demanded interpersonal social behavior, were different. All of a sudden, players became individuals known to each other. We therefore categorize interactions among players after the speed chatting game as those that occurred postsocialization.

The Voting Game

Following on the heels of the speed chatting game, the 2009 voting game was designed to procure information about trust and pure

QUESTIONNAIRE SUR LE JEU DE CONVERSATION
PROJET «COMPORTEMENTS DE JEU DES HABITANTS DE L'ILE DE FRANCE»
(Sciences-Po Paris, Université Paris 1 Panthéon Sorbonne, Université de Stanford)

Numéro d'identification : _____

Simone

Questions	L'avez-vous **deviné** ou **appris** durant le jeu de conversation?	Indiquez sur une échelle de 1 à 10 votre degré de certitude dans votre réponse (1 signifie que vous doutez beaucoup de votre réponse, 10 signifie que vous en êtes complètement certain)
1. Quel âge a cette personne? _____	Deviné / Appris	1 2 3 4 5 6 7 8 9 10
2. Quelle est sa religion? _____	Deviné / Appris	1 2 3 4 5 6 7 8 9 10
3. Travaille-t-elle à son compte? OUI / NON	Deviné / Appris	1 2 3 4 5 6 7 8 9 10
4. A-t-elle le Baccalauréat? OUI / NON	Deviné / Appris	1 2 3 4 5 6 7 8 9 10
5. Dans quel pays est-elle née? _____	Deviné / Appris	1 2 3 4 5 6 7 8 9 10
6. Dans quel arrondissement habite-t-elle? Si elle n'habite pas Paris, marquez "NP": _____	Deviné / Appris	1 2 3 4 5 6 7 8 9 10
7. Est-elle mariée? OUI / NON	Deviné / Appris	1 2 3 4 5 6 7 8 9 10
8. Quel est son loisir préféré? _____	Deviné / Appris	1 2 3 4 5 6 7 8 9 10

Figure 5.1. Sample sheet of the 2009 speed chatting game. From Claire L. Adida, David D. Laitin, and Marie-Anne Valfort, "Religious Homophily in a Secular Country: Evidence from a Voting Game in France," *Economic Inquiry* 53, no. 2 (2015), Figure 5, p. 1199. Copyright © 2015 Western Economic Association International.

altruism toward other players. Each player in each of the two teams of five players formed during the speed chatting game was asked to play two roles, sequentially.

First, each player was to be a voter, that is, to choose one leader from the other team, knowing that the leader would have the responsibility of dividing thirty euros between herself and her electorate in any way she wanted (including keeping it all to herself). Each voter received a printed handout with the pictures of each of the five candidates she was to rank in order of preference for the role of leader. Figure 5.2 illustrates a sample sheet for the voting decision.

Second, on a separate printed handout, each player had to indicate how much she would allocate to each of the members of her electorate, were she to be elected the leader. The player with the highest ranking in votes in each team became the leader, and her allocations were distributed between herself and the members of the other team and computed on their accounts that accumulated after each game. Figure 5.3 illustrates a sample sheet for the allocation decision.

As indicated, the voting game was meant to measure taste-based discrimination and/or statistical discrimination after the speed chatting socialization phase. Consider a mythical winner, Paul, and a voter, Jane. Clearly, Jane's decision to rank Paul first can be motivated by pure altruism toward Paul (that is, the willingness to increase the chance for Paul of being elected and of getting thirty euros no matter how Paul might allocate the award). It can also be motivated by trust, which is the belief that Paul is most likely to return a larger share of his thirty euros to the electorate or to certain members of his electorate. Similarly, Paul's decision, in his role as leader, to allocate a strictly positive amount to Jane can also be motivated by pure altruism toward Jane (that is, the willingness to increase Jane's payoff irrespective of Jane's electoral choice). It can also be motivated by belief-based reciprocal altruism, that is, the willingness of Paul to reward Jane based on the belief that Jane voted for him to be the leader.

The Dictator Game

After the voting game, subjects were ushered into a single room to play a dictator game. In this classic experimental game introduced by Kahneman, Knetsch, and Thaler (1986), players (the "donors") view pictures of people whom they have never met and are given money either to keep for themselves or to share with the person (the "recipient") whose picture they are viewing (being assured that the amounts accruing to each recipient will actually be transferred to them). There is no penalty for keeping the entire amount, and no

CHOIX DU CHEF DE GROUPE PARMI LES JOUEURS B
PROJET «COMPORTEMENT DE JEU DES HABITANTS DE L'ILE DE FRANCE»
(Sciences-Po Paris, Université Paris 1 Panthéon Sorbonne, Université de Stanford)

Numéro d'identification: ______________

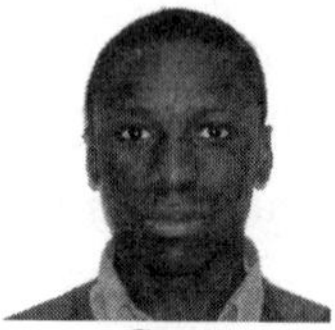
Gaston
____

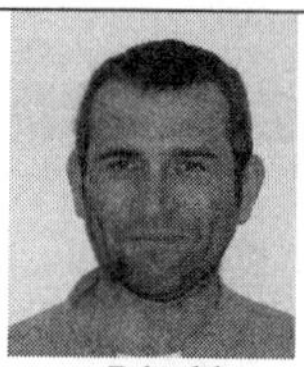
Rénald
____

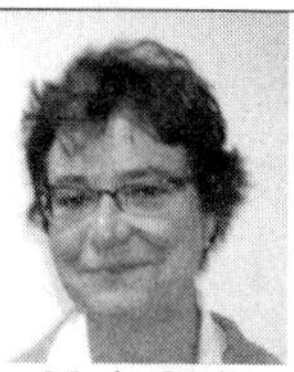
Marie-Cécile
____

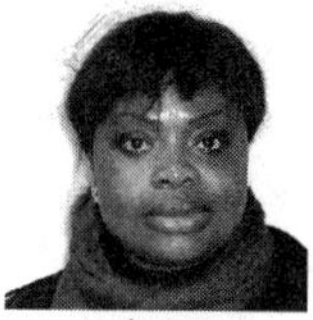
Astou
____

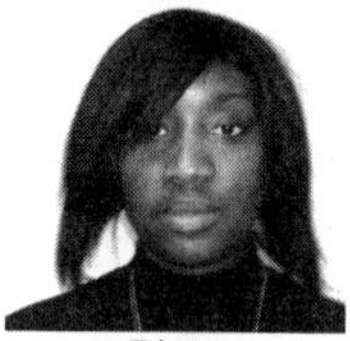
Bintou
____

1. Classez ces candidats au statut "de chef de groupe" par ordre de préférence:

   Rang 1 (votre candidat préféré): ______________
   Rang 2: ______________
   Rang 3: ______________
   Rang 4: ______________
   Rang 5 (le candidat que vous préférez le moins): ______________

2. Pour lequel de ces candidats décidez-vous de voter? ______________

Figure 5.2. Sample sheet of the voting decision in the 2009 voting game. From Claire L. Adida, David D. Laitin, and Marie-Anne Valfort, "Religious Homophily in a Secular Country: Evidence from a Voting Game in France," *Economic Inquiry* 53, no. 2 (2015), Figure 2, p. 1192. Copyright © 2015 Western Economic Association International.

DECISION D'ALLOCATION DU CHEF DE GROUPE PARMI LES JOUEURS A
PROJET «COMPORTEMENTS DE JEU DES HABITANTS DE L'ILE DE FRANCE»
(Sciences-Po Paris, Université Paris 1 Panthéon Sorbonne, Université de Stanford)

Numéro d'identification : ___________________

Imaginez que vous venez de recevoir 30 euros. Indiquez le montant que vous souhaitez donner à chacun de ces participants.

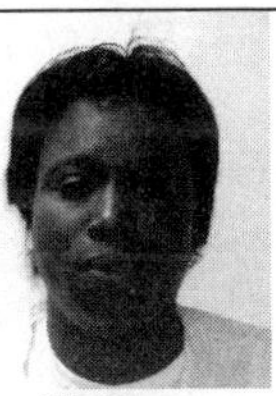 Thérèse _________	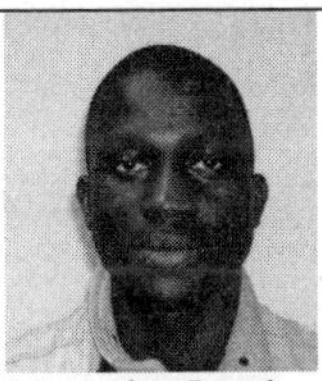 Mamadou Lamine _________
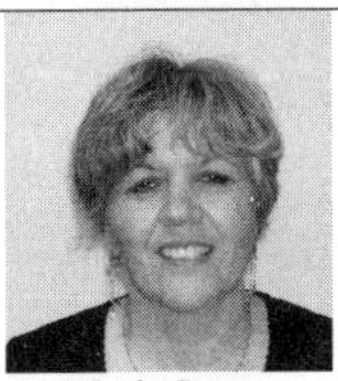 Marie-Laure _________	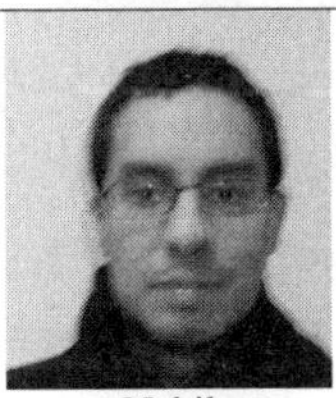 Nabil _________
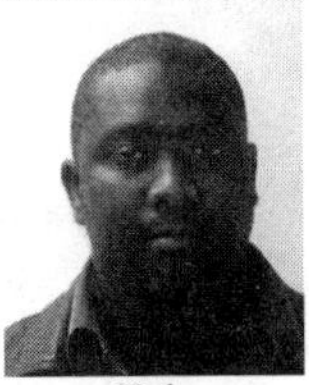 Kals _________	

Figure 5.3. Sample sheet of the allocation decision in the 2009 voting game. From Claire L. Adida, David D. Laitin, and Marie-Anne Valfort, "Religious Homophily in a Secular Country: Evidence from a Voting Game in France," *Economic Inquiry* 53, no. 2 (2015), Figure 3, p. 1193. Copyright © 2015 Western Economic Association International.

one can influence the players' donations: they are therefore, effectively, "dictators." This dictator game is the cleanest test of pure altruism toward others. Players indeed contribute money from their accounts to the account of someone they never met, whom they see only as a photo, and who has no say in the game. We can therefore compare the degree to which FFF players give to an African face with a Muslim ascribed name as compared with that very same face with a Christian ascribed name. The difference can only be one of taste, provided the donor's perception of the recipient's need does not vary across these two recipients.

In our adaptation of this classic game, all players were shown sequentially the same set of six partners (that is, the recipients) on a large screen revealing only their faces and ascribed first names, which we strategically altered as is commonly done in correspondence tests (see our résumé experiment in Chapter 2). Among the six recipients, two were apparent FFFs with Christian names, two were ambiguous with alternatively Muslim and Christian names, such that players could reasonably think they were FFFs with Christian names or North Africans with Muslim names, and two were apparent black Africans. For half of the sessions, subjects viewed one of the ambiguous recipients and one of the Senegalese recipients with a Christian name and the other ambiguous recipient as well as the other Senegalese recipient with a Muslim name; for the other half of the sessions, this was reversed. By doing so, we avoid any confound between the ethnic type of the recipient and the face of the recipient. Put differently, the fact that donors in different sessions see the same Senegalese face with alternated religious identities (one Christian, the other Muslim) allows us to hold the face of the recipient (and thus any donor's reaction to purely physical characteristics) constant in our analysis. Figure 5.4 illustrates the faces and alternating first names of our recipients in the dictator game.

The four non-Senegalese recipients were recruited from the Nineteenth District of Paris in a similar way as the 2009 players. As for the Senegalese recipients, they were recruited outside Île-de-France in order to ensure that they would not be recognized by our Senegalese donors. None of the recipients ever participated in our game sessions, and none was ever known personally by any of the donors. The donors saw the sequence of recipients only once and

V. 1	Sylvie	Georges	Khadija	Jean-Marc	Farida	Michel
V. 2	Sylvie	Mohammed	Joséphine	Jean-Marc	Christine	Aboubacar
Type	FFF	FFF/North African	SM/SX	FFF	FFF/North African	SX/SM

Figure 5.4. Variations in the ethnoreligious identity of the recipients in the 2009 dictator game. From Claire L. Adida, David D. Laitin, and Marie-Anne Valfort, "Gender Norms, Muslim Immigrants, and Economic Integration in France," *Economics and Politics* 26, no. 1 (2014), Figure 1, p. 84. Copyright © 2013 John Wiley & Sons Ltd.

were asked to make a decision to allocate $a = \{0, 1, 2, 3, 4, 5\}$ euros to each recipient—out of five euros allotted to them for each face. Again, given that the recipient has no say in the dictator game and that the dictator game was organized after the speed chatting game, differences in the donor's donation to the various recipients should be interpreted as differences in pure altruism after the socialization phase (again, provided the donor's perception of the recipient's need does not vary, a condition we verify in our analyses in Part III).

The Strategic Dictator Game

The 2009 strategic dictator game immediately followed the 2009 dictator game. The strategic dictator game consisted of asking players to guess the amount allocated in the dictator game to each of the recipients by one of the session's players—who unbeknownst to the players was always an FFF whom we call the "model."[4] Players were also told that the player who guessed closest to the actual decisions of this model would receive a prize of thirty euros. Players therefore faced a clear incentive to guess the model's allocation decisions as accurately as possible, guided only by their beliefs about FFF pure altruism toward different types of players.

The strategic dictator game therefore helps us determine the beliefs of our 2009 players about FFF pure altruism toward the various recipients in the 2009 dictator game. More precisely, it allows us to test whether SMs distrust FFFs more than do SXs, that is, whether SM expectations about FFF pure altruism toward SMs are significantly lower than SX expectations about FFF pure altruism toward SXs.

Additional Reflections on
Our 2009 Experimental Protocols

Three elements of our experimental protocol need to be made transparent, as they permit us to make our claims with greater confidence. First, the players of our games received substantial monetary rewards, assuring us that they were not merely giving answers at random or to comply with social desirability. For example, in the 2009 strategic dictator game, we asked one player (Player A) to guess how many euros a player in her session (Player B) gave to another player (Player C) in that same session. If we did not provide a reward for a correct answer (that is, what the actual transfer was), Player A has every incentive to guess randomly, as nothing is at stake. But a reward for guessing correctly changes matters profoundly. Player A now has an incentive to look at Players B and C and to think about how Player B might be assessing Player C. In other words, the reward allows for a revelation of Player A's true beliefs about Player B. Note that the substantial monetary rewards received by our players were also justified by the fact that each session of the games lasted about two and a half hours. It was thus important, in order to guarantee their continued focus, that the players could expect to be compensated for the time devoted to our experiments. Thus, each participant was able to win up to 148 euros, the equivalent, on a per-hour basis, of 8.5 times France's net minimum salary of about seven euros in 2009.

Second, we could never fully explain to the players the precise objectives of the games they were playing. We told them at recruitment that we were interested in how residents of Île-de-France behave when monetary rewards are offered, which of course is true. But they were not told that the experiment had anything to do with how FFFs interact with others based on those others' religion.[5] Moreover, throughout the experiment, we never primed religion. We simply allowed for the given names that were pasted on the players' chests to help players identify their game partners' religion.

Revealing our objective would have made the experiments too distant from the actualities of life in France, where others' religion may be known, but people are not programmed to condition their behavior on religious similarity or difference. Telling Player A that it mattered to us that Player B was of a different religion would have certainly induced Player A to wonder whether he was expected to behave differently toward Player B as compared with how he would have behaved in real life. We did not want to arouse these expectations, as they would contaminate our experiments. Fortunately, we were successful at hiding the real purpose of our research. After each session of the games, we asked players what goal they thought the experiments fulfilled. Only one of our eighty players voiced a suspicion that the experiment had something to do with interactions among individuals of a different religion.

Third, the sequencing of our games may raise a concern with contamination effects of previous games on players' behavior during the subsequent games. This is likely to occur if players learned about other players' game decisions once they were allowed to interact and communicate freely (during the speed chatting game). In our protocols, such contamination was highly unlikely. During our initial presentation of the experiments to the players, we emphasized that all game decisions would remain anonymous and private at all times. Notably, players were informed about their earnings and received them only after all the games had been played. Moreover, in our instructions for the speed chatting game, we stressed that players were to get to know—in French, "faire connaissance avec"—their speed chatting partners, meaning that players were instructed to find out information about who their partners were outside of the lab, not what their partners did during the previous game. Finally, we instructed all players to keep notes of their speed chatting conversations. In these notes, there is no evidence that game-behavior information was exchanged during player conversations.

Experimental Games of 2010

Our experimental results of 2009 left several key interpretive questions unanswered about how the FFFs might have been conditioning their behavior in the games we administered. We therefore went back into the "field" in March 2010 to resolve those issues. Here we describe the protocols for the five games we administered to FFF subjects sitting in front of a computerized set of tasks. The five games to be described below are (1) the names game; (2) the beauty game; (3) the strategic dictator game; (4) the double strategic dictator game; and (5) the incomes game. These games lasted roughly forty-five minutes and allowed the players to earn between 18.5 and 90.5 euros.

The Names Game

Because SX and SM players were indistinguishable to us on the research team in terms of dress and appearance, the only observable signals clearly differentiating our Senegalese players were their first names, which were written on a label pasted on their chests. The names of our SM and SX players are listed in Table 5.1. As should be

Table 5.1   First names of the 2009 Senegalese Muslim (SM) and Senegalese Christian (SX) players

SM player first names	SX player first names
Amadou	Cécile
Amie	Christine
Astou	Daniel
Awa	Ephigénie
Ciré	Gaston
Fatoumata	Hélène
Ibou	Louis
Ibrahima	Mamadou Jean
Kals	Nina
Khady	Robert Antoine
Mamadou Lamine	Thérèse
Moustapha	
Ndeye	
Ousmane	
Sidy	
Siré	
Tamsir	
Yacine	

Table source: Claire L. Adida, David D. Laitin, and Marie-Anne Valfort, "Muslims in France: Identifying a Discriminatory Equilibrium," *Journal of Population Economics* 27, no. 4 (2014), Table 8, p. 1060. Copyright © 2014 Springer-Verlag Berlin Heidelberg.

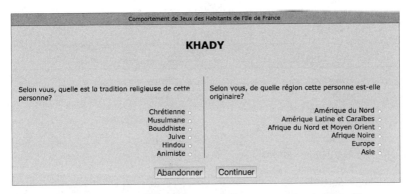

Figure 5.5. Sample screenshot for the 2010 name game. From Claire L. Adida, David D. Laitin, and Marie-Anne Valfort, "Muslims in France: Identifying a Discriminatory Equilibrium," *Journal of Population Economics* 27, no. 4 (2014), Figure 1, p. 1061. Copyright © 2014 Springer-Verlag Berlin Heidelberg.

apparent, all the SX players had names that are from the New Testament (which are common French names and no longer have a religious connotation), but none of the Muslim players did. From the point of view of the FFFs, therefore, the SXs had French names. However, the SMs all had foreign names, some of them sounding Muslim, others sounding more African. This raises a question: did SM and SX first names adequately signal their religious affiliation, or might they have signaled something else, such as foreignness? If we want to say something about the integration of Muslims in France, it is critical to test whether FFF behavior toward SMs is a response to SM Muslimness or to SM foreignness.

The names game helps us distinguish between these two possibilities.[6] The fifty FFF participants in our 2010 experiments were presented, sequentially, with a series of names among which appeared the names of our 2009 SM and SX players. For purposes of expediency, a random half of FFF players were shown half of SM and SX players' first names; the other half were shown the rest. For each name, FFF players were asked to guess the religious heritage of the person in question (Christian, Muslim, Buddhist, Jewish, Hindu, Animist). Figure 5.5 illustrates a sample screenshot of the names game.

The 2010 names game informs us that SX were unambiguously identified as Christians, consistent with the fact that they had names

Table 5.2   Categorization of the 2009 SM players' first names as SMM or
              SMA by our 2010 FFF players

SMM player first names	SMA player first names
Amadou	Amie
Awa	Astou
Fatoumata	Ciré
Ibrahima	Ibou
Khady	Kals
Mamadou Lamine	Sidy
Moustapha	Siré
Ndeye	Tamsir
Ousmane	
Yacine	

Table source: Claire L. Adida, David D. Laitin, and Marie-Anne Valfort, "Muslims in
France: Identifying a Discriminatory Equilibrium," *Journal of Population Economics* 27,
no. 4 (2014), Table 9, p. 1062. Copyright © 2014 Springer-Verlag Berlin Heidelberg.
   Notes: SM = Senegalese Muslim; SMM = Senegalese Muslims with Muslim names;
SMA = Senegalese Muslims with African names; FFF = French-born, French-born
parents, French-born grandparents.

that are common French names from the Christian Bible. However,
SMs were not unambiguously characterized as Muslims. More precisely, the names game allowed us to compute, for each SM first
name, the percentage of FFFs who identified it as a "Muslim" name.
Using this information, we created two subgroups among SMs:
SMM ("Senegalese Muslims with Muslim names") were those whose
first names were guessed as "Muslim" by more than 50% of the FFFs
answering that question; SMA ("Senegalese Muslims with African
names") were the remaining SMs. Table 5.2 shows that most of those
with first names of Arabic origin were considered as Muslims
(SMM).[7] By contrast, the remaining SMs (SMA) were considered as
Christians or affiliated with traditional religions.

   With this classification, we are able to compare, based on our 2009
data, how FFFs interact with those Senegalese they see as Christians,
those whom they see as Muslims, and those who are Muslims but,
due to their names, are not recognized as such. This allows us to
determine whether any discrimination is simply directed to nonas-
similated individuals (that is, those not having a name from the New
Testament) or whether it more specifically targets Muslims.

The Beauty Game

Results from the 2009 simultaneous trust game may be biased by the influence of facial traits. In an original interpretation of data from the trust game, Eckel and Wilson (2006) showed that attractive receivers are viewed as more trustworthy: they are trusted at higher rates by the sender and as a consequence receive more from him or her.

To estimate this bias, we asked FFF participants in our 2010 experiments to examine pictures of our 2009 players and evaluate their beauty, friendliness, and trustworthiness. More precisely, in this beauty game, FFF players were shown, sequentially, a series of photographs of our Senegalese and FFF participants in our 2009 experiments.[8] For each photograph, FFF players were asked to choose, for each of three pairs of adjectives (attractive/unattractive; friendly/unfriendly; trustworthy/untrustworthy), which adjective best corresponded to the photographed player. Six options were available for each pair. For instance, for the pair (friendly/unfriendly), the player could select: "very friendly," "friendly," "somewhat friendly," "somewhat unfriendly," "unfriendly," "very unfriendly." Figure 5.6 illustrates a sample screenshot of the beauty game.

We assign to each Senegalese and FFF player from our 2009 experiments the average beauty, friendliness, and trustworthiness scores assigned to them by our 2010 FFF players. This allows us to neutralize the influence of facial traits in our analysis of the 2009 simultaneous trust game.

The 2010 Strategic Dictator Game

In our 2009 protocol, we learned the beliefs of our Senegalese targets about how a typical FFF would allocate money to recipients of different religions. Absent was any information on the beliefs of the FFF players about how SMs and SXs would allocate to these recipients, which could have influenced their own allocation decisions.

We remedied this gap in the 2010 strategic dictator game in which the 50 FFF players were shown, sequentially, the photographs of

Figure 5.6. Sample screenshot for the 2010 beauty game. From Claire L. Adida, David D. Laitin, and Marie-Anne Valfort, "Muslims in France: Identifying a Discriminatory Equilibrium," *Journal of Population Economics* 27, no. 4 (2014), Figure 2, p. 1080. Copyright © 2014 Springer-Verlag Berlin Heidelberg.

some of our 2009 Senegalese players. Underneath the photograph, they were also shown the photographs of the six recipients from the 2009 dictator game. FFF players were asked to guess the donation of the pictured 2009 donor to each of the six recipients. Players received fifty centimes for each correct answer (and twenty-five centimes for any answer they gave for interactions that did not actually occur in 2009). Figure 5.7 illustrates a sample screenshot of the 2010 strategic dictator game.

Two versions of the game were prepared, but only one of them (randomly chosen) was selected for each player. The same Senegalese donor was ascribed a Muslim name in one version and a Christian

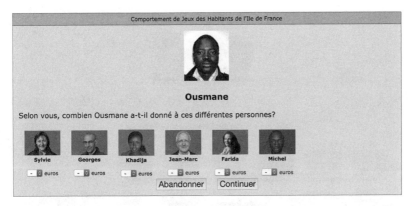

Figure 5.7. Sample screenshot for the 2010 strategic dictator game. From Claire L. Adida, David D. Laitin, and Marie-Anne Valfort, "Muslims in France: Identifying a Discriminatory Equilibrium," *Journal of Population Economics* 27, no. 4 (2014), Appendix, Figure A3. Copyright © 2014 Springer-Verlag Berlin Heidelberg.

name in the other. This allowed us to hold the face of the donor constant when we compared FFF guesses about SM donations to FFF recipients with FFF guesses about SX donations to FFF recipients. This comparison enables us to determine whether FFFs expect SMs (as compared with SXs) to show lower levels of pure altruism toward FFF recipients before socialization. Our 2010 FFF players were unaware that a speed chatting game had occurred before the 2009 dictator game.

The Double Strategic Dictator Game

The 2010 strategic dictator game provides information on what is known in the game theory literature as "first-order beliefs," for example, what an FFF player believes about the pure altruism of a SM donor toward an FFF recipient. But we wished to dig deeper than that and explore "second-order beliefs." In this case, we wanted to know FFF beliefs about Senegalese beliefs concerning FFFs. In other words, do FFFs expect SM beliefs about FFF pure altruism toward SMs to be more pessimistic than SX beliefs about FFF pure altruism toward SXs? If they do hold such second-order beliefs, this would

Figure 5.8. Sample screenshot for the 2010 double strategic dictator game. From Claire L. Adida, David D. Laitin, and Marie-Anne Valfort, "Muslims in France: Identifying a Discriminatory Equilibrium," *Journal of Population Economics* 27, no. 4 (2014), Appendix, Figure A4. Copyright © 2014 Springer-Verlag Berlin Heidelberg.

be indirect evidence of a form of statistical discrimination, in that FFFs would be basing their behavior toward Senegalese on their beliefs about how different Senegalese (Christian and Muslim) perceive FFF behavior toward them.

To implement this protocol, the 50 FFF players were shown the photographs of two of our 2009 Senegalese female donors, as well as of two of our 2009 FFF female donors. Underneath these photographs, they were also shown the photographs of the six recipients from the 2009 dictator game. Our 2010 FFF players were asked to guess the guesses of the 2009 Senegalese female players during the 2009 strategic dictator game about the amount that the 2009 FFF donor had transferred to each of the six recipients from the 2009 dictator game. Players received fifty centimes for each correct answer and twenty-five centimes for any answer for an interaction that did not actually occur. Figure 5.8 illustrates a sample screenshot of the 2010 double strategic dictator game.

As with the strategic dictator game in 2010, two versions of the game were prepared, but only one of them (randomly chosen) was selected for each player. In order to run an analysis that holds the face of the Senegalese player constant, we ascribed the same 2009

Senegalese player the Muslim first name "Aisha" in one version and the Christian first name "Monique" in the other.

The 2010 Incomes Game

We interpreted the results from our 2009 dictator game as reflecting altruism that differed across the religions of the recipients. But we could not rule out the possibility that the FFF donation was based at least in part on assumptions of the neediness of the recipients. In this case, observing that FFFs give less to SM recipients than to SX recipients may simply reflect that FFF view SX recipients as more needy than SM recipients, not that FFFs feel a stronger "distaste" toward SM recipients.

The purpose of the incomes game was therefore to get FFF beliefs about the relative neediness of the different recipients. In this game, we showed our 2010 FFF players the pictures of the six recipients from the 2009 dictator game with their ascribed first names and asked them to guess the monthly income of each of these individuals. Half of the FFF players saw the picture of the Senegalese female recipient and the picture of the Senegalese male recipient with the ascribed first names "Khadija" and "Michel," respectively, and half saw the picture of the Senegalese female recipient and the picture of the Senegalese male recipient with the ascribed first names "Joséphine" and "Aboubacar," respectively. This experimental setup allowed us to test whether, holding the picture of the Senegalese constant, FFFs reveal different beliefs about SM versus SX neediness. It thus permitted us to examine whether differences in allocation in the 2009 dictator game were explained by differences in pure altruism or rather by differences in perceived neediness.

Conclusion

We have now completed a description of the research that we conducted in France in 2009 and in 2010. We have described the identification strategy allowing us to make causal statements about the effects of Muslim religious heritage on integration in France (in Chapter 3). We then described the methods we used to procure samples of the identified actors, such that we could generalize our findings beyond the narrow group of subjects who participated in our studies (in Chapter 4). Finally, here in Chapter 5, we described the research protocols themselves. Readers will be able to refer back to these protocols when in Part III of this book we analyze the data allowing us to specify the mechanisms driving anti-Muslim discrimination in France.

PART III

Why Is There Religious Discrimination in France?

THERE IS DISCRIMINATION in France directed toward Muslims (as demonstrated in Chapter 2). We have systematically described a research plan (in Chapters 3–5) that would allow us to answer why that is. Part III, implementing that research plan, is devoted to an answer. In Chapter 6, the focus is on Muslims. Looking at the resources they bring to the table and at their norms, we analyze those that can legitimately be considered as problematic for a French firm's productivity and esprit de corps and are indeed claimed to be so by French recruiters. From this perspective, rational Islamophobia is apparent and has the potential to play a role in accounting for anti-Muslim discrimination. In Chapter 7, we focus on those whose families go back at least three generations in the French hexagon (the FFFs). There we find evidence of distaste for Muslims qua Muslims, meaning that FFFs discriminate against Muslims even when they do not expect any particular hostility from Muslims with whom they interact. In other words, Islamophobia is also nonrational.

Bringing together these findings in Chapter 8, we show that Muslims and rooted French jointly bear the responsibility for Muslims' integration failure in France: Muslims behave in a way that induces statistical discrimination, while rooted French distaste induces Muslims to sustain practices that the French find problematic. In other words, rooted French and Muslims are locked in a discriminatory equilibrium that leads to continued relative failure of Muslims (compared with matched Christians) to fully integrate into France.

6

Muslim Characteristics That Feed Rational Islamophobia

LET US RETURN to the poll first noted in Chapter 1 on "the image of Islam in France" that was conducted in 2012 by the French newspaper *Le Figaro*. In this survey, a representative sample of 1,736 from the French population were asked whether people of Muslim origin were well integrated in French society. Two-thirds of the respondents answered "no." Respondents were then asked whether French society was sufficiently open in welcoming Muslims. Here 69% answered "yes," meaning that the large majority of French shift the blame for the failure of Muslim integration in France on Muslims themselves. And indeed, among the reasons for this failure to integrate successfully (respondents could give several answers), "Muslims' refusal to integrate themselves" was pointed to by the largest share (68%) of respondents. Although it would be easy to write this off as unfounded prejudice, it is important to examine whether there is an empirical foundation for this viewpoint, to help explain the discrimination Muslims face.

In this chapter, we consider three elements of the Muslim presence in France that typically lead to a sense among French employers in particular and rooted French in general that Muslims are a threat to French firms and French society. The first has to do with their religious norms. The second has to do with their gender norms. The third has to do with their mastery of the host population's language.

Religious Norms

Although we dub France as a Christian-heritage society, the facts on the ground for it (and for nearly all Christian-heritage societies in the advanced industrial world) reveal a virtual absence of religious practice. As an illustration, although more than two-thirds of the French population identify as Christians, only 4.5% go to church every Sunday.[1] Moreover, according to the World Values Survey (2006), the average position of French respondents on a 1 to 10 scale, where 1 means that God has the least importance in one's life and 10 denotes the greatest importance, is 3.1. This is in marked contrast to the average Muslim respondent worldwide who, as shown by Fish (2011), is more religious than the average Christian respondent: the score of the former on the 1 to 10 scale is 9.5, against 8.1 for the latter.[2] Our 2009 survey confirms that Muslim immigrants are distinctive from their Christian counterparts in terms of religiosity. The mean score of SMs on the 1 to 10 scale is 9.0 against 7.6 for SXs.[3] The gap in religiosity between SMs and SXs is not specific to second- and third-generation immigrants. Relying on questions that ask them to report on the first migrant in their family, we find that SM first migrants were more likely to go to the mosque than SX first migrants were to go to the church.

This difference in religiosity has implications for integration, in particular in the labor market. In a work entitled *Allah a-t-il sa place dans l'entreprise?* (Does Allah have a place in the Firm?), Dounia Bouzar and Lylia Bouzar (2009), through a representative survey of French firms, analyze the ways in which Islam is understood in the workplace. Their study is based on 350 interviews with HR directors responsible for hiring and overseeing work teams. In these interviews, HR respondents reported proselytization and sanctioning of coreligionists for not meeting high religious standards among their Muslim workers only. One manager reported, "I have a team advisor *[conseiller]* who fasts and was aggressive to one of his colleagues [also a Muslim] who was not fasting when she brought and drank a hot chocolate in front of her work station. He downright insulted her for having dared to disrespect him. Afterwards, the team advisor needed to manage [the conflict]. . . . That disorganized the entire service for several hours. And then there is the issue of security, one never knows, things can slip *[ça peux déraper]*" (Bouzar and Bouzar 2009, 122). Another manager reported on a Muslim worker at a call center who turned the lights out for all work posts when the fast broke and demanded that fellow workers cease taking calls (Bouzar and Bouzar 2009, 122). To be sure, these examples are rare and extreme. A May 2013 survey of workers and managers organized by l'Observatoire du Fait Religieux en Entreprise (OFRE) and the contract staffing firm Randstad found that only a minority—28% of HR managers and 14% of floor managers— were confronted with these sorts of religious conflicts in their workplaces.[4] All but 6% of the problems were immediately solved on the floor. Still, these conflicts exist and are prevalent in the minds of HR recruiters. They can partly explain why Marie Diouf was systematically favored over Khadija Diouf in our 2009 correspondence test.

But French recruiters do not only fear proselytization. They also worry that Muslim workers, because they are more religious than their Christian counterparts, are more likely to advertise their religious affiliation. Expression of religious affiliation in public places, even if not ostentatious, is indeed considered by many in France as an unacceptable violation of laïcité. To be sure, 56% of French respondents define laïcité as "the possibility for each citizen to practice his/her religion."[5] But a large majority also believe that such expressions should be confined to the private sphere. As an illustration, the 2014 edition of the OFRE/Randstad survey reveals that 61% of respondents think that religious symbols must be proscribed from the workplace.[6] Bouzar and Bouzar (2009) confirmed that this view is widespread. They underlined the fact that only 10% of their interviewees defined laïcité as a juridical concept spurred by the 1905 law guaranteeing to all individuals liberty of conscience. For the others, laïcité is understood as an antireligious disposition validating the fact that all manifestation of religious beliefs by an individual is necessarily a threat to the freedom of conscience for all.[7] The following excerpts taken from the interviews are illustrative of the rather extremist view on this "essentially contested concept" (Gallie 1964) that prevails in the French firm:

> "La laïcité? C'est simple: pas de religion" [Laïcité? It is simple: no religion] (Bouzar and Bouzar 2009, 80)

> "Moi, je suis contre la religion, je suis laïque" [Me, I am against religion, I am secular] (Bouzar and Bouzar 2009, 81)

> "Attention, moi je suis choqué si je surprends quelqu'un qui prie. . . . Je ne laisse pas passer . . . Parce que je suis laïque. La loi de 1905 n'a pas été mise en place pour rien. On nous a demandé de laisser tomber toutes nos croyances et ça marche bien. On a bien réussi à s'en séparer." [I'm shocked if I pass by someone praying. I don't let this happen because I'm laïque. The 1905 law was not implemented for nothing. We are asked to drop all our [religious] beliefs and all is well. We do well by separating ourselves from these beliefs.] (Bouzar and Bouzar 2009, 81)

Muslims are today's principal victims of this radical view of laïcité. They are not only more religious than their Christian counterparts; expression of their religious affiliation is also more visible, even when it does not aim to be ostentatious. It is the foulard (headscarf) that set off a torrent of anger among FFFs.[8] To be sure, Christian women were asked by Paul to cover their head while praying.[9] But today, this has no relevance to public behavior in the Christian-heritage societies of the West. However, Muslim culture today follows more closely the admonitions of two suras in the Qur'an and an admonition in the Hadith asking women to remain covered in the public sphere. The visibility of the headscarf that is worn by nearly one-third of religious Muslim women in France (IFOP 2011, 27) triggers hostility among HR managers and workers. Bouzar and Bouzar (2009) reported on a union petition to management in regard to an employee wearing a headscarf: "The good diversity in the enterprise begins with the acceptance of diversity of opinions; yet, wearing a headscarf is like imposing your opinions" (Bouzar and Bouzar 2009, 105). One recruiter even reported that a young girl appearing at a job interview wearing a veil is his "nightmare" *(cauchemar)*. He recalled making up false reasons to dismiss her from the interview, such as "you live too far away," just to move on to the next applicant (Bouzar and Bouzar 2009, 60). Hostility toward the headscarf is not confined to French firms. It also concerns broader French society. In a survey conducted by IFOP in March 2013 (IFOP 2013), 84% of French respondents were opposed to the wearing of the Islamic headscarf by women working in places that are open to the public (among others, commercial enterprises, supermarkets, medical offices, nursery schools, and private schools).

Muslims' higher level of religiosity feeds Islamophobia. Notably, from the viewpoint of French recruiters, it poses a threat to the firm's esprit de corps that indeed induces among non-Muslim employees a radical view of laïcité. But the nature itself of Muslim religious practices also constitutes a source of statistical discrimination. Practices such as the fast, the call to prayer five times each day, and dietary restrictions can erect obstacles to the productivity and cohesion of the workforce in a way that is not matched by Christian religious practices. Although, as we show in Chapter 7, a considerable part of this perceived threat is exaggerated and thereby contains a non-rational component, we see here that there is a rational foundation to these concerns by French recruiters.

Let us begin with the Ramadan fast. More than 70% of French Muslims of both sexes and across the age spread claim to fast for the entire month, and this number is evidently growing by the year (IFOP 2011, 8). Bouzar and Bouzar reported on several complaints in regard to workers in their firm adhering to the fast. A manager of a call center with a significant labor force of Muslims reported that the number of calls that were administered declined by 10% to 15% during the month of Ramadan (Bouzar and Bouzar 2009, 77). The head of a building site told Bouzar and Bouzar (2009, 77) that a person who is lacking both food and drink (as typically occurs during Ramadan) is more susceptible to accidents, not only hurting himself but others as well. A team leader reported that he had to face up to a tired workforce during the fast. Overall, and especially in jobs where there is a need for precision or sustained activity, HR personnel fear that Muslims may fail to perform at acceptable standards for one month of the year. This fear is not matched for religious Christians. Notably, Catholics traditionally fast at the start and end of Lent,[10] but that practice in France has fallen into desuetude.

Daily prayer presents an equal challenge to HR personnel. To be sure, it is much less widely practiced, and much less so for the younger generation than the fast. Indeed, only about 39% of Muslims in France adhere to the strict regimen of five prayer interludes each day (IFOP, 2011). However, even with small numbers of enthusiasts, Muslim daily prayer presents a specific issue for managers. For them, the frequency of praying is not in itself consequential. After all, they easily accommodate smokers or coffee addicts who need more regular work pauses than religious Muslims. The conditions required for praying matter, however. Christian prayer during the day tends to be private; Muslim prayer requires paraphernalia and designated space that present a burden on managers, especially as the numbers of Muslims in the firm increase.

Food restrictions raise further issues for managers. As Max Weber (1946, 42) recognized in his writings on the sociology of religion, rules of commensality constitute a mechanism of ethnic separation and exclusion. Muslim practices permit consumption of meat only if the animals have been slaughtered according to Muslim rites (and designated as halal) and prohibit the consumption of alcoholic beverages or pork. These practices are widespread among Muslims in France: 74% report regularly buying only halal meats, and 67% of those who buy halal meats report that they are vigilant about other food products as to whether they meet religious standards (IFOP 2011, 17–21). Having Muslims in the workforce, as some managers claim, therefore means bearing the costs of proposing different menus when the firm has its own cafeteria. When there is no firm restaurant, having Muslims in the workforce is also costly, to the extent that Muslims are less likely to have lunch with their non-Muslim colleagues due to their different eating habits. This creates systematic separation within the work team at a time, lunch break, when a work team's esprit de corps is typically nurtured. This separation may be particularly strong in France where authentic French food is a hot-button issue. When one fast food chain in Marseille and other spots with a substantial Muslim population advertised that all its hamburgers would be halal, there was a brouhaha in the French media, as if this restaurant chain was the last bastion upholding French cuisine (Destelle 2010). This outrage as exhibited by the rooted French is well perceived by Muslim workers who share a sense that they are considered non-French if they deny themselves the foods and drinks many French see as essential for their national culture. In our ethnographic interviews, this theme received recurrent mention. One respondent, Abou (a Muslim Joola), reported: "I was working at an internship. . . . My hosts invited their friends over for a glass of champagne. Except that I do not drink champagne. There was a brief silence and discomfort. The host was a bit annoyed that I do not drink with them. Also, they often made me a dish with pork. I felt a certain irritation [among my hosts] when I told them that I don't eat it. There was a real discomfort."

Finally, Muslim holidays deviate from the French calendar. In the Christian-heritage societies of the West, religious festivals such as Christmas and Easter have become highly secularized and are treated as national holidays in which workers can celebrate without taking vacation days off. This is not the same for non-Christian religious holidays such as Yom Kippur for the Jews or 'Iid for Muslims. One HR manager in the transport sector reported to Bouzar and Bouzar (2009, 113), "For us, the management of the 'Iid festival is truly an annoyance [casse-tête]. In my network, half of my drivers ask to be absent at that time, how can I be assured of 100 percent service?" Here the HR manager might well want to limit hiring of Muslims to the benefit of Christians. Otherwise, he could be forced to operate under reduced service on days that are not public holidays and where, consequently, customers do not expect reduced service. In sum, Muslim prayer, Muslim fasting, Muslim culinary restrictions, and Muslim holidays are all incommensurate with the norms in a Christian-heritage society and present constraints to working together.

Gender Norms

In nearly all surveys that we have conducted or consulted, cultural (rather than political) norms reveal the most significant differences between Christians and Muslims. Norris and Inglehart (2003), in combining data from two waves (from 1995 to 2001) of the World Values Survey, created a normalized scale from 0 to 100 on a set of cultural values. On whether respondents approve of gender equality, the mean score for Western Christian respondents is 82; for Muslim respondents, it is 55. For approval of homosexuality, for Western Christian respondents, the mean score is 53; for Muslim respondents, it is 12. For approval of abortion, it is 48 for Western Christian respondents and 25 for Muslim respondents. Finally, for approval of divorce, it is 60 for Western Christian respondents and 35 for Muslim respondents. Using statistical tests comparing these means, the differences are highly significant. Most of these cultural issues revolve around issues of gender. Fish (2011), relying on the World Values Survey, found statistically different results across societies between Muslims and Christians when asked questions as to whether a university education is more important for a boy than for a girl; or whether men, when jobs are scarce, should have more right to a job than women; or whether, on the whole, men make better political leaders than women. In all these cases, Muslims show less favor to women. Brouard and Tiberj (2005, 88–89), relying on similar questions as in the World Values Survey but sampling solely in France, found a sharp relationship between the Muslim religion of respondents and conservative views about women's role in society.[11]

Our 2009 survey data, better able to identify a Muslim effect than is possible with the World Values Survey, reveal similar patterns. On questions such as whether men ought to get precedence for jobs when they are scarce, our SM respondents were much more likely to approve than were our SX respondents. But do these attitudes translate into differences in behavior toward woman? Here, it is in the 2009 dictator game that we have our most original and powerful results (see Chapter 5 for the protocols).[12] As readers might recall, each group of ten players sat before a screen that showed sequentially pictures of people to whom they were invited to contribute some (or no) part of the five euros given to them for each face. Figure 5.4 illustrated the faces and alternating names of our recipients. It shows, for example, that a random half of our donors could choose to give money to Khadija and Michel, while the other random half could choose to give money to Joséphine and Aboubacar. Khadija and Joséphine on one hand and Michel and Aboubacar on the other are exactly the same recipient: the only parameter that varies is their first name, one that signals a Muslim affiliation (Khadija and Aboubacar) and one that signals a Christian affiliation (Joséphine and Michel). This protocol thus allows us to measure, all else equal, pure altruism of FFF, SM, and SX donors toward (1) FFF recipients, both male (Jean-Marc, Georges) and female (Sylvie, Christine); (2) North African recipients, both male (Mohammed) and female (Farida); and (3) male and female recipients who are coethnics: Abou-bacar and Khadija for SMs, Michel and Joséphine for SXs, and Jean-Marc and Georges as well as Sylvie and Christine for FFFs.

Our analysis compares the extent to which SM and SX donors diverge from FFF donors in their donations to female versus male recipients. By so doing, it identifies—if it exists—the Muslim effect on behavior toward women. Our results, illustrated in Figure 6.1, reveal that SM donors (especially men) distinguish themselves from FFF donors in a way that SX donors do not: while both FFF and SX donors tend to favor women over men in several different contexts, male SM donors and female SM donors, marginally so, favor men over women instead.

These bar graphs tell a clear story of SM gender bias favoring males. Consider Figure 6.1, focusing on the three bar graphs down the left column (6.1A, 6.1C, and 6.1E), all reporting on male donations. We see that SM male donors consistently give more money to men than to women, whether the recipient is an average recipient (Figure 6.1A), a fellow SM (that is, a coethnic recipient) (Figure 6.1C), or an FFF recipient (6.1E). By contrast, both SX and FFF male donors consis-tently give more money to women. More precisely, SM donors give twenty-seven cents on average to women and seventy cents to men. Meanwhile, SX donors give 1.67 euros to women and 1.53 euros on average to men. These results hold up statistically in what is called a difference-in-difference test—comparing both SM and SX with FFF donors, the SM donors are significantly more generous to men, while the SX donors are not only more generous to women but statistically no different from the behavior of the FFF donors.

The trends are the same for SM and SX behavior toward rooted French (Figure 6.1E). Senegalese Christian and rooted French male

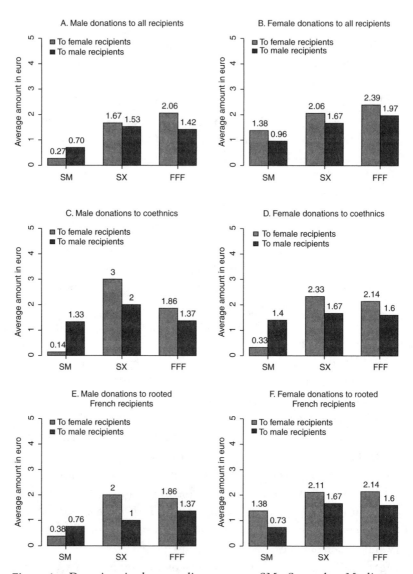

Figure 6.1. Donations in the 2009 dictator game. SM = Senegalese Muslim; SX = Senegalese Christian; FFF = French born, French parents, French grandparents.

donors both favor rooted French women over rooted French men: Senegalese Christian male donors give them on average one more euro, while rooted French male donors give them on average forty-nine more centimes. By contrast, SM male donors exhibit the opposite tendency, giving FFF men an average twice what they give to

FFF women. On average, SX and FFF behavior toward women converge, while SM behavior toward women diverges from the FFF norm.

Figures 6.1B, 6.1D, and 6.1F report on the donations of female donors. These average patterns are also revealing: SM, SX, and FFF female donors all tend to favor women over men—and thus do not differ significantly in this regard—except when it comes to coethnic donations. Here, SM female donors favor coethnic men over coethnic women, while both SX and FFF female donors favor coethnic women over coethnic men. More specifically, female SM donors give on average thirty-three cents to SM females, while giving 1.40 euros on average to SM men. Compare that with SX women. They give on average 2.33 euros to SX women and 1.67 euros to SX men. Just as with the men, the donation of SX women donors to SX recipients is not statistically different from that of FFF female donors to FFF recipients. The dictator game data thereby confirm that SM female donors diverge in their treatment of coethnic women from both SX and FFF female donors.

Our experimental data therefore complement survey-based results. Muslims do not only have less favorable attitudes toward women, they also act less generously toward them than do matched Christians.[13] Recruiters in French firms insist on the fact that these differences in gender norms matter for the productivity and esprit de corps of their enterprises, hence for their hiring decisions. One HR manager interviewed by Bouzar and Bouzar reported, "I have a coworker on my team who refuses to shake hands with a female. This creates enormous tensions in relationships. To shake one's hand, it's merely politeness" (Bouzar and Bouzar 2009, 122). Another reported that a worker "harasses his colleagues. To those women who wear skirts that are too short, he sends messages of reprimand or insult" (Bouzar and Bouzar 2009, 122). To be sure, these cases are rare, but the stories circulate like viruses, infecting religious relations throughout society. In this context, many FFF workers interpret the headscarf as a confirming signal of female submission to male dominance (and here we are bordering on the nonrational exaggerations that are the focus of Chapter 7). One respondent told Bouzar and Bouzar, "I am against carrying the veil because I'm for male/female equality, and against the submission of women" (Bouzar and Bouzar 2009, 94).

Another viewed the headscarf as attracting "attention [from a male supervisor, that] I am not your equal and I wear the veil to protect me from any impulses you might have" (Bouzar and Bouzar 2009, 94). A third expressed horror at the "bastards" [*salauds*] from Afghanistan who march down the street with a troop of women veiled in black behind them and concluded from this that "Never would I accept in my firm anything complicit with that" (Bouzar and Bouzar 2009, 95). The fact that Muslims show, on average, different gender norms therefore forms a basis for statistical discrimination on the part of French recruiters but also of the host society as a whole, which sees gender equality increasingly as one of its core untouchable values.

Language

Linguistic competence is also considered a sine qua non for most jobs.[14] Hence, if Muslims in France are less fluent in French than matched Christians, this would justify a rational basis for their disadvantage on the labor market. Two factors suggest that Muslims in France might indeed be less fluent in French relative to matched Christians. Former French colonies make up a substantial part of immigration to France from the global south. Whereas Muslims in these colonies were more likely to have enrolled in a madrasa (where Arabic would be the medium of instruction), the Christians flocked to mission schools that were operated through the French medium. As an illustration, data from Afrobarometer in Senegal confirm that the SXs master French more successfully than the SMs.[15] And once in France, Muslim immigrants pray in mosques where the language of prayer is Arabic; meanwhile, Christian immigrants frequent the church (far more than do the FFFs), where they are exposed to French. However, the church as a conduit for everyday social interactions between immigrants and rooted French turns out to be weak. In our ethnographic interviews, we learned that our SX informants who went to church reported that they rarely, if ever, see or meet FFFs on Sundays. As noted above, survey data show that very few FFFs visit the church on their day of worship.

It is not then surprising that our data provide only a weak support for a linguistic deficit by SMs as compared with the SXs. In our speed chatting game (see Chapter 5 to review the protocols), FFFs interacted with both SXs and SMs for three-minute conversations to get to know one another. We expected that the SXs, due in part to their linguistic advantage, would be better able to learn about FFFs and transmit personal information to FFFs than would the SMs. But our results reveal that FFFs performed equally well when quizzed about SM partners and SX partners. As for SM and SX players, they also performed equally well overall when quizzed about FFF partners. We detected a statistically significant difference in only one of the eight questions of the speed chatting quiz (the question on whether the game partner achieved a *baccaularéat*). In this case, SXs perform better than SMs at guessing whether their FFF partner had obtained their baccalauréat.[16] As for the 2009 survey, it is also only weakly supportive of the fact that SXs show higher proficiency in French. When we asked our surveyors about the language competence (in French) of their respondents, the SXs were judged to be more competent. On a scale from 1 (signifying weak mastery of French) to 3 (signifying normal competence in French), the mean score for the SMs was 2.909 while the mean score for the SXs was 2.969. Although this is statistically significant (at the 95% confidence level), the substantive difference is miniscule.

But let us put these limited findings from our linguistic competence data in perspective. For several reasons, these results are likely an underestimate of the Muslim effect in France. For one, in our experimental games, participants were selected in part based on their ability to follow instructions in French, which biased the SM sample in favor of French fluency. Moreover, as we emphasized in Chapter 3, our choice of Senegal for our sample was based on the historical observation that the French colonial state bent over backward to educate Muslims in French schools, and this was not the case elsewhere in the empire, where Christians flocked to missionary schools and Muslims to madrasas. Potential employers of a Khadija (from an immigrant background) could therefore infer that her mastery of French was inferior to the standard required for successful marketing skills, while inferring that Marie's linguistic competence in French, despite the immigrant background, would meet that standard. It thus remains a possibility that differences in the mastery of French favoring Christian immigrants from the former French empire remains a source of statistical discrimination disfavoring Muslims.

Conclusion

This chapter has focused on Muslim traits that could provide a rational basis for Muslims' relative failure in the French job market. On the one hand, high levels of religiosity in a self-proclaimed laïc society, male-favored gender norms in a society in which women have struggled for equal rights for a half century, and French linguistic weakness in a society that glorifies its language all feed into beliefs that Muslims will present problems as coworkers in French firms. These beliefs give HR personnel a sense that, all else being equal, Muslims will perform less well in their firms compared with Christians.

On the other hand, the radical view on laïcité enunciated by many French survey respondents is suspect. It has not much to do with the spirit of the 1905 law that was supposed to allow each citizen to practice his or her religion. Although the majority of French know the content of this law,[17] their persistence in interpreting it as requiring rejection of religious symbols in the public sphere, as we discuss in the Appendix, may well be a way for them to exclude Muslims from their midst out of distaste for them. In the name of laïcité, workers and managers in private firms are suspicious of women wearing the headscarf. In mid-summer 2014, also in the name of laïcité, the mayor of a city in a Paris suburb banned the presence of women wearing the headscarf at a popular leisure spot.[18] One can infer that it is distaste against Muslims that leads to these interpretations of laïcité that justify discriminatory behavior. Here in Chapter 6, our focus was on the rational foundation for anti-Muslim bias in France. In Chapter 7, we investigate whether the host population's distaste for Muslims constitutes a supplementary mechanism behind the Muslim disadvantage in France.

7

Evidence of Nonrational
Islamophobia

When there's one [Muslim], that's OK; it's when there's a lot of
them that there are problems.

—Brice Hortefeux, former French minister of interior[1]

WE LEARNED in Chapter 6 that there are Muslim traits
that feed statistical discrimination against Muslims. But is anti-
Muslim discrimination also taste based? Do we observe that rooted
French discriminate against Muslims even when they do not expect
any particular hostility from Muslims with whom they interact?

Our answer, as we develop it in this chapter, is yes. We proceed as
follows. In the first section, to identify whether anti-Muslim discrimination is taste based, we analyze the behavior of our subjects as
they played the simultaneous trust game. Our results show that,
while our FFF players do not distrust the SMs more than the SXs,
they are more altruistic to their coreligionists (the SXs) than they
are to those with whom they do not share a religion (the SMs). In
the second section, we examine FFF behavior toward SMs and SXs
after a period in which they met each other in informal discussions,
meeting the criteria of a potentially prejudice-reducing level of group
contact. We show that FFF distaste toward SMs (relative to SXs) is

somewhat ameliorated but still significant. Moreover, and this is shown in the third section, FFF distaste for Muslims is regenerated when the proportion of Muslims around them increases. Overall, we find strong evidence that Islamophobia in France cannot be deemed (and justified) as being only a rational response to differences in Muslim cultural norms and practices.

The Simultaneous Trust Game: A Matter of Taste

Social psychology has revealed a tendency among human beings to nonrationally discriminate against non coethnics from an outgroup. People tend to be more hostile toward outgroup members, even when they do not expect these out-group members to represent any real threat to them. Henri Tajfel (1970), a prominent social psychologist, demonstrated this tendency in a famous experiment (followed by a series of others) in which he showed his subjects a set of juxtaposed reproductions from the paintings of Wassily Kandinsky and Paul Klee. These subjects were asked for each Klee–Kandinsky pairing which painting they preferred. He then created two teams, one in which subjects preferred Klee's paintings in the majority of cases (this team was called the "Klee team") and one in which subjects preferred Kandinsky's in a majority of cases (this team was called the "Kandinsky team"). Subjects were informed of the logic behind this sorting. They therefore knew that group membership was not based on anything cultural, ethnic, or intellectual; it was as good as a random sorting. Third, each subject was given cash to distribute to two fellow players—one from each team—to reward them for their collective work. The results were unambiguous: subjects gave a larger share of the offering to members of their own team. In other words, the Klees discriminated against the Kandinskys (and vice versa) based on nothing other than a recently created identity reflecting no antagonism between the teams.

Do we observe a similar pattern in our experiments?[2] Do FFFs side with SXs (on their religion team) rather than with SMs even if they do not expect more cooperation from SXs than from SMs? We begin to address this question by relying on the first of our experimental games, the simultaneous trust game (see Chapter 5 for the protocols). In its basic outline, from our experimental group of ten players, we selected pairs of players from a protocol that allowed us to match every SM and SX with an FFF in both roles, as that of a sender and that of a receiver. Players were not told how many times they would play, with whom, or in what role. Recall that the sender was allocated three euros into her account and could give the receiver (sitting right across her at a table) any integer from zero to three euros but without the receiver seeing (or ever knowing) how much was sent. The receiver was then allocated three times what was sent by the sender, and this was deposited into his account. Simultaneously, the receiver had to decide whether to send any money back to the sender, from 0, to 1/3, to 2/3, or all of his tripled allocation.

In conventional interpretations of this game, as we outlined in Chapter 5, the amount sent by the sender is considered as a sign of trust, hence the name of this game. Conversely, the amount sent back by the receiver is interpreted as a signal of pure altruism and/or belief-based reciprocal altruism. Pure altruism refers to the receiver's willingness to be generous to the sender irrespective of what the sender does. Belief-based reciprocal altruism describes the receiver's willingness to be generous to the sender because the receiver believes the sender is being kind to him, that is, the sender is sending a strictly positive amount to the receiver.

As already emphasized in Chapter 5, differences in pure altruism by the receiver should reveal taste-based discrimination. By contrast, differences in trust on the side of the sender and differences in belief-based reciprocal altruism on the side of the receiver should reveal statistical discrimination. Hence, if we observe that FFFs discriminate against SMs as receivers but not as senders, then this will reveal FFF taste-based discrimination against Muslims.

We indeed found that FFFs did not distrust the SMs more than the SXs. On average, they sent 2.50 euros to the SX receivers and 2.48 euros to the SM receivers, an almost identical amount. However, the FFFs discriminated against the SMs in their role as receiver. They returned on average 39% of what they were sent by SM senders and 48% of what they were sent by SX senders (this difference is statistically significant).[3]

To further assure ourselves that FFFs did not hold different beliefs about the probability of SM as opposed to SX pure altruism toward FFFs, we ran a new experiment in 2010 (see Chapter 5 for the protocol for the 2010 strategic dictator game). In this game, we asked a new set of FFFs (with the same social and geographic characteristics of our original players) to guess how much each of the SM and SX donors gave to each of the faces in the previous year's dictator game. We learn from this game that FFFs did not hold different beliefs about SM and SX donors' pure altruism toward FFF recipients. These one-year-later complementary results add to our confidence that it was not beliefs about SM trustworthiness that was holding back the levels of return by FFFs to SMs in the trust game; rather, it was more a matter of pure altruism—or taste—in favor of the SXs.[4]

A possible objection can be raised with our interpretation that differences in FFF pure altruism toward SMs and SXs reflect differences in "taste." Perhaps FFF behavior in the simultaneous trust game is accounted for by the fact that FFFs view SXs as more needy than SMs. We therefore asked our second crop of FFF players (those recruited in 2010) to indicate what they thought was the monthly income of those SM and SX players whose pictures they saw on their computer screens. Our results reveal that FFFs guessed about equally across SM and SX players. This confirms that the lower amount sent back by FFF receivers to SM senders in the simultaneous trust game reflects taste-based discrimination, not difference in assumptions of the neediness of the sender.

There is one final worry in interpreting our simultaneous trust game results. How can we be sure that FFFs are conditioning their discriminatory behavior on the religion of their interlocutor? Recall from Chapter 5 that all the SXs had names that are from the New Testament (which are common French names), but none of the Muslim players did. From the point of view of the FFFs, therefore, the SXs had French names. However, the SMs all had foreign names, some of them sounding Muslim, others sounding more African. This raises a question: did SM and SX first names adequately signal their religious affiliation, or might they have signaled something else, such as foreignness? The names game that we conducted in 2010 again among our second crop of FFFs allows us to distinguish between two subgroups among SMs: SMM (Senegalese Muslims with Muslim names) were those whose first names were guessed as "Muslim" by more than 50% of the 2010 FFF participants; SMA (Senegalese Muslims with African names) were the remaining SMs. Our results were unambiguous. We found that FFF receivers sent back the same amount to SXs as they did to SMA (48% on average); however, they sent back only 33% to SMM. These results confirm that the difference in behavior of the FFFs toward SMs and SXs is based on a distaste specifically targeting Muslims, not simply those with foreign-sounding names.[5]

FFF Behavior Postsocialization: The Voting Game

FFFs display a distaste against Muslim players relative to matched Christians in one-shot interactions in which they know close to nothing about their game partners. Is this behavior altered by socialization? After the simultaneous trust game, our players got to know one another in the game we called "speed chatting." Although the goal of this game was to see whether communication was more effective among coreligionists (FFF and SX) than across religions (FFF and SM) possibly explaining why SXs did better in the French labor market, the game had a second purpose, namely, to provide a context of social contact between FFFs and SMs in which, perhaps, earlier prejudices would be ameliorated. We thus interpret the speed chatting experiment as a socialization treatment, especially oriented toward our FFF players.

After this socialization treatment, we administered our voting game. Here, as we foreshadowed in Chapter 2, our players were asked to vote for a team leader among the five other players they had just met in speed chatting. This leader would receive thirty euros in his or her account and could distribute it among those who voted (keeping as much as she or he wanted for him- or herself). Players were then required to indicate how much they would allocate to each of the members of their electorate, were they to be elected the leader. The player with the highest ranking in votes in each team became the leader, and her allocations were distributed between herself and the members of her electorate and added onto their accounts that accumulated after each game.

If the socialization phase had no impact on FFF distaste toward SMs, we would observe that (1) FFF voters were less likely to vote for SM than for SX candidates and that (2) FFF leaders allocated less to SM than to SX voters. If the socialization phase erased such distaste, FFFs would behave similarly toward SMs and SXs in the voting game, in both roles.

In fact, socialization did have a noticeable effect in reducing anti-Muslim discrimination on the part of FFFs. To be sure, there remained consequential coethnic favoritism, as we revealed in Chapter 2. This tendency did not escape FFF voters: an SX had a 27% chance of being chosen by an FFF voter compared with a 14% chance for an SM. However, in terms of allocation of funds, we find that socialization matters. Indeed, there was no substantive difference in the amount FFF leaders allocate to SM as compared with SX players. These allocation decisions reveal that differences in pure altruism of FFFs toward SMs and SXs were ameliorated, at least to some extent, after the socialization phase.

Bringing together our results from the simultaneous trust game and from the voting game, taste-based discrimination emerges in the form of lower pure altruism before our speed chatting game. But after the speed chatting game, which involves socialization, such discrimination appears to be milder: players simply seek to associate with people with whom they share a religion, though they are no longer more altruistic toward them, as the absence of difference in the amount allocated by FFF leaders to SM and SX voters indicates. This finding is in line with intergroup contact theory (Allport 1954), which predicts that contact opportunities with the outgroup attenuate prejudice toward the outgroup.

Reactivation of Distaste toward Muslims with Muslim Outgroup Salience: The Dictator Game

Yet, this amelioration of taste-based anti-Muslim discrimination by FFFs was short-lived. In the dictator game, which followed the voting game, we confirmed that FFF donors were as generous toward SM recipients as they were toward SX recipients. But this equal treatment by FFF donors was conditional. Indeed, an examination of the change in FFF behavior when there were changes in their environment—namely, the number of SMs in their session—yields evocative results.

We now ask what happens to FFF behavior once the proportion of SMs and SXs in the game session varies, in other words, when "Muslim outgroup salience" changes.[6] Here we aim at testing intergroup contact theory against group threat theory. Intergroup contact theory predicts that an increase in the relative size of Muslims attenuates FFF prejudice against them by providing more contact opportunities between FFFs and Muslims during the speed chatting game. By contrast, group threat theory (Blalock 1967) predicts that an increase in the relative size of Muslims should exacerbate FFF distaste toward Muslims. To determine which theory wins out, we took advantage of the fact that the number of SMs and SXs in our game sessions varied. This approach allows us to capture the effect of outgroup salience, by comparing the change in FFF donors' donation toward SM recipients when the number of SMs increases, with the change in FFF donors' donation toward SX recipients when the number of SXs increases. The number of SMs varied from one (in two sessions) to three (also in two sessions), whereas the number of SXs varied from one (in five sessions) to two (in three sessions).[7]

Did FFF donors behave systematically differently when they were in the room with one SM than when they were in the room with two or three SMs? We present results in Figure 7.1, relying on difference-of-means tests.[8] In Figure 7.1A, we find that a marginal increase in the number of SMs, holding the number of SXs constant at one, decreases FFF donations to SM recipients monotonically from 2.83 euros in sessions with one SM to 1.60 euros in sessions with two SMs to 0.75 euros in sessions with three SMs, while FFF donations to SX recipients do not evolve in any ordered form. In Figure 7.1B, the marginal increase in the number of SMs, holding constant the number of SXs at two, again yields a decrease in FFF donations toward SMs. By contrast, Figures 7.1C and 7.1D indicate inconsistent patterns of FFF generosity toward SXs when the number of SXs increases, holding constant the number of SMs. These difference-of-means tests bring to light a consistent decrease in FFF altruism toward SMs as SM numbers increase but no consistent change in FFF behavior toward SXs as SX numbers increase.

Yet, it is not certain that these results reflect an activation of FFF distaste against Muslims with Muslim outgroup salience. It could be that the decrease in FFF generosity toward SMs when SM numbers

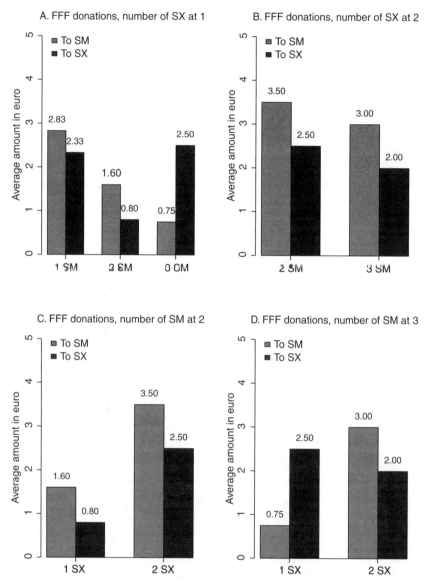

Figure 7.1. Donations of FFFs in the 2009 dictator game when the number of SMs and SXs in the room varies. FFF = French born, French parents, French grandparents; SX = Senegalese Christian; SM = Senegalese Muslim.

increase is a response to FFF expectations about a change in the behavior of other donors when SM numbers increase. Our data are not supportive of this story. FFF donors were indeed the only donors in the dictator game who changed their behavior when Muslim numbers increased. Still, FFF donors may wrongly believe that their change in behavior is not unique. Notably, FFFs might expect that SM donors are less purely altruistic toward FFF recipients than are SX donors because of higher coethnic generosity. This would impel FFF donors to give more to FFF recipients and hence less to SM recipients in order to compensate FFF recipients for decreasing donations when SM numbers increase. Again, our data are not supportive of this interpretation, as shown by the 2010 strategic dictator game (see Chapter 5 for the relevant protocol). This game allowed us to tease out FFF beliefs about SM and SX donors' donation in the 2009 dictator game. The analysis of such beliefs shows that FFFs expected the same intragroup generosity among SMs and SXs as well as the same generosity of SM and SX donors toward FFF recipients.

Our data are hence supportive of the fact that the presence of one additional SM in the room is enough to reactivate FFF distaste toward SMs after the socialization phase. We portray this result as the "Hortefeux effect." In 2009, then serving as minister of interior in the government of President Nicolas Sarkozy, Brice Hortefeux was attending a summer program to train party militants. At a photo op, he found himself in an intense political discussion with a young militant of North African origin, Hamid. Someone pointed out to the minister that Hamid appeared as French as any French person—that is, he ate pork and drank beer. This may have been an indirect way to criticize President Sarkozy's government for policies that appeared hostile to Muslims.[9] Mr. Hortefeux responded that Hamid "does not correspond at all to the prototype." Hortefeux's further reflection on Muslims—namely, on the problems that accrue when there are more than one of them, as quoted in the epigraph to this chapter—is precisely the reaction revealed by our data: a sense of nonrational cultural threat not when there is a single Muslim in one's social milieu but when there is more than one.

It is important to stress that, based on the 2009 strategic dictator game (see Chapter 5 for the protocol), we are able to test whether

FFF players were aware of the Hortefeux effect on FFF behavior. The 2009 strategic dictator game indeed allows us to tease out our players', and hence FFF players', beliefs about FFF donors' donation in the 2009 dictator game. The analysis of such beliefs shows that FFF anticipation of the impact of SM outgroup salience on FFF behavior toward SM recipients is significantly more negative than the impact of SX outgroup salience on FFF generosity toward SX recipients.[10] That FFFs believe that other members of their group behave like them has an important implication. It may provide implicit justification for all FFFs to act in conformity with the expected prejudicial behavior of coethnic members with an increase in Muslim outgroup salience. In other words, FFFs may consider discriminatory behavior toward Muslims in an environment with several Muslims around them as normal—so normal that former Minister Hortefeux could state it in a self-assured and unreflective manner.

The Sources of Distaste

Whereas Stigler and Becker (1977), as we noted in Chapter 1, were silent on the sources of distaste, we have conceived of these sources in terms of exaggerated fears of cultural threat, often leading to conspiracy theories as to what is likely to happen if a group begins to assert its will on the larger society. This sense of threat is reflected in a 2013 survey of a stratified sample of 1,189 respondents in France, in which 73% of the respondents revealed a negative image of Islam. This was far greater than any of the other religions that were presented to respondents. The results of this survey are graphically exemplified in a word cloud that compiled associations articulated by respondents to an open-ended question about the Muslim religion. In the cloud of compiled responses, the prominent words that appear are "fundamentalism," "intolerance," "fanaticism," and "terrorism," along with frequent mentions of "attacks" and "women." Hardly a positive image was recorded.[11]

The rhetoric of the Front National captures the exaggeration on the macro level. It pushes the center right to mimic its stereotyped vision, as exemplified by remarks attributed to Jacques Chirac, then serving as mayor of Paris but also a former prime minister and future president. Seeking to show sympathy for the typical French worker, Chirac imagined him on his front porch watching an immigrant family (clearly North African) "with a father, three or four wives, some twenty kids, drawing 50,000 francs in benefits—naturally without working. If you add to that the noise and the odor, the worker . . . goes nuts."[12] The Hortefeux effect captures this phenomenon on the micro level.

However, it is legitimate to ask how exaggerated is the threat? To be sure, and as we have already demonstrated, there are cultural differences between SMs and SXs, and these differences weigh heavily on HR personnel fearing threats to labor productivity. We might think it a clear and present danger to French society as reflected in the field notes from interviews of HR personnel as reported by Bouzar and Bouzar (2009). But this threat for firms in particular and FFFs in general is based on a distortion of cultural differences, a distortion that treats Muslim and French culture as polar opposites. A sober reading of the data, both ours and by other survey researchers, clearly shows that Muslim cultural differences do not translate into what Huntington (1997) has famously called "a clash of civilizations." Indeed, survey data suggest that Bouzar and Bouzar might be reflecting what Tversky and Kahneman (1982, 11–14) have labeled the "availability bias," which means overweighing one's expectations of the likelihood of an event based on a few spectacular instances of its previous occurrences.

Here we take two elements of the cultural threat discussed in Chapter 6 and evaluate their magnitude based on data from our 2009 survey. First we consider the notion of laïcité. Chapter 6 has shown that Muslims tend to be more religiously observant than are matched Christians. The question we pose here is whether this greater religiosity clashes with French laïcité. To answer this question, we turn to a measure in our 2009 survey that asked Serer and Joola respondents whether they think that laïcité is an obstacle to religious liberty. The four-point scale ranges from 1 (completely agree) to 4 (completely disagree). Our results are illuminating: SM respondents scored an average 2.94, compared with 3.07 for SX respondents. It is important to note that this difference is not statistically significant. It therefore hardly justifies a fear that Muslims qua Muslims are a threat to France's republican traditions.

Furthermore, in the more general survey of Muslim immigrants conducted by Brouard and Tiberj (2005, 37), the authors report that over 80% of their Muslim respondents see the term "laïcité" as either very or rather positive. Their findings indicate overwhelming support among French Muslims that "in France, only *laïcité* allows people of different beliefs to live together." They conclude by saying that "the equation 'more religious = less secular' does not generally work for French Muslims." Finally, although Brouard and Tiberj (2005, 27–28) confirm a greater intensity of religious feeling among the Muslims they sampled, they found no difference in frequency of worship across Muslims and Christians from immigrant backgrounds. Their general finding, along the lines of their book's title, is that Muslim immigrants, though distinctive in some respects, are otherwise "French like the others."

The second issue that reflects a genuine cultural difference is that of gender norms. Indeed, we reported from our experimental games significant differences in generosity toward women for our SM and SX players, with SMs favoring men and SXs—just like the rooted French players—favoring women. However, we should be careful to report that these substantive differences do not amount to opposing civilizational views or reflect incarceration of young women under male domination, as grotesquely exaggerated accounts would describe it. Consider the data from our 2009 survey. We asked a random half of our sample what level of education they aspired to for their senior daughters (or, if they did not have a daughter, imagining that they had one). The other half were asked precisely the same question about their sons. The answers ranged on a scale from 1 (no diploma) to 8 (diploma of higher education).[13] The mean score for SX and SM respondents for their sons was virtually the same, with slightly (but not significantly) higher expectations from the Muslim respondents: 7.43 for SMs and 7.33 for SXs. Meanwhile, the mean scores for SX and SM respondents for their daughters also did not differ significantly, though here the SXs reported slightly higher expectation levels: 7.53 for SXs and 7.34 for SMs. Even if one massaged the data with controls to establish a significant difference in gendered expectations of educational attainment across this religious divide, it would be a gross exaggeration to imagine these differences as justifying the stereotyped view of Muslims as misogynists. To be sure, there are cultural differences concerning gender, but these do not amount to a polarized divide between SMs and SXs.

Conclusion

In Chapter 6, we showed that there is room for statistical discrimination against Muslims in the French labor market: we identified Muslim traits, such as Muslims' higher religiosity, different gender norms, and poorer mastery of the French language—all of which can legitimately be claimed as problematic in the labor market and are claimed to be so by French recruiters. These findings are consistent with the widely shared view among the rooted population according to which Islamophobia is rational. However, putting all the blame of Muslims' integration failure in France on Muslims themselves does not take into account the full range of data. In this chapter, we therefore investigated whether Islamophobia is also unprovoked, or nonrational. To do so, we relied on experimental games. Our results are eloquent. First, we found that rooted French are indeed guilty of discriminating against Muslims even when they do not expect any particular hostility from the Muslims with whom they interact. Second, although a socialization phase mitigates FFF prejudice against Muslims, a subtler form of distaste persists: FFF players seek to associate with people with whom they share a religion, though they are no longer more altruistic toward them. Third, even after a socialization phase, FFF distaste toward Muslims is reactivated when the number of Muslims in their midst increases, in what we call the Hortefeux effect.

The results reported in this chapter have important implications for Muslims' integration in the French labor market. First, they establish that anti-Muslim discrimination is not only statistical; it is also taste based. This means that, even if French recruiters considered Muslim candidates as strictly identical to Christian candidates in terms of productive characteristics, they would still discriminate against Muslims, out of pure distaste. Second, the fact that distaste persists even after a socialization phase challenges the view, as we discuss in Chapter 10, that the anonymous résumé could be a solution to anti-Muslim discrimination. Surely, the anonymous ré-sumé is likely to increase Muslims' chances to be called for a job in-terview. However, we are skeptical that this tool could increase Muslims' chances of ultimately being hired. As indicated by our experimental results, French recruiters would likely keep on seeking to associate with coreligionists even after a job interview.

Third, based on the "Hortefeux effect" and its correct anticipa-tion by FFFs, it is likely that French recruiters also anticipate that an open employment policy would activate discriminatory behavior among their firm's employees and customers, with deleterious effect on these employees' and customers' comfort. In other words, even a French employer who has no particular distaste against Muslims will have a clear economic incentive to limit the number of Muslims in his firm. This "Hortefeux effect" therefore provides part of the an-swer to our question as to why Khadija fared less well in her ap-plications for a job on the French labor market, as documented in Chapter 2. We can now interpret firm behavior at least in part as stemming from a concern that if Khadija were hired, this would open opportunities for other Muslims. After some threshold of Muslim hiring is reached, managers would fear that the token Muslim would become a cascade, threatening the integrity of French cultural prac-tices that are the foundation of any firm's esprit de corps.

The research in this chapter suggests that there is a strong taste-based component to the discrimination by the FFFs toward Mus-lims. To be sure, Muslim gender and religious norms yield rational concerns about how well Muslims will integrate into French society. But these concerns reveal themselves in a grotesquely exaggerated form in France today as just reported. These reactions support our interpretation that discrimination against Muslims in France, as with the Catholic threat in seventeenth-century England (as noted in Chapter 1), is in part a matter of distaste.

And like the case of Catholics in England, the French have their own conspiracy theories. A novel published by Michel Houellebecq on the day of the January 2015 *Charlie Hebdo* attacks, called *Soumis-sion*, imagines France in the year 2022 when the Muslim Brother-hood, funded by Arab Gulf states, wins the presidential election, and inter alia the Sorbonne becomes the Islamic University of Paris-

Sorbonne; female faculty lose their positions; and those male faculty who convert to Islam can retain their tenure and take on several wives. This false equivalency between "Muslim" and "intolerance," and thus the nonrational discrimination that the French harbor against Muslims, is likely to be reinforced by events like the double massacre in Paris in January 2015 perpetrated by those claiming to act in the name of Islam.[14] The nonrational behaviors described in this chapter, we are suggesting, emerge from the unfounded exaggerations of small differences across cultures with conspiracy-based stories feeding fear and distaste. Although not rational (that is, not based on reasonable projections of evidence), there is, despite the claims of Stigler and Becker (1977), an accounting for (dis)taste.

8

A Discriminatory Equilibrium

Bᴿɪɴɢɪɴɢ ᴛᴏɢᴇᴛʜᴇʀ Chapters 6 and 7, we find that both Muslims and rooted French jointly bear the responsibility for Muslims' integration failure in France: Muslims display characteristics that leave room for statistical discrimination, while rooted French show not only statistical but also taste-based discrimination disfavoring Muslims.[1] In this chapter, we show that rooted French and Muslims are locked in a discriminatory equilibrium.[2]

By "discriminatory equilibrium" we mean a vicious circle in which both FFFs and Muslims in France are acting negatively toward one another in ways that are mutually reinforcing. We describe this equilibrium as follows: (1) Muslim immigrants display behaviors that feed into French statistical discrimination against them in the labor market (Chapter 6); (2) rooted French exhibit unprovoked taste-based discrimination against Muslims (chapter 7); and (3) Muslims, perceiving more hostility in France, separate more from the host society than do their Christian counterparts.

The purpose of this chapter is to demonstrate Point 3. We first provide evidence that Muslims perceive more hostility in France than do their Christian counterparts. We then show that, as a result, Muslims separate more from the host society. Finally, we stress the self-reinforcing nature of this discriminatory equilibrium: the Muslim disadvantage is not being ameliorated over time, and there is no prospect on the horizon for improvement in the relative Muslim position in French society (compared with their counterpart Christians) unless a strong intervention impels an equilibrium shift.

More Hostility Perceived by Muslim than by Christian Immigrants in France

All of our project methods—from experimental games to ethnographic interviews and a survey—demonstrate a perception of hostility by FFFs felt by SMs more so than by SXs.

Perceived Discrimination in the Strategic Dictator Game

The 2009 strategic dictator game (see Chapter 5 for the protocol) helps us determine the beliefs of our 2009 players about FFF generosity toward the various recipients in the conventional dictator game previously played. In Chapter 7, we discussed expectations of FFF players about a model FFF donor's behavior toward SM and SX recipients. Here we look at Senegalese players' beliefs about the amount FFF donors gave to SM and SX recipients.

Our results show that SM expectations about FFF generosity toward SMs were significantly lower than SX expectations about FFF generosity toward SXs. After neutralizing the impact of a wide range of confounds, we estimate that SMs expected about 1.06 euros less given to a SM guise from an FFF as compared with what an SX expected an FFF to give to an SX guise. This difference is statistically significant and substantively rather large, given that the range of possible donations spans from zero to five euros. In other words, our results reveal that SMs have less confidence in FFF generosity toward them than do SXs.

Interestingly, however, our data also reveal that this sense of SM higher distrust toward FFFs was not accompanied by SM expectations of FFF discrimination against uniquely themselves. More precisely, SMs did not expect FFFs to be less generous toward SMs than toward SXs. They simply expected, more than did SXs, lower FFF pure altruism toward both SMs and SXs.

Perceived Discrimination in Our
Ethnographic Interviews

This last result is consistent with the lessons we were able to draw from our ethnographic interviews. These interviews as discussed in Chapter 5 were conducted in 2009 and covered the assimilation patterns of nineteen SM families and twenty-two SX families in the four zones previously noted. In these interviews, only one of our SM contacts (Pape, a Muslim Joola) considered religion directly as the reason for the discrimination he keenly felt. In his interview, he dismissed the state's purported neutrality, telling us that the state and the media get very worked up when a Jew or a Christian is attacked, but they do not show the same concern when a Muslim is attacked. The state bans Muslim girls from veiling, but skullcaps and crosses are not as rigorously regulated, he emphasized. A few other of our informants, as will be discussed shortly, expressed keen awareness that their Muslim given names were a signal of foreignness facilitating FFF discrimination against them.

But in the bulk of our ethnographic interviews, religion rarely came into play for our SM informants. Abba, a middle-aged Muslim Joola, pointed out that while young Muslims often flaunt their religion, most people at work do not know that he is Muslim, and he is not going to go around broadcasting the fact. The majority of the stories concerning discrimination centered on the difficulties the respondents have had professionally, and nearly all were connected to race rather than religion. Skin color as a signal for discrimination was a common theme in nearly all our ethnographic interviews, should they involve SM or SX respondents. Robert (a Christian Serer) is a highly successful lawyer. Yet he is frequently mistaken for a lower-level lawyer in courtrooms instead of the lawyer in charge of his case. What really bothers him, though, is when he wins a case for a white client, and the client thinks—or so Robert surmises—he could have gotten a better outcome with a white lawyer.

Despite recurrent attributions of racial discrimination articulated by both SMs and SXs, our SM respondents were more likely to report on a vague sense of being unwanted in France. Mama (a Muslim Joola) was granted her citizenship by the socialist president François

Mitterrand for her work on women's rights when in Senegal. Although she says that France has been generous and has welcomed her, she feels she will always be a stranger in France. Maïmouna (a Muslim Joola) hopes for more success with French men. She feels that marrying a French man will give her more security: "It's not that a white man is better. It's that, here, they are at home and if we want to stay in their country, we must live with them, share our lives and even our beds!" This sense of being an eternal foreigner unless they do something drastic was a theme addressed almost uniquely by Muslims.

In sum, although SM respondents were more likely to report a sense of being unwanted in France as compared with SX respondents, only one of our SM respondents considered religion as the reason for such discrimination. By contrast, for those who reported the experience of discrimination, race was highlighted by a majority of SMs as the reason underlying that discrimination in France. This difficulty of SMs to figure out on which ground they are discriminated against by FFFs is easily understandable: as emphasized in Chapter 1, research on discrimination itself has so far been unable to disentangle a religious effect from other possible confounds such as race. Nonetheless, our ethnographies reveal that although they may misread the intentions of FFFs, they correctly expect more hostility from FFFs than do SXs when asked in open-ended interviews about feelings of discrimination in France.

Perceived Discrimination in Our Survey

Consistent with our experimental results and interpretation of the ethnographic interviews, SM respondents revealed higher levels of distrust toward French institutions than did their matched SX respondents in our 2009 survey.[3] We asked the respondents to report on the degree of trust they had for a set of seven different institutions. We then asked, for an overlapping set of institutions, whether they agreed with the claim that "French institutions treat individuals on an equal basis." Both sets of questions permitted answers that were scaled from one to four. For the trust question, a 1 means "fully trusts"; a 4 means "fully distrusts." For the question on equal treatment, a 1 signifies "fully agrees"; and a 4 signifies "fully disagrees."

Table 8.1   Level of SM and SX distrust in French institutions

Institution	SX (a)	SM (b)	Raw difference (b) − (a)	Regression-adjusted difference (b) − (a)
Schooling system	1.646	1.876	0.230***	0.380***
	(n = 127)	(n = 339)	(n = 466)	(n = 295)
Police	2.659	2.722	0.063	0.166
	(n = 126)	(n = 338)	(n = 464)	(n = 295)
Parliament	2.646	2.820	0.174*	0.313**
	(n = 127)	(n = 333)	(n = 460)	(n = 293)
Administration	2.183	2.473	0.290***	0.426***
	(n = 126)	(n = 334)	(n = 460)	(n = 295)
Judicial system	3.230	2.982	−0.248	0.357***
	(n = 126)	(n = 334)	(n = 460)	(n = 295)
Trade unions	2.024	2.291	0.267***	0.209**
	(n = 126)	(n = 326)	(n = 452)	(n = 289)
Private firms	2.206	2.385	0.179**	0.277**
	(n = 126)	(n = 330)	(n = 456)	(n = 291)

Source: Adapted from Claire L. Adida, David D. Laitin, and Marie-Anne Valfort, "Muslims in France: Identifying a Discriminatory Equilibrium," *Journal of Population Economics* 27, no. 4 (2014), Table 13, p. 1076.

Notes: Columns 1 and 2 report the mean value for Senegalese Christians (SXs) and Senegalese Muslims (SMs), respectively. Column 3 reports the difference between the mean values in Columns 1 and 2. Column 4 reports the difference between the mean values in Columns 1 and 2 once the impact of differences between SXs and SMs in terms of gender, age, education, and time elapsed since arrival of the first migrant to France is neutralized. Scale ranges from 1 (trust entirely) to 4 (distrust entirely). *, **, and *** indicate significance at the 90%, 95%, and 99% confidence levels, respectively.

To assess relative levels of trust toward French institutions, we asked about the schooling system, the police, the parliament, the administration, the judicial system, the trade unions, and private firms. Social segregation in France often implies very little interaction between FFFs and Senegalese. As a consequence, Senegalese rarely have clear opinions about FFFs as people. However, immigrants are constantly in touch with officials in state institutions and in private firms. Thus these responses about institutional treatment are good indicators of the SM and SX experience of acceptance by official France. Difference-of-means results are reported in

Table 8.2 Comparing SM and SX agreement that French institutions treat all on equal basis

Institution	SX (a)	SM (b)	Raw difference (b) − (a)	Regression-adjusted difference (b) − (a)
Police	1.910	1.825	−0.085	−0.218*
	(n = 122)	(n = 331)	(n = 453)	(n = 293)
Immigration authorities	2.034	1.923	−0.111	−0.265**
	(n = 117)	(n = 323)	(n = 440)	(n = 286)
Prefecture	2.458	2.265	−0.193*	−0.445***
	(n = 120)	(n = 324)	(n = 444)	(n = 289)
Judicial system	2.468	2.268	−0.200**	−0.318***
	(n = 124)	(n = 325)	(n = 449)	(n = 293)
Schooling system	3.112	2.825	−0.287***	−0.432***
	(n = 125)	(n = 331)	(n = 456)	(n = 292)
Pôle Emploi	2.669	2.461	−0.208**	−0.263**
	(n = 118)	(n = 310)	(n = 428)	(n = 274)

Source: Adapted from Claire L. Adida, David D. Laitin, and Marie-Anne Valfort, "Muslims in France: Identifying a Discriminatory Equilibrium," *Journal of Population Economics* 27, no. 4 (2014), Table 14, p. 1077.

Notes: Columns 1 and 2 report the mean value for Senegalese Christians (SXs) and Senegalese Muslims (SMs), respectively. Column 3 reports the difference between the mean values in Columns 1 and 2. Column 4 reports the difference between the mean values in Columns 1 and 2 once the impact of differences between SXs and SMs in terms of gender, age, education, and time elapsed since arrival of the first migrant to France is neutralized. Scale ranges from 4 (Yes, the institution very much treats all people equally) to 1 (No, the institution does not at all treat people equally). *, **, and *** indicate significance at the 90%, 95%, and 99% confidence levels, respectively.

Tables 8.1 and 8.2. As can be observed in Table 8.1, of the seven institutions we asked about, SMs in all cases were more distrusting, and in six of them, this difference was statistically significant with at least a 95% level of confidence.

As for whether the respondent considers that French institutions treat individuals on an equal basis, we inquired about the following six institutions: the police, the immigration authorities, the prefecture, the judicial system, the schooling system, and the Pôle Emploi, the French national employment agency whose advertisements we used for our correspondence test described in Chapter 2. Table 8.2 shows that, for all these institutions, SMs are less likely than SXs to agree that these institutions treat individuals on an equal basis. The raw differences are significant for four of them, that is, for a majority of the institutions. These difference-of-means results are reinforced when we run a regression analysis that allows us to hold constant the potential effect of SM and SX characteristics such as their gender, age, education, and time of arrival in France. The results increase in significance, showing on average that SMs are less likely to evaluate core French institutions positively in terms of equal treatment to all.

The results from the strategic dictator game and the survey reveal that SMs feel greater hostility from FFFs and French institutions compared with their SX counterparts. As we observe from our ethnographic interviews, perhaps SMs do not see this as a consequence of being Muslim and see it more in terms of their race (as Africans). But compared with the SXs (who are also Africans), it is the SMs who express more distrust toward French institutions.

Less Attachment to French Society and Greater Attachment to Home Country by Muslims

Muslims perceive more hostility in France than do their Christian counterparts. Does this induce Muslims to separate more from France than do Christians? Along with Constant, Gataullina, and Zimmermann (2009), we analyze immigrant insertion as the product of two dimensions: attachment to one's home country and attachment to one's host country. For these authors, the welfare-maximizing option is integration, which they define as strong commitment to the home as well as the host country, as this is the source of cultural enrichment for both immigrant and host populations. By contrast, marginalization captures a situation in which ties to the home country weaken but those to the host country do not develop. Assimilation is defined as the situation where ties to the home country erode but are strengthened in that of the host. Finally, when ties remain strong with the home society but never develop in that of the host, Constant, Gataullina, and Zimmermann (2009) call this separation.

Our survey data reveal that for the SMs, the logic of separation is powerful. Compared with SXs, SMs maintain stronger ties to Senegal and weaker ties to France. To be sure, this is an expected result when one focuses on first-generation SMs and SXs. After all, cultural differences between SM immigrants and the host population are objectively greater upon arrival as immigrants to France, as compared with cultural differences between SXs and the host population. Contrary to SMs, SXs share a common religion with the host population.

Data from our 2009 survey confirm a difference in integration between SM and SX first migrants. When asked about the first migrant in their family, SM second- and third-generation immigrants report, as compared with their Christian counterparts, a higher probability that this first migrant married (1) an African woman and (2) a coreligionist.

A similar pattern of SM withdrawal is observed in our 2009 experimental games in which mainly first-generation SM and SX immigrants participated: SM not only showed lower levels of trust but also lower levels of pure altruism toward their game partners in France, be they FFF, SM, SX, or other ethnic groups. As donors, SMs gave indiscriminately less to all recipients in the dictator game, despite the fact that SM and SX players were similar in terms of income and hence ability to donate.[4] This behavior is consistent with SMs being more attached to their country of origin and hence seeking to send or bring as much money as possible back to their community in Senegal.

One could offer an alternative explanation though. Maybe Muslims are simply inherently less altruistic than are Christians, which could constitute an additional source of statistical discrimination by French recruiters and society beyond those analyzed in Chapter 6. But experimental research to date provides no support for this interpretation. Notably, when dictator games were conducted in fifteen diverse communities in Latin America, Oceania, and sub-Saharan Africa, Henrich et al. (2010) found no difference in donations between Christian and Muslim subjects. Moreover, as we shall shortly see, SMs are at least as generous, if not more so, than SX when sending remittances back to Senegal.

In sum, data from the 2009 survey indicate a difference in integration pattern between SM and SX first-generation immigrants, which is confirmed by our 2009 experimental games. However, the 2009 survey also provides strong evidence that this difference in integration patterns is not confined to first-generation SM and SX immigrants. It also extends to second- and third-generation SM and SX immigrants. This is a surprising result given that convergence to the values of the host society is typically observed among the descendants of first migrants (see Giavazzi, Petkov, and Schiantarelli 2014). This finding suggests that SM higher separation in the second- and third-generation is, at least partly, a consequence of the discrimination they face and perceive in France.

But let us now detail these differences in integration between second- and third-generation immigrants. Table 8.3 reports differences in attachment to the country of origin between SM and SX respondents based on nine separate questions: whether they had ever been to Africa; whether they send remittances to Africa; the degree of sympathy they have toward Senegalese living in Senegal; whether the grandparents of the respondent's best friend originate from Africa; whether any of their civic association memberships are related to Africa; whether they believe they share much in common with people of the same country of origin as their family; whether they want to be buried in Senegal or in Africa as opposed to France; whether they own a home in Africa; and whether they disapprove of a Senegalese student who chooses not to renounce a scholarship in a top French university to take care of a sick mother in Senegal.

Our survey results show a consistent pattern of higher SM attachment to their home country relative to SXs. On all nine questions measuring attachment to the ancestral homeland—whether it be Senegal or Africa—SM respondents reported higher levels of attachment (and this includes remittances, a sign that SMs are not inherently ungenerous), with statistical significance for six of these indicators. The question of where the respondent hopes to be buried captures the heart of African beliefs as to their real identities (Attias-Donfut 2006, 74). On this question, 76.7% of SMs but only 43.7% of SXs answered Senegal (or Africa) as opposed to France. Equally impressive is the level of SM investment in their home communities even though they are on average poorer than the SXs. The number of SMs who report owning a home in Africa is nearly ten percentage points more than for SXs. And the number who report sending back remittances is 6.4 percentage points greater among the SMs.

Table 8.3 Comparing average SM and SX attachment to the country or continent of origin

Measure	SX (a)	SM (b)	Raw difference	Regression-adjusted difference (b)−(a)
(1) Visit: whether respondent has ever been to Africa	0.850 (n=127)	0.920 (n=339)	0.070** (n=466)	0.105** (n=295)
(2) Remit: whether respondent sends remittances to Africa	0.520 (n=127)	0.584 (n=339)	0.064 (n=466)	0.102* (n=295)
(3) Sympathy: degree of sympathy respondent has toward Senegalese living in Senegal	8.268 (n=127)	8.298 (n=329)	0.030 (n=456)	0.048 (n=292)
(4) Best friend: whether grandparents of respondent's best friend originate from Africa	0.504 (n=127)	0.634 (n=328)	0.130** (n=455)	0.188*** (n=290)
(5) Association: whether association to which respondent belongs is related to Africa	0.286 (n=42)	0.425 (n=134)	0.139* (n=176)	0.265*** (n=127)
(6) Commonalities: commonalities respondent believes s/he shares with people from Senegal	2.969 (n=127)	3.175 (n=338)	0.206** (n=465)	0.217** (n=295)
(7) Burial: whether respondent wants to be buried in Africa	0.437 (n=103)	0.767 (n=287)	0.330*** (n=390)	0.386*** (n=250)
(8) Home: whether respondent owns a home in Africa	0.795 (n=127)	0.891 (n=339)	0.096** (n=466)	0.134** (n=295)
(9) Sick mother: whether respondent disapproves of Senegalese student who does not renounce a scholarship in a top French university to take care of a sick mother in Senegal	2.276 (n=127)	2.361 (n=332)	0.085 (n=459)	0.096 (n=292)

Table source: Claire L. Adida, David D. Laitin, and Marie-Anne Valfort, "Muslims in France: Identifying a Discriminatory Equilibrium," *Journal of Population Economics* 27, no. 4 (2014), Table 1, p. 1046. Copyright © 2014 Springer-Verlag Berlin Heidelberg.

Notes: Columns 1 and 2 report the mean value for Senegalese Christians (SXs) and Senegalese Muslims (SMs), respectively. Column 3 reports the difference between the mean values in Columns 1 and 2. Column 4 reports the difference between the mean values in Columns 1 and 2 once the impact of differences between SXs and SMs in terms of gender, age, education, and time elapsed since arrival of the first migrant to France is neutralized. *Sympathy* is measured on a scale from 1 to 10. *Commonalities* is measured on a scale from 1 to 4. *Sick mother* is measured on a scale from 1 to 3. *, **, and *** indicate significance at the 90%, 95%, and 99% confidence levels, respectively.

Table 8.4 Comparing average SM and SX identification with French culture and society

Measure	SX (a)	SM (b)	Raw difference (b) – (a)	Regression-adjusted difference (b) – (a)
(1) Sympathy: degree of sympathy respondent has toward French people	7.619 (n=126)	7.404 (n=329)	−0.215 (n=455)	−0.673*** (n=291)
(2) No conflict: whether respondent believes immigrants should do everything possible to avoid conflict with host society	0.593 (n=123)	0.500 (n=326)	−0.093* (n=449)	−0.135** (n=286)
(3) Best friend: whether grandparents of respondent's best friend originate from France	0.394 (n=127)	0.201 (n=328)	−0.193*** (n=455)	−0.262*** (n=290)
(4) Left-right: whether respondent's political preferences can be positioned on typical left-wing/right-wing scale	0.752 (n=117)	0.615 (n=312)	−0.137*** (n=429)	−0.176*** (n=276)
(5) Commonalities: commonalities respondent believes s/he shares with French people	2.888 (n=125)	2.713 (n=335)	−0.175** (n=460)	−0.173* (n=292)
(6) Burial: whether respondent wants to be buried in France	0.485 (n=103)	0.160 (n=287)	−0.325*** (n=390)	−0.357*** (n=250)
(7) Hide father: whether respondent approves of a man of Senegalese origin who hides from his white son's friends so they may believe son is rooted French	1.325 (n=126)	1.203 (n=335)	−0.122*** (n=461)	−0.223*** (n=294)

Table source: Claire L. Adida, David D. Laitin, and Marie-Anne Valfort, "Muslims in France: Identifying a Discriminatory Equilibrium," *Journal of Population Economics* 27, no. 4 (2014), Table 2, p. 1047. Copyright © 2014 Springer-Verlag Berlin Heidelberg.

Notes: Columns 1 and 2 report the mean value for Senegalese Christians (SXs) and Senegalese Muslims (SMs), respectively. Column 3 reports the difference between the mean values in Columns 1 and 2. Column 4 reports the difference between the mean values in Columns 1 and 2 once the impact of differences between SXs and SMs in terms of gender, age, education, and time elapsed since arrival of the first migrant to France is neutralized. *Sympathy* is measured on a scale from 1 to 10. *Commonalities* is measured on a scale from 1 to 4. *Hide father* is measured on a scale from 1 to 3. *, **, and *** indicate significance at the 90%, 95%, and 99% confidence levels, respectively.

Let us now analyze our respondents' identification with French culture and society. Such identification constitutes the second dimension that allows us to characterize the insertion of SM and SX immigrants in France. This dimension is based on seven questions capturing the degree of sympathy the respondent has toward French people: whether the respondent believes that immigrants should do whatever possible to avoid conflict with the host society; whether the grandparents of the respondent's best friend originate from France; whether the respondent shows political preferences that can be positioned on a typical left-wing/right-wing scale, reflecting an understanding of the political divide in European politics; whether the respondent considers that he or she shares much in common with French people; whether the respondent wants to be buried in France; and whether the respondent approves of a scenario whereby a man of Senegalese origin hides from his white son's friends so that they may believe the son is rooted French.

Answers to all seven questions are reported in Table 8.4. They reveal a closer (and statistically significant) identification with French culture and society by the SXs as compared with the SMs. Particularly noticeable is the nineteen percentage points higher likelihood of the SX respondents to report that their best friend comes from a rooted French household.

The strength of the respondent's identification with the host culture and society is further captured by the respondent's degree of secularization. We include measures of secularization because this is a key area of cultural difference between Senegal (the home country) and France (the host country). The World Values Survey (2006) reported that 13% of French respondents say that religion is very important to their lives; by contrast, the Afrobarometer Survey (2008), relying on the identical question, reported that 98.5% of Senegalese respondents say that religion is very important to their lives.[5] Therefore, immigrants who claim that religion is less important to their lives are plausibly identifying with the norms of contemporary French society. The degree of secularization in our survey is based on six questions: the importance of God in the respondent's life; whether the respondent would disapprove of his or her child marrying a religious other; the degree of sympathy the respondent

Table 8.5 Comparing average SM and SX identification with secular norms

Measure	SX (a)	SM (b)	Raw difference (b) – (a)	Regression-adjusted difference (b) – (a)
(1) God: importance of God in respondent's life	7.592 ($n = 125$)	9.006 ($n = 330$)	1.414*** ($n = 455$)	1.456*** ($n = 291$)
(2) Exogamy: whether respondent disapproves of child marrying religious other	1.880 ($n = 125$)	2.075 ($n = 335$)	0.195*** ($n = 460$)	0.174** ($n = 293$)
(3) Sympathy: degree of sympathy respondent has toward people of same religion	8.073 ($n = 124$)	8.360 ($n = 331$)	0.287 ($n = 455$)	0.331 ($n = 291$)
(4) Best friend: whether respondent's best friend is of same religion	0.589 ($n = 124$)	0.675 ($n = 320$)	0.086* ($n = 444$)	0.107* ($n = 287$)
(5) Association: whether the association respondent belongs to is related to religion	0.071 ($n = 42$)	0.127 ($n = 134$)	0.056 ($n = 176$)	0.048 ($n = 127$)
(6) Commonalities: whether respondent believes s/he shares commonalities with people of same religion	2.912 ($n = 125$)	3.190 ($n = 336$)	0.278*** ($n = 461$)	0.272** ($n = 291$)

Table source: Claire L. Adida, David D. Laitin, and Marie-Anne Valfort, "Muslims in France: Identifying a Discriminatory Equilibrium," *Journal of Population Economics* 27, no. 4 (2014), Table 3, p. 1048. Copyright © 2014 Springer-Verlag Berlin Heidelberg.

Notes: Columns 1 and 2 report the mean value for Senegalese Christians (SXs) and Senegalese Muslims (SMs), respectively. Column 3 reports the difference between the mean values in Columns 1 and 2. Column 4 reports the difference between the mean values in Columns 1 and 2 once the impact of differences between SXs and SMs in terms of gender, age, education, and time elapsed since arrival of the first migrant to France is neutralized. *God* is measured on a scale from 1 to 10. *Exogamy* is measured on a scale from 1 to 3. *Sympathy* is measured on a scale from 1 to 10. *Commonalities* is measured on a scale from 1 to 4. *, **, and *** indicate significance at the 90%, 95%, and 99% confidence levels, respectively.

has toward people sharing the same religion; whether the best friend of the respondent is of the same religion; whether the association the respondent belongs to is related to religion; and whether the respondent believes he or she shares much in common with people of the same religion. In regard to identification with contemporary French norms about secularization, again we found that SM respondents are further from today's France.

On all six questions (see Table 8.5), and four of them significantly so, the SM respondents reveal less acceptance of secular norms than do the SX respondents. SMs reported the importance of God in their lives at about 1.4 points higher (on a ten-point scale) than did the SXs.

Our survey and experimental games tell a clear story. Compared with their SX compatriots, the SMs exhibit greater attachment to the homeland of their ancestors, a lower identification with French society, and lower adoption of the host country's secular norms. In sum, Muslims are separated from and therefore not fully integrated into France and its society.[6]

A Self-Sustaining Failure of Muslim Integration in France

The pattern according to which SMs separate more from France than do SXs is observed not only among first- but also among second- and third-generation immigrants. This suggests that Muslims' logic of separation is, at least partly, a consequence of the discrimination they face and perceive in France. In other words, that both FFFs and Muslims in France are acting negatively toward one another in ways that are mutually reinforcing captures the favorable conditions for a discriminatory equilibrium to emerge. If this interpretation is correct, we should observe that the integration deficit of descendants of the first Muslim migrants does not improve and even worsens with the time elapsed since arrival of these first migrants to France.

This is indeed what our data reveal. If anything, the gap between SM and SX integration tends to widen over time.[7] In Table 8.6, dividing our 2009 survey population at the median year of arrival of the family's first migrant to France (which is 1970), we can compare

Table 8.6 The evolution of SM and SX integration over time

Measure	Respondent family's first migrant arrived after 1970 (a)	Respondent family's first migrant arrived before 1970 (b)	Difference (b) − (a)	Difference-in-difference $(b-a)_{SM} - (b-a)_{SX}$
Importance of God				
SM	8.693	8.965	0.272	0.753*
SX	7.592	7.111	−0.481	
Whether men, when jobs are scarce, should have more rights to a job than women				
SM	3.052	3.186	0.134*	0.163**
SX	2.918	2.889	−0.029	
Mastery of French				
SM	2.948	2.915	−0.033	0.011
SX	3.000	2.956	−0.044	
Probability of sending remittances				
SM	0.574	0.720	0.146**	0.290**
SX	0.633	0.489	−0.144	
Probability of owning a home in Africa				
SM	0.870	0.932	0.062	0.166**
SX	0.837	0.733	−0.104	

Source: Adapted from Claire L. Adida, David D. Laitin, and Marie-Anne Valfort, "Muslims in France: Identifying a Discriminatory Equilibrium," *Journal of Population Economics* 27, no. 4 (2014), Table 4, p. 1050. Copyright © 2014 Springer-Verlag Berlin Heidelberg.

Notes: Columns 1 and 2 report the mean value for immigrants (SM and SX) whose first family migrant arrived in France after 1970 and before 1970, respectively. Column 3 reports the difference between immigrants whose first migrant arrived before 1970 and immigrants whose first migrant arrived after 1970. Column 4 reports the difference-in-difference between Senegalese Muslim (SM) immigrants whose first family migrant arrived before 1970 versus after 1970 and Senegalese Christian (SX) immigrants whose first family migrant arrived before 1970 versus after 1970, controlling for the immigrant's age, gender, and education level. It thus captures the evolution over time for SMs versus SXs. Scale ranges from 1 (not important at all) to 10 (extremely important) for the importance of God, from 1 (women should always have priority) to 5 (men should always have priority) for jobs, from 1 (very weak) to 3 (normal) for mastery of French, from 0 (sends no remittances) to 1 (sends remittances) for remittances, and from 0 (does not own a home) to 1 (owns a home) for owning a home in Africa. * and ** indicate significance at the 90% and 95% confidence levels, respectively.

intergenerational trends in values and behavior. Table 8.6 reports on these intergenerational trends, and on four of the five dimensions highlighted in the table, the gap between SMs and SXs widens across generations.

Take the importance immigrants attach to God. Over time (captured as the difference between b and a), this increases for SMs (from 8.693 to 8.965 on a 1 to 10 scale), while it decreases (from 7.592 to 7.111) for SXs. The difference in these over-time-differences, between SMs and SXs, is statistically significant at the 90% level of confidence.

On the question concerning whether men should have greater access to jobs than women when economic conditions are poor, we know that SM interviewees were more likely to report that "the men ought to have the first opportunities in such a case." What Table 8.6 reveals is that this trend is exacerbated with time (from 3.052 to 3.186 on a 1 to 5 scale) for SMs but alleviated with time (from 2.918 to 2.889) for SXs. The widening gap between the SMs and SXs is here significant at the 95% level of confidence.

On connections to one's homeland, the gap between SMs and SXs also widens significantly. Whereas SMs are more likely to send remittances home and to own a home in Senegal with time, among the SXs the trend is in the opposite direction. Therefore, the widening gap between SMs and SXs on both these measures is quite significant at the 95% level of confidence.

Finally, we note one area where patterns over time are not consistent with a widening gap between SMs and SXs: the immigrant's mastery of the French language. This variable, coded by our survey team, seems to move very little over time for both SM and SX immigrants.

Overall, the integration gap between SMs and SXs in France is widening, revealing a self-reinforcing separation of SMs from French society.

Conclusion

Chapters 6 and 7 have shown that rooted French exhibit statistical and taste-based discrimination against Muslims. Here in Chapter 8 we provide evidence that Muslims, perceiving more hostility in France, separate more from the host society than do their Christian counterparts. The conditions are therefore fulfilled for a discriminatory equilibrium to emerge in which both Muslims and rooted French act to reinforce beliefs that separation of the two groups will persist. And indeed, Muslims' rates of integration do not improve—they even worsen relative to their Christian counterparts—with the time they spend in France. Seeking a route out of that trap ought to be a principal public policy concern.

PART IV

Looking Beyond, Looking Ahead

In our previous chapters, we have shown that Muslim immigrants qua Muslims are discriminated against in the French labor market and that Muslims and the host population jointly bear the responsibility for this disturbing situation. Moreover, our results allow us to establish that rooted French and Muslims are locked in a discriminatory equilibrium whereby (1) rooted French exhibit taste-based and statistical discrimination against Muslims and (2) Muslims, perceiving more hostility in France, separate more from the host society than do their Christian counterparts. Consistent with this discriminatory equilibrium, a final result emerges in Chapter 8: Muslims' separation from France does not improve over time and even worsens.

In Chapter 9, we address whether these conclusions (at least those we are able to test) go beyond France. Have we identified a deep problem unique to France? Or can evidence of a discriminatory equilibrium be inferred from data collected more widely in Christian-heritage societies? By relying on studies that were not designed to rigorously identify a Muslim effect, we cannot make strong claims about religious discrimination faced by Muslims in these other societies. Nonetheless, as we develop in Chapter 9, our substantial results hold in the two regions in which information on immigrants from Muslim-majority countries was collected: Western Europe and the United States. These results support a more general understanding than what could be concluded from our France-based study, namely, that Muslim integration into Christian heritage societies of the West is by and large a failure.

What are the implications of our findings for public policy? That is the question motivating Chapter 10. The goal is to infer from the discriminatory equilibrium that we have uncovered what is most likely to lower the barriers to successful integration for Muslims in Christian-heritage societies. We examine policies at three different levels: the micro, the meso, and the macro. The take-away from this chapter is that an equilibrium shift requires positive action from both the host society and Muslim immigrants. Specific recommendations are then provided.

9

Beyond France: Muslim
Immigrants in Western Europe
and in the United States

THIS CHAPTER RELIES on two surveys that allow us to compare the integration patterns of Muslim and Christian immigrants from Muslim-majority countries. This strategy permits us to isolate a Muslim effect because it consists in holding the region of origin of the immigrants constant (Muslim-majority countries) while allowing their religion to vary (Christian versus Muslim). The first of these is the European Social Survey (ESS). Conducted every two years since 2001, this survey measures the attitudes, beliefs, and behavior patterns of a representative sample of respondents in seventeen Western European countries.[1] The second of these surveys is the Detroit Arab American Study (DAAS), a research project led by scholars at the University of Michigan. It was conducted in 2003 among a sample of 1,016 Arab American Muslims and Christians ages eighteen and older and living in the Detroit metropolitan area. The purpose of this survey was to analyze Arab Americans' attitudes and experiences since September 11.

With these data we are able to test whether two of our findings for France hold elsewhere: (1) Muslims qua Muslims are discriminated against; and (2) Muslims' separation from their host country does not improve over time, which is consistent with the existence of a discriminatory equilibrium. ESS and DAAS data confirm that both findings are observed in other Western European countries and in the United States. France is therefore not unique among Christian-heritage societies in which Muslim immigrants experience more discrimination and integrate less rapidly than do comparable Christians.

Integration of Muslims in Western Europe

The ESS data contain information on the country of birth of the respondent, as well as on the country of birth of the respondent's parents. These data therefore allow us to focus on first- and second-generation migrants from Muslim-majority countries now living in Western European countries. We define a first-generation migrant as someone who was not born in the Western European host country where the interview was conducted but who now lives in this country. A second-generation migrant is someone born in the Western European host country where the interview is conducted, with at least one parent born abroad. From these survey data, we isolate Christian and Muslim immigrants from Muslim-majority countries in order to compare their integration patterns. Our sample is composed of 2,604 respondents: 1,585 Muslims and 1,019 Christians.

Discrimination Faced by Muslims in the Host Country

Two variables in the ESS are related to the discrimination that immigrants may face in Western European countries. The first variable is subjective. It measures the perception of discrimination by the respondent. It is equal to one if the respondent "would describe [him- or herself] as being a member of a group that is discriminated against" in the country where the interview was conducted and zero otherwise. The second variable is more objective. It indicates the employment status of the respondent, which is likely to be affected by discrimination. It is equal to one if the respondent is unemployed or inactive and zero if she or he is employed. Indeed, discrimination may not only prevent people actively looking for a job from finding one (that is, the unemployed). It may also increase their probability of being "inactive" by encouraging them to exit the labor force, either to pursue further education or vocational training to improve their job opportunities or to simply abandon their search for a job (for example, by becoming a homemaker or retiring earlier).[2]

To be sure, neither the "felt discrimination" nor the "unemployed/ inactive" measure is fully satisfying. The perception of discrimination is problematic given that a group's feeling of being discriminated against may be disconnected from any actual discrimination. Moreover, discrimination is obviously only one of the many factors that influence individuals' employment status. We therefore rely on a third variable that combines the two previous measures in order to better capture the actual level of discrimination faced in Western Europe by immigrants from Muslim-majority countries. This third variable—which we claim is tantamount to actual discrimination— is equal to one if the respondent "would describe [him- or herself] as being a member of a group that is discriminated against" and if the respondent is unemployed or inactive. This variable is equal to zero otherwise.[3]

The values on this third variable for each subgroup of the ESS sample—the Muslim immigrant populations, the Christian immigrant populations, and the host populations (defined as the set of individuals with no recent immigrant background, meaning that they and their parents were born in the Western European country where the survey was conducted)—are displayed in Figure 9.1.[4]

Not surprisingly, we observe that Muslim and Christian immigrants show a higher mean value on each of these variables than does the host population, with the differences between the host population and each of the immigrant groups statistically significant at the 99% confidence level. But more important for our concerns, a clear Muslim effect emerges: Muslim immigrants from Muslim-majority countries face systematically higher discrimination than do their Christian counterparts; their joint probability of feeling discriminated against and of being unemployed or inactive is 11% (against 7% for Christians). This difference is also statistically significant at the 99% confidence level.

Still, one may worry that the results shown in Figure 9.1 are biased by the fact that Christian immigrants from Muslim-majority

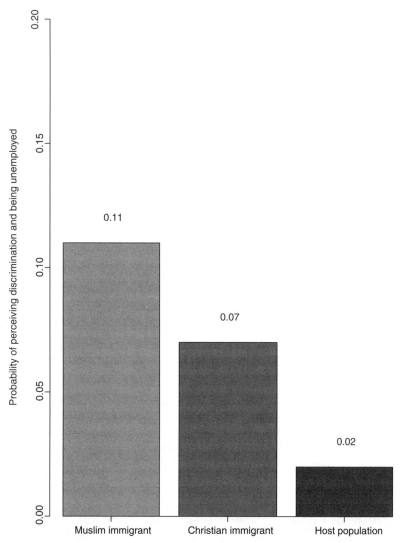

Figure 9.1. Comparing discrimination by host populations in Western Europe against Muslim and Christian immigrants from Muslim-majority countries.

countries are in fact "Europeans" by origin who either settled there since the colonial period or whose parents or grandparents did so in an earlier era. For instance, Christians from Muslim-majority countries in France who report that at least one of their parents was born in Algeria may be descendants of *pieds noirs*, that is, of French citizens who lived in French Algeria before independence. If this is the case, then our approach does not allow us to isolate a Muslim effect because it would also capture a broader cultural effect. Indeed, Muslim and Christian immigrants from Muslim-majority countries would differ not only on religion but also on their region of ancestry.

Of the forty-seven Muslim-majority countries reported in Table 1.1 (see Chapter 1), thirty-four are former colonies from one of the seventeen Western European host countries in our sample. Of these thirty-four countries, thirty-one (91%) were colonized by either France or the United Kingdom. The remaining three are former colonies of the Netherlands (Indonesia), Italy (Libya), and Spain (Western Sahara). To avoid the possibility that the results displayed in Figure 9.1 are driven by a colonial effect, we rerun our analysis after having excluded France and the United Kingdom from the set of host countries as well as Indonesia, Libya, and Western Sahara from the set of Muslim-majority countries of origin. Results that support Figure 9.1 remain unchanged after this exclusion, confirming that our strategy to isolate a Muslim effect is not threatened by the existence of former colonial relationships between the host and the home countries.

One last worry concerns the minority/majority status of immigrants in their country of origin. When we estimate the religion effect, Christian immigrants from Muslim-majority countries have minority status, whereas Muslim immigrants from Muslim-majority countries do not. Yet, belonging to the minority (rather than to the majority) in one's country of origin is likely to affect one's cultural adaptation skills. It may be that belonging to the minority sharpens such skills by forcing one to adapt to the culture of the majority. If this is the case, results displayed in Figure 9.1 would capture not necessarily a Muslim effect but simply the fact that as a minority in their home countries, Christians from Muslim-majority countries have developed a capacity for adaptation to the dominant culture better than their Muslim homologues.

To address this concern, we compare the integration patterns of Christians and Muslims from Bosnia-Herzegovina on one hand and from Lebanon on the other hand. Bosnia-Herzegovina and Lebanon

are indeed the two countries worldwide that have roughly equal proportions of Christians and Muslims. With this approach, we not
only hold the country of origin constant; we also neutralize the potential effects on integration that majority or minority status in the
home country may have. Note, however, that, while analyzing the
integration patterns of Muslim and Christian immigrants from
Bosnia-Herzegovina, we take care to drop from our analysis those
first-generation migrants who emigrated in the period of the Bosnian War (1992–1995). Indeed, by inflicting considerable suffering
on Bosniaks (Bosnian Muslims), this war is likely to have made them
feel more insecure than their Christian counterparts, not only in
their country of origin but also abroad. Such a feeling of insecurity is
expected to be associated with a higher perception of discrimination.
But such a feeling may also affect individuals' probability of being
unemployed due to lower self-confidence. To avoid this confound, we
focus on second-generation migrants and only those first-generation
migrants who arrived in Western Europe before 1992. Unfortunately,
due to a lack of precise information on the year of arrival of migrants
in the host country, we are unable to replicate this approach for Lebanon. We therefore use the entire Lebanon sample not knowing
whether they arrived before or after the Lebanese Civil War of 1975–
1990. But this is less of a worry given that this war, unlike the one in
Bosnia, did not bring special suffering to Muslims.

Although we are working on a small sample (roughly fifty and
seventy immigrants from Bosnia-Herzegovina and Lebanon, respectively), our results confirm the Muslim effect highlighted in Figure 9.1.
They show that Muslim immigrants from Bosnia-Herzegovina
and Lebanon are significantly more discriminated against in Western
Europe than are their Christian counterparts. The joint probability
of feeling discriminated against and of being unemployed or inactive
is 11.8% for Muslim immigrants from Bosnia-Herzegovina and
25.5% for Muslim immigrants from Lebanon. By contrast, this
joint probability is equal to zero for their Christian counterparts.
This difference between Muslim and Christian immigrants is
strongly statistically significant in both cases.[5]

Results from the ESS confirm that Muslims qua Muslims are discriminated against, not only in France but also in other Western

European countries.[6] Do they also show that Muslims' separation from their host country remains unchanged and even worsens over time, which would be consistent with the existence of a self-reinforcing discriminatory equilibrium beyond France? We address this question in the next section.

The Evolution of Muslims' Separation from the Host Country over Time

Muslim immigrants in France, as shown in Chapters 6 and 8, separate from their host country more than do their Christian counterparts by showing (1) lower secularization; (2) lower support for gender equality; (3) lower mastery of the French language; (4) lower attachment to France; and (5) higher attachment to their country of origin. The ESS allows us to test whether Outcomes 1 and 2 hold for other Western European populations whose modal citizens, like the French, are culturally secular and believers in gender equality. Beyond average differences, the ESS permits us to analyze how religious and gender norms of Muslims and Christians from Muslim-majority countries evolve over time.

To run this analysis, we rely on two questions. The first question asks the respondent how religious he or she is. The answer to this question is coded from 0 (very religious) to 10 (not at all religious). The second question asks the respondent whether he or she agrees or disagrees with the following statement: "When jobs are scarce, men should have more rights to a job than women," a probe widely used to assess gender norms among Muslims, as shown in Chapter 6. The answer to this question is coded from 1 (agree strongly) to 5 (disagree strongly).

Figure 9.2 compares the answers to both questions of Muslim and Christian immigrants from Muslim-majority countries and each of the host populations, controlling again for their gender, age, education level, household income, number of household members, year of interview, and host country characteristics. We observe that Muslim and Christian immigrants are more religious and less supportive of gender equality as compared with the host populations. Moreover, Figure 9.2 confirms the lessons from Chapter 6. Muslims

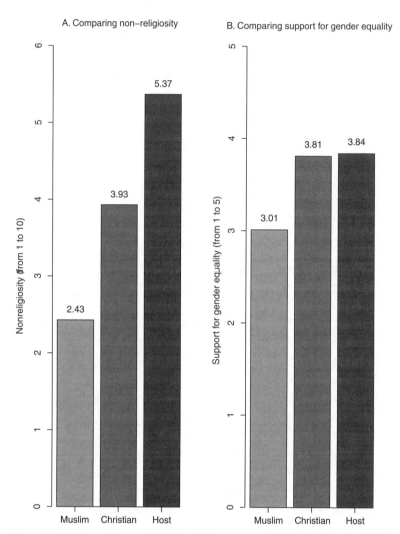

Figure 9.2. Comparing gender and religious norms in Western Europe of Muslim and Christian immigrants from Muslim-majority countries.

are distinctive with respect to their religious and gender norms as compared with their Christian counterparts. The Muslim immigrant's mean score on secularism (Figure 9.2A) is 2.43 as opposed to 3.93 for Christians. Meanwhile, the Muslim immigrant mean support for gender equality (Figure 9.2B) is 3.01 as opposed to 3.81 for Christians (whose score is not significantly different from that of their host populations). Both differences between the Muslim and Christian immigrant samples are statistically significant at least at the 99% confidence level.

Figure 9.2 clearly illustrates that, compared with their Christian counterparts, Muslim immigrants separate more from the host society in terms of religious and gender norms. And statistical tests confirm what we see. But how does this separation evolve over time? To address this question, one would be tempted to focus on first-generation Muslim and Christian immigrants only and to examine the impact of the time elapsed since their arrival in the host country. But we would not be sure of the validity of our results, which could be driven by a "dynamic selection bias," whereby differences in integration skills of Christians and Muslims who decide to migrate to the host country vary with their time of arrival. For instance, there is the possibility that Muslims who arrived earlier initially showed lower integration skills as compared with their Christian counterparts than did Muslims who arrived later. In this case, we would observe that the time elapsed since arrival in the host country coincides with an exacerbation of the difference in integration between Christian and Muslim immigrants. However, this would not necessarily capture a causal impact of the time spent in the host country. It could simply reflect the fact that differences in integration skills between Muslims and Christians vary with their date of arrival in the host country.

Instead of comparing different groups of first-generation immigrants based on their date of arrival in the host country, we compare first- with second-generation immigrants. To be sure, second-generation immigrants are likely to be descendants of first-generation immigrants who arrived before those first-generation immigrants who were surveyed by the ESS. This premise is confirmed by the fact that the age of first- and later-generation immigrants is about the same. In this context, if the parents of second-generation immigrants arrived in the host country with integration skills different from the integration skills of the first-generation immigrants surveyed by the ESS, meaning that a dynamic selection bias exists, our approach will still not allow us to fully identify the effect. Indeed, cultural values are transmitted from one generation to another. Still, to the extent that such cultural transmission from one generation to another is partial, we maintain that comparing the different generations of immigrants remains more promising than comparing groups of first-generation immigrants who settled at different times.[7] Children's values are not only inherited from their parents; the host country environment also shapes them (Nunn and Wantchekon 2011; Voors et al. 2012). In sum, as in previous studies (Bisin et al. 2008; Algan et al. 2010; Giavazzi, Petkov, and Schiantarelli 2014), our approach is not a panacea in that it does not allow us to completely solve the dynamic selection bias if it exists. Nonetheless, it does allow us to mitigate it.

How do differences in religious and gender norms evolve across first- and second-generation Muslim and Christian immigrants? Figure 9.3 displays differences in secularization and support for gender equality between Muslim and Christian immigrants from Muslim-majority countries, conditional on whether they belong to the first or second generation of immigrants, relying on the same set of controls as discussed for Figures 9.1 and 9.2. For Figure 9.3, we illustrate the mean value (on secularization and gender) for first-generation as well as second-generation Muslim and Christian immigrants.

The results reveal that the gap increases between the Muslims and Christians across generations. For secularism (Figure 9.3A), the mean gap is −0.99 for first-generation immigrants and −2.66 for the second generation. In this case, the second-generation Christian immigrants become more secular while the second-generation Muslims become less secular and even further from the host country mean. For secularism, the gap between Muslim and Christian immigrants is strongly significant for both generations, and the increasing distance between the two immigrant communities is also strongly significant, that is, the gap between the groups in the second generation is significantly higher (with an increase in distance of 1.67 points on the 10-point scale across generations) than the gap between the groups in the first generation.

As for gender norms (Figure 9.3B), we see again a significant difference between Muslims and Christians for both generations. Note that for both Muslims and Christians, second-generation migrants

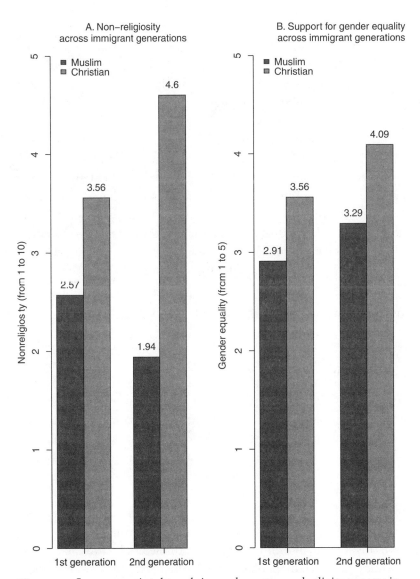

Figure 9.3. Intergenerational trends in gender norms and religious norms in Western Europe of Muslim and Christian immigrants from Muslim-majority countries.

are more supportive of gender equality than their first-generation coreligionists. However, second-generation Christians move more quickly in the second generation toward the host country norm than do the second-generation Muslims, and therefore the gap between Muslims and Christians is greater in the second generation than in the first. However, this increase in distance (of only 0.15 on the five-point scale) is not statistically significant.

We therefore find evidence in the ESS that Muslims not only separate more from the host country than do their Christian counterparts but also that this logic of separation does not improve and even worsens with the time these immigrants' families have spent in the host country. This finding is consistent with the fact that, as in France, Muslim immigrants and the host population in other Western European countries are locked in a discriminatory equilibrium.

Integration of Muslims in the United States

The question as to whether America is Islamophobic was posed on the cover of *Time* magazine in its August 30, 2010, edition, and the lead story focused on a wave of antimosque movements across the country. In *Time*'s poll of more than a thousand respondents, 25% doubted the patriotism of U.S. Muslims, and 61% said they opposed the construction of a mosque in the vicinity of Ground Zero, the site of the 9/11 attack on the World Trade Center. Journalist Bobby Ghosh (2010, 26), writing from Dearborn, Michigan, after reviewing examples of altruism toward American Muslims in distress, nonetheless concluded that "when it comes to Muslims and Islam, America's better angels are not always so accommodating."

In this section, by examining data from the DAAS, we can address the question of Islamophobia in the United States in a more systematic way. This study allows us to compare the perceived discrimination from the host society as well as the integration patterns of Muslim and Christian immigrants originating from the same region of origin (Middle East and North Africa). Among the original sample (1,016 individuals), 952 respondents reported their religion, their country of birth, and their parents' country of birth. Of these, 41% are Muslim (59% Christian). Moreover, the majority ($n = 691$) are first-generation immigrants (second- and third-generation immigrants comprise 261 individuals).

Is Detroit representative of the U.S. Muslim population? Our answer is that this is an exemplary population, and we cannot generalize to the entire United States from this.[8] Howell and Jamal's (2009) estimates reveal that Detroit has 42% Muslims among its Arab Americans; in the United States, this proportion ranges from 23% to 33%. In terms of concentration, 35% of the town of Dearborn, which is in the study area (population 99,000), is Arab American; no other city has a comparable Arab American concentration. As an example, for cities in America with populations of more than 100,000, the highest percentage of Arabs outside the study area is Sterling Heights, Michigan, with 3.69%. Detroit Arabs compared with Arab Americans nationally are less well educated and have arrived to the U.S. more recently. Only 72% of Detroit's Arabs have high school degrees, compared with 88% nationally; only 23% of Detroit's Arabs have an advanced degree while 43% of Arabs nationally do; 25% of Detroit's Arabs report annual income greater than $100,000 compared with 36% nationally; 24% have an income of less than $20,000 compared with 7% nationally. Yet, despite lower education, Howell and Jamal (2009, 75) point to the fact that in terms of public service, Detroit's Arab Americans "have a higher level of representation in municipal, county, and state government," but no national comparisons are provided. We therefore cannot see this study as representative of Arab Americans nationally, but we can see this as a possible bellwether of Arab American integration patterns in the United States.

Discrimination Faced by Muslims in the United States

Sixteen questions allow us to measure a respondent's perceived discrimination from the host society. Moreover, the DAAS contains a question on the employment status of the respondent (unemployed/inactive versus employed).

Arab American Muslims (as compared with their Christian Arab counterparts in the Detroit area) perceive higher levels of discrimination from their host society, as revealed in the data in Table 9.1. This table reports the difference in average answers to these questions

Table 9.1 Comparing Muslim and Christian Arab Americans on discrimination from the host society

Variable	Average		Difference
	Muslim	Christian	
A: Perceived discrimination from the host society			
(1) Distrust legal: how much respondent distrusts the U.S. legal system	2.20	2.11	0.09
(2) Distrust police: how much respondent distrusts the local police	1.88	1.68	0.20**
(3) Distrust Wash.: how much respondent distrusts the government in Washington	2.57	2.30	0.27***
(4) Biased news: how much respondent believes that news coverage of Arab Americans is biased	2.60	2.23	0.37***
(5) No respect Arab Am.: how much respondent believes that Arab Americans are not respected by American society	3.28	2.99	0.29**
(6) No respect co-rel.: how much respondent believes that coreligionists are not respected by American society	3.27	2.24	1.03***
(7) Verbal insult: whether respondent has experienced verbal insults	0.23	0.17	0.06
(8) Threat: whether respondent has experienced threatening words	0.11	0.08	0.03
(9) Physical attack: whether respondent has experienced physical attacks	0.00	0.00	0.00
(10) Vandalism: whether respondent has experienced vandalism	0.01	0.00	0.01
(11) Emp. loss: whether respondent has experienced loss of employment	0.03	0.00	0.03***
(12) Land of opp.: how much respondent disagrees with claim that United States is land of equal opportunity	1.90	1.58	0.32***
(13) Bad exp.: whether respondent has had a bad experience since 9/11	0.20	0.09	0.11***
(14) Not at home: how much respondent feels not at home in the United States	1.83	1.57	0.26***
(15) Feeling change: whether the feeling of not feeling at home in the United States has changed since 9/11	0.30	0.19	0.11**
(16) Suspicion: how much respondent seemed guarded, nervous or suspicious about the interview	1.49	1.39	0.10
B: Employment status: whether respondent is unemployed or inactive versus employed	0.44	0.29	0.15***

Notes: Across answers, observations range from 563 to 785. *Distrust legal*, *Distrust police*, and *Distrust Wash.* range from 1 to 4. *Biased news* ranges from 1 to 3. *No respect Arab Am.*, *No respect co-rel.*, *Land of opp.*, and *Not at home* range from 1 to 5. *Verbal insult*, *Threat*, *Physical attack*, *Vandalism*, *Emp. loss*, *Bad exp.*, *Feeling change*, and *Unemployed* are binary. ** and *** indicate significance at the 95% and 99% confidence levels, respectively.

provided by Arab American Muslims and Christians, pooling across all generations of immigrants. We control for their gender, age, education level, household income, number of household members, generation in the United States, and country of origin. This difference is statistically significant at conventional confidence levels for eleven of our seventeen tests. A typical result is exemplified on Line 6, which captures whether the respondent feels that coreligionists are not respected by American society. On a scale from 1 (reflecting respect) to 5 (reflecting no respect), the average score for Muslim Arabs in Detroit is 3.27; for their matched (through controls) Christian Arab counterparts, the average score is 2.24. The 1.03 difference is statistically significant at the 99% level of confidence. Moreover, Arab American Muslims are more likely to be unemployed or inactive than are Arab American Christians. On this question, 44% of the Muslim Arabs report unemployment or inactivity, whereas only 29% of matched (through controls) Christians report similarly. This difference of fifteen percentage points is also statistically significant at the 99% level of confidence.

Results from the DAAS suggest that Muslims qua Muslims sense that they are discriminated against in the United States. Do they also reveal that Muslims integrate less successfully, as would be shown if there were no catch-up over time with the level of integration of matched Christians?

The Evolution of Muslims' Separation from the United States over Time

ESS data allowed us to test whether Muslim immigrants in Western European countries indeed show lower secularization and lower support for gender equality than do their Christian counterparts. The DAAS permit us to go one step further and test the robustness of the following three additional results found for France: Muslims show (1) lower mastery of the host country's language; (2) lower attachment to the host country; and (3) higher attachment to their country of origin. Analysis of these three dimensions is reported in Figures 9.4 and 9.5 and Table 9.2, where we again control for the respondent's gender, age, education level, household income, number

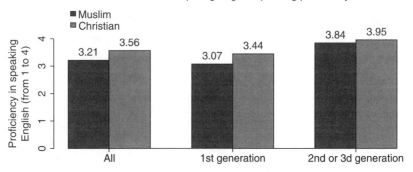

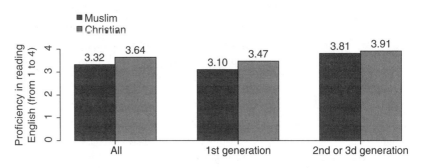

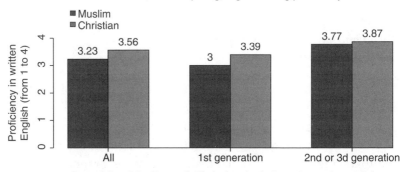

Figure 9.4. Comparing Muslim and Christian Arab Americans on proficiency in English.

of household members, generation in the United States, and country of origin.

Consider first the issue of language proficiency illustrated in the three panels of Figure 9.4. We see that on a four-point scale on language proficiency, first-generation Muslim immigrants have on average nearly a 0.4-point difference on speaking proficiency (Figure 9.4A), on reading proficiency (Figure 9.4B), and on writing proficiency (Figure 9.4C). These differences largely disappear in the combined second- and third-generation sample (with about a 0.1-point difference), though it remains barely significant for reading in English. In this case, we see some catch-up for Muslims across generations, as has been the case for language assimilation for all groups of immigrants in the United States since the earliest settlers.[9]

A somewhat less successful (but not strongly different) integration story for Muslims can be told for survey answers on Arab American Muslim and Christian attachment to the United States, their host country, as illustrated in Figure 9.5. On three of the four questions, whether having to do with the respondent seeing him- or herself as white (rather than as an Arab), or watching American news on television, or being proud to be an American, there is for both first- and later-generation respondents a significantly greater sense of attachment to the host country among the Christian Arabs. (There is virtually no evidence of exogamy for either group, so there are no differences to report on whether they had a spouse of American origin.) Worthy of mention (see Figure 9.5A) is our result on whether the respondent considers her- or himself of the white race: across generations the proportion of Christians who answer yes jumps from 74% to 78%. Meanwhile, the proportion of Muslims who answer yes falls from 58% to 48%.

The other two indicators, on whether respondents watch news on television (on a 0 to 1 scale and illustrated in Figure 9.5B) and on whether they are proud to be Americans (now on a four-point scale and illustrated in Figure 9.5C), show greater intergenerational catch-up by Muslim Arabs in America. On watching news, the gap drops from a difference of .05 points to one of .02 points. On the issue of pride to be American, both religious groups reveal greater pride in later generations, but the improvement from the first to the second

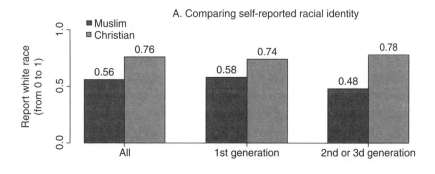

A. Comparing self-reported racial identity

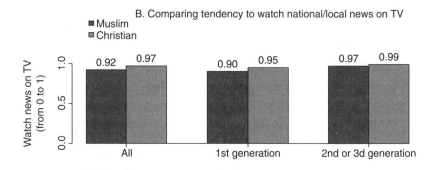

B. Comparing tendency to watch national/local news on TV

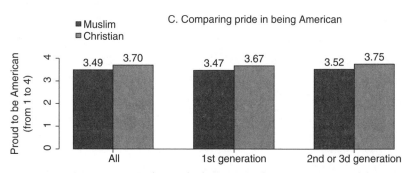

C. Comparing pride in being American

Figure 9.5. Comparing Muslim and Christian Arab Americans on attachment to America.

or third generation is greater for the Christian Arabs. The change across generations is not significantly different, but the base differences are at least maintained across generations.

On the third element of integration, having to do with attachment to their region of origin, we refer readers to Table 9.2. (With ten separate questions, presenting these materials is more efficient using a table.) In general, attachment to home country and culture is greater for Muslims than for Christians, and in several cases the differences between the two religious groups significantly increase across generations. Most prominently is the reported attitude on the importance of speaking Arabic. On a four-point scale, Muslims of the first generation are barely more supportive than Christians (3.55 compared with 3.52 on average). However, the Muslims of the later generations maintain virtually the same attachment to Arabic (with an average score of 3.44 on the importance of speaking Arabic), whereas the Christians drop to an average of 2.82. The evolutionary change in the difference is 0.59, and that is significant with a 99% confidence level. On the question of whether the respondent's spouse is of Arab-origin, the first-generation Muslims are more likely to say yes (98% versus 89%, and this is significant); and over time, this drops by five percentage points for Muslims but by twenty percentage points for Christians. This difference is substantively (but not statistically, due to low numbers who responded to this question) significant.

Overall, on the three elements of integration, Muslims show lower mastery of English language, lower attachment to the United States, and higher attachment to their region of origin. Moreover, comparisons across generations indicate that, in most instances, the significant differences we have identified between Arab American Muslims and Christians hold for both first-generation immigrants and second- and third-generation immigrants. Finally, Muslim higher separation remains largely unchanged from one generation of immigrant to another.[10]

Lessons from the DAAS therefore echo those from the ESS and from our research project in France: (1) Muslims qua Muslims are discriminated against; and (2) Muslims' separation from their host country does not improve at rates similar to non-Muslims, and in some cases the differences worsen over time. The data are therefore consistent with the existence of a discriminatory equilibrium.

Table 9.2 Comparing Muslim and Christian Arab Americans on attachment to their region of origin

Variable	All (a) (1)	1st generation (b) (2)	2nd or 3rd generation (c) (3)	Evolution (c) − (b) (4)
(1) Arab race: whether respondent reports to be Arab rather than white or any other race	0.36 − 0.21 = 0.15***	0.33 − 0.22 = 0.11**	0.49 − 0.20 = 0.29***	+0.18*
(2) Arabic TV: whether respondent watches any TV news broadcast in Arabic	0.77 − 0.52 = 0.25***	0.85 − 0.63 = 0.22***	0.49 − 0.27 = 0.22**	0.00
(3) Arabic radio: whether respondent listens to any radio news in Arabic	0.32 − 0.23 = 0.09	0.44 − 0.35 = 0.09	0.16 − 0.06 = 0.09	0.00
(4) Arabic newspaper: whether respondent reads any news-paper in Arabic	0.38 − 0.16 = 0.22***	0.60 − 0.27 = 0.33***	0.04 − 0.05 = −0.01	−0.34*
(5) Arabic Internet: whether respondent reads any news item in Arabic on Internet	0.02 − 0.00 = 0.02**	0.09 − 0.02 = 0.07**	0.00 − 0.00 = 0.0	−0.07
(6) Important speak Arabic: how important it is for respondent to speak Arabic	3.51 − 3.34 = 0.17*	3.55 − 3.52 = 0.03	3.44 − 2.82 = 0.62***	+0.59***
(7) Marry Arab: how important it is for respondent to marry someone of Arabic background	3.44 − 3.16 = 0.28**	3.51 − 3.29 = 0.22**	3.26 − 2.80 = 0.46**	+0.24
(8) Important visit home: how important it is for respondent to visit family's country of ancestry	3.01 − 3.05 = −0.04	3.11 − 3.20 = −0.09	2.76 − 2.63 = 0.13	+0.22
(9) Arabic at home: whether respondent speaks Arabic at home in addition to English	0.98 − 0.87 = 0.11***	0.99 − 0.95 = 0.04***	0.87 − 0.50* = 0.37***	+0.33
(10) Arab spouse: whether the respondent's spouse/partner is of Arab origin	0.98 − 0.86 = 0.12***	0.98 − 0.89 = 0.09***	0.93 − 0.69 = 0.24**	+0.15

Notes: Across answers, observations range from 284 to 780. *Arab race, Arabic TV, Arabic radio, Arabic newspaper, Arabic Internet,* and *Arabic at home* are binary. *Important speak Arabic, Marry Arab,* and *Important visit home* range from 1 to 4. *, **, and *** indicate significance at the 90%, 95%, and 99% confidence levels ,respectively.

Conclusion

The two data sets exploited in this chapter—one a set of cross-national surveys conducted in seventeen Western European countries, the other a unique data set of Arab Americans in the Detroit metropolitan area—show similar patterns. Wherever we identify Muslim and Christian immigrant populations in the Christian-heritage societies of the West that are similar in most respects but differ on religion, we observe a significant and intergenerationally robust disadvantage faced by the Muslims. The equilibrium we identified in France—one in which distaste for mixing with Muslims on the part of the rooted populations coincides with a feeling by Muslims that their future in the host society is not secure—may well be operating throughout Europe and the United States. Thus, we get survey results in the United States and across Europe that are consistent with our survey and experimental results from France. It is now incumbent on us to identify routes out of this discriminatory trap. This we do in Chapter 10.

10

What Is to Be Done?

Governments of Christian-heritage societies, at both the local and national levels, recognize the failures of Muslim integration that we have documented in this book. Yet they have no consistent vision about how best to ameliorate a deeply challenging social issue with grave consequences for the well-being of all their citizens. Two stories appearing in the American press in late 2014 illustrate the horns of a deep policy dilemma. On October 20, the *Washington Post* reported on a policy by the government of Aarhus, Denmark. The city, to the chagrin of many parliamentarians, was providing free psychological counseling and job placement services for citizens who are returning jihadists, having fought for an Islamic state on the borders of Syria and Iraq. On the next day, October 21, the *New York Times* reported that officials at the Paris National Opera, in compliance with the state's law against the wearing of full veils in public places, had one of their attendants demand that a woman wearing a burka remove it or leave the audience. A spokesperson from France's Collective against Islamophobia declared the episode an outrage, but officials at both the opera and the Théâtre du Châtelet insisted that it is their responsibility to uphold the law. In one case (Aarhus), we see Europe flailing to the side of accommodation; in the other case (Paris), we see Europe flailing to the side of confrontation.[1] The question we ask in this chapter is whether our analyses can provide a more coherent line of policy recommendations than is currently in practice across Europe and other Christian-heritage societies.

We believe that our analyses throughout this book provide guide-lines in answering this fundamental policy question: What is to be done? Recognition of a discriminatory "equilibrium" (Chapter 8) provides clues as to why discrimination persists—that is, no party has an incentive to unilaterally change its behavior. The rooted French see their stereotypes confirmed when they observe that Muslims from immigrant backgrounds retain cultural norms that diverge from the national mode. Hence, they can rationalize their discriminatory behavior against Muslims. Meanwhile, Muslims sense the nonrational elements of the discrimination they face from rooted French and French institutions. They sense this because they face discriminatory behavior irrespective of whether they show cooperation toward FFFs with whom they interact. They sense it as well because the rational elements of anti-Muslim discrimination, having to do with their gender and religious norms, even if highly exaggerated in FFF interpretations of those norms, would remain. Hence, Muslims are reluctant to seek integration into French so-ciety. Each group's reaction to the other, as we conclude in Chapter 8, helps sustain a discriminatory equilibrium.

Moreover, the fact that FFF discrimination has both a taste-based and statistical component adds a greater challenge for a positive equi-librium shift. Indeed, solutions to discrimination based on both statis-tical and taste-based assessments present a greater burden on public policy. Petit (2007) identified beliefs driving gender discrimination, such as the fear that women would quickly take parental leave and thus the firm would not yield its full investment in job training. There appeared to be little resistance based on taste. Therefore, state inter-ventions concerning parental leave were able to provide a more equal playing field for women in the competition for jobs. But the task be-fore us, where statistical and taste-based discrimination support each other, presents a new challenge. Policies aimed at only one element of the equilibrium—either the rational or the nonrational elements of discrimination—are not likely to generate an equilibrium shift.

In this chapter, we propose simultaneous interventions at three levels of French society: the micro (focusing on the individual cit-izen), the meso (focusing on societal institutions), and the macro (focusing on the state) levels. Devised to appear as beneficial to all relevant populations, the interventions we propose have the potential to generate exit from the discriminatory trap in which France is locked. These interventions should also inspire other Christian-heritage societies to work toward exit from their discriminatory equilibria.

The Micro Level (The Level of the Individual Citizen)

Attitudes and behaviors are hard to change. But, as a new generation of economists has demonstrated, making small changes in an individual's environment, or what economists call "nudging," may induce substantial shifts in behavior and contribute to solving large social problems (Thaler and Sunstein 2008). As an illustration, it is possible to nudge kids to reduce their risk of obesity. Simple changes in the presentation and layout of the food service in school cafeterias have indeed been shown to push kids to select and eat low-fat and more nutritious foods (see Hanks, Just, and Wansink 2013). The premise behind nudge theory is that individuals have behavioral biases that lead them to make certain decisions. Nudge theory takes advantage of such biases to lead individuals toward the right decision. If a food is more convenient to reach in a lunch line than a close and preferred substitute, individuals will be more prone to choose the convenient option. If the apples are easier to reach than the cookies, kids are nudged, on the margin successfully so, to take the apples.

We believe nudges can also be used to challenge religious discrimination. In what follows, we explain how we expect to provoke both the host and the immigrant Muslim communities out of their discriminatory equilibrium with nudges.

Broadcast That Part of Anti-Muslim Discrimination That Is Nonrational

Pope, Price, and Wolfers (2014) have recently shown the benefits of broadcasting research findings on discrimination, especially in an institutional environment committed to fair play (as with our case in France). These authors refer to the considerable media attention given to one of their papers published in 2010. In that article, they documented that personal fouls were relatively more likely to be called against professional basketball players when they were officiated by an opposite-race refereeing crew. Yet, personal fouls are objectively not more frequent when a player faces an officiating crew of a different race. Pope, Price, and Wolfers (2014) showed that media coverage durably erased referees' expression of their nonrational (and unconscious) racial bias. This finding suggests that individuals are prone to change their behavior when they are shown it is nonrational and violating institutional norms. We believe it is possible to take advantage of this tendency. Broadcasting that rooted populations discriminate against Muslims even when they do not expect any particular hostility from them may help citizens (recruiters included) resist more effectively their present tendencies toward discriminatory behavior.

This nudge needs to target not only adults but also children at school. There, various recreational games, such as the Klee/Kandinsky experiment reported in Chapter 7, could be played in the classroom to make children aware of their tendency to nonrationally discriminate against members of the outgroup. To address more specifically religious discrimination, these interventions could be complemented by easily digestible sessions on the history of world religions. By emphasizing that these world religions stem from the same cradle, these sessions may nudge children of Christian, Muslim, and Jewish religious background to see each other as coethnics.[2]

Highlight That Retaining Exclusively Muslim Names Is Nonrational for Muslims

It was not lost on the Senegalese we interviewed that rooted populations are more likely to cooperate with individuals bearing names that sound familiar to them. Abou (a Muslim from the Joola ethnic group) had no doubt that Catholic given names would win out for jobs. "Etienne X [using the first name of a member of our ethnographic team, with the respondent's own surname, here withheld] is going to advance farther [than if I kept my first name], this is evident, as [your name, Etienne] is a name belonging here." He added that many Muslim families are beginning to give Christian names to their children so that they won't be burdened with a Muslim name in France. It is, he reasoned, "a form of protection against anti-Muslim feelings." As for Souleymane (a Muslim from the Serer ethnic group), he let his wife look for apartments and conduct more official business because her name, Sokhna, does not sound as Muslim to the rooted French with whom she interacts. He told Etienne, "Up till now when I have to take steps, it's my wife who takes the lead. I stay in my corner because my first name is my first big enemy." Another of our interviewees shared a revealing anecdote. One day he had to call the mayor's office, and he introduced himself as Gormack X, his actual first name. The secretary told him the mayor was on vacation for two weeks. He then called back, introducing himself instead as Jean-Christophe X, and was talking to the mayor a few minutes later.

Indeed, Muslims can make it harder for members of the host society to identify them as "Muslims" and discriminate against them by retaining names that are not exclusively Muslim. In a correspondence test briefly mentioned in Chapter 1, Duguet et al. (2010) showed that the callback rate of a French applicant with a French first name and surname is four times higher than the callback rate of a French applicant with a Moroccan first name and surname. However, the gap substantially reduces when the French applicant with a Moroccan surname changes his Moroccan first name to a French one. In this case, this French applicant with a French first name and Moroccan surname is "only" 2.5 times less likely than the French applicant with a French first name and surname to be called back by the recruiter for an interview.

We recognize there are costs to the abandonment of Muslim first names. To many in their communities, such behavior might be considered a near conversion and a loss of cultural identity. If those costs are higher than any economic benefits of becoming a "Jean-Baptiste," giving a Christian name to one's child is hardly rational. However, Muslims could be nudged into choosing names for their children that are consistent with Muslim culture but are not exclusively Muslim, or perhaps to adopt a dual name structure, one for official France and the other for home and community.[3] Each of these strategies would make it more difficult for rooted French to automatically discriminate based on a signal of Muslimness. Moreover, it might also reveal to those French who could still infer a Muslim identity that this particular Muslim is coming from a family that is committed to integration into France. These strategies do not prevent the rooted French from finding other clues for Muslim identity. However, this nudge on naming could well serve as a transitional tactic to induce an equilibrium shift.

To be sure, a nonnegligible proportion of (Muslim) immigrants from Muslim-majority countries already implement this strategy. Relying on the French Labor Force Survey, which reports the first names of the respondent's household members, children included, Algan, Mayer, and Thoenig (2013) analyzed the naming decision in France of parents with Arabic names. It appears that this decision is fairly balanced between Arabic and non-Arabic first names. Of parents with Arabic names, 51.1% give an Arabic first name to their offspring, while the remaining transmit to their children a first name that sounds more traditional (that is, national rather than religious) or more neutral relative to French culture. In particular, the generic first names that are most frequently selected are Adam or Yanis for boys and Ines or Sarah for girls. These are names that can be attached to different cultures and are also common choices among rooted French parents. Broadcasting the rationality of giving such names to one's children or of retaining Muslim names only for family or community is likely to be a powerful nudge to further increase the proportion of Muslims adopting such strategies.

The Meso Level (The Level of French Secondary Institutions)

Simultaneous with information campaigns and nudges on the individual level, our research points to the need for effective regulations at the level of secondary institutions—standing in between the family and the central state. Here we have in mind interventions at the level of the firm and at the level of the educational system. Let us begin with firms.

Overcoming Anti-Muslim Discrimination
in the Labor Market

Good Intentions; Bad Ideas Common answers to discrimination in the labor market are quotas and the requirement of the "anonymous résumé."[4] Yet, we are doubtful about the promise of these policy treatments.

Quotas in France already exist for handicapped persons. Yet the impact of these quotas on the incorporation of handicapped applicants in the labor market is far from encouraging. In a law of July 10, 1987, all enterprises with at least twenty workers had to dedicate 6% of their positions to handicapped persons. After a quarter century, handicapped workers stand for less than 3% of the workforce in targeted firms. Put differently, these firms prefer to pay the fine associated with not abiding by the quota than to abide by it. We see no reason for a different pattern to emerge should quotas for ethnoreligious minorities be instituted.[5]

Even if the fines were augmented to raise the costs of discrimination, meaning that firms would be nearly "forced" to abide by ethnoreligious quotas, these quotas would not likely serve as a solution to anti-Muslim discrimination. They are in fact likely to bring resentment among the rooted French we have been calling FFFs. To be sure, it would be difficult for FFFs to consider in good faith ethnoreligious quotas as unfair in the case where those rooted French candidates and candidates from ethnoreligious minorities (Muslims from Muslim-majority countries particularly) apply to positions with equal productivity levels. Should this condition hold, it would be unquestionable that the religious composition of the firm should reflect the religious composition of the employment area where the firm is located. However, legitimate resentment would emerge among FFFs if this condition of equal productivity is violated. Yet, as shown in the next section, which stresses the failure of the French educational system to ensure equality of opportunity, this condition of equal productivity is not likely to be fulfilled. FFF candidates are typically better qualified, at least with formal credentials, than Muslim candidates from Muslim-majority countries. In other words, so long as equality of opportunity at the level of education is not reached, quotas for ethnoreligious minorities on the labor market would yield FFF resentment against such minorities, especially for skilled employment. Low representation of Muslims in the workforce, the main symptom of anti-Muslim hiring discrimination in the labor market, might not be visible any more thanks to these quotas. But, from the viewpoint of the host population, such quotas would incentivize anti-Muslim discrimination at other stages of Muslims' professional career advancement or even discrimination in other aspects of social life, such as access to housing or to candidacy for electoral office as determined by political parties. Instituting fines leveled at firms who fail to hire candidates of a religious minority who are likely on average to be less qualified cannot be expected to free France from its discriminatory trap.

Another common policy recommendation is the anonymous résumé. Indeed on March 31, 2006, the French government announced a requirement for the anonymous résumé applied to all enterprises of more than fifty employees. But as of this writing, the State Council has not set the rules for the administration of this decree, and it therefore remains in bureaucratic limbo.

At first sight, one may be optimistic regarding the anonymous résumé's effectiveness against taste-based discrimination. After all, the job interview resembles a socialization phase that could substantially reduce distaste toward the outgroup. However, our results (notably those from the voting game—see Chapters 2 and 7) challenge this optimistic view. They reveal that FFF distaste toward Muslims persists after the socialization phase. They suggest that, even after a job interview, French recruiters (to the extent that they act as did our FFF subjects) would show a preference to select coreligionists, at least after a few token Muslims were hired.

Moreover, there is no reason why the job interview should alleviate recruiters' concerns about the risk of proselytism or of problematic relationships with female colleagues they associate with Muslims. Statistical discrimination should still be in effect after the job interview because recruiters surely know that candidates' attitudes during a job interview are only an imperfect indication of what their behavior in the firm would be once they are hired. Hence, although the anonymous résumé will give Christian and Muslim applicants with equivalent paper qualifications equal likelihood of obtaining a job interview, it does not ensure equal chance of being hired.

There are other reasons to be skeptical as to whether the rollout of this law would help France attain a nondiscriminatory equilibrium. There is a big difference between Muslims voluntarily changing their names in order to obtain better opportunities and the state instituting policies based on the forced obfuscation of identity. Such a decree would send a strong signal to members of the immigrant community that their adopted country admits that the only way they would get opportunities in France is if they could erase any element of their identities. This can hardly be seen as a welcoming gesture; indeed, the message to immigrants with this treatment is that France seeks diversity on the labor market by concealing it. More generally, by admitting that discrimination can be addressed only if those with immigrant backgrounds hide their identities, this approach could further widen the trust deficit in France, which is already reported to be large, both in French society as a whole (Algan and Cahuc 2007; Algan, Cahuc, and Zylberberg 2012) and in the workplace (Institut Montaigne 2014a).

All in all, the returns to the anonymous résumé seem negative: not only is it unlikely to improve a Muslim applicant's chance of being hired, it risks severely undermining Muslims' self-esteem by sending the state-sponsored message that Muslims must dissimulate their entire identity (not only their first names) in order to improve their chances of being interviewed.

A Better Alternative: Diversity Training within the Firm To fight against anti-Muslim discrimination, French firms should provide their recruitment teams[6] and managers[7] with diversity training sessions. The purpose of these sessions would consist in making these employees aware (1) of their tendency to nonrationally discriminate against members of the outgroup and hence (2) of the necessity to resist such tendency for the sake of the firm's economic performance. Indeed, eliminating discriminatory behavior within the firm can improve economic performance through three channels.

STRESSING THE ECONOMIC BENEFIT OF GIVING UP ANTI-MUSLIM DISCRIMINATION The first channel that would work to the benefit of the firm is to actively hunt down discriminatory behavior. This would allow firms to protect themselves against legal risks. Indeed, participants in diversity training sessions would be reminded that Article 225-1 of the Penal Code defines twenty categories that are protected from discrimination, and these include origin (ethnic, national, and racial) and religion. Religious discrimination in labor market recruitment, for example, is punishable by three years of imprisonment and a 45,000 euro fine. Furthermore, in order to convey to recruiters the message that such legislation represents a credible threat to discriminatory firms—and thus that it is not in their interest to underestimate the probability that their discriminatory practices will be detected—recruiter diversity training should highlight the fact that the 2006 French law on equal opportunity recognizes correspondence tests and audit studies as admissible evidence of discrimination. One need only demonstrate that for two equally qualified candidates, the Christian candidate's probability of receiving an interview callback and of receiving a job offer by a given firm is systematically higher than that of the Muslim candidate for this firm to face the legal ramifications of its religious discrimination.

One concrete way in which this threat can be made more credible to discriminating recruiters is via the creation of a public institution whose objective is to regularly verify and test the recruiting practices of French firms through correspondence tests and audit studies. An example of such an institution already exists in Défenseur des Droits, an independent constitutionally mandated authority (since 2008) charged with ensuring the protection of citizens' rights and liberties and promoting equality.[8] In sum, firms can and should take advantage of the legal framework in which they operate to fight against discriminatory practices through diversity training.

A second channel through which firms stand to gain from fighting discriminatory practices is via the firm's reputation. We envision the emergence of a nongovernmental organization that can award a "diversity-compliant" label to firms whose ethnoreligious composition matches that of the employment area in which they are located (information on individuals' country of ancestry has been available from the National Institute of Statistics and Economic Studies, as we discuss below, since 2005).[9] These firms would have demonstrated their commitment to not discriminate based on ethnicity and religion.

Receiving such a label would be rewarding for firms that are listed in the stock exchange. Indeed, appearing as socially responsible can be a way for them to attract investors. Moreover, the label "diversity-compliant" could become a valued stamp on merchandise sold at the retail level, even for unlisted companies, at least for some (and often the most affluent) customers. This model has been successful for the production of environmentally friendly products, for example, where labels such as Energy Star have set new standards for energy efficiency since the 1990s. Similarly, since the late 1980s, consumers concerned about fair trade, environmental, and labor practices can prioritize Fair Trade products in their purchasing decisions.[10]

Appearing as socially responsible offers an additional, often ignored benefit for all firms. Research suggests that socially responsible firms attract socially responsible employees (Nyborg 2014). Such employees should be desirable to firms because they (1) claim themselves willing to accept lower wages for the opportunity of working in a socially responsible environment and (2) are more productive because of their ability to cooperate with one another. An authoritative and credible label that signals to potential employees that firms are socially responsible is thus one key for this mutually beneficial scenario to be achieved.

But workplace diversity can be assessed only if it can be measured (Institute Montaigne 2014b). It is therefore urgent that unneeded constraints on "sensitive" data collection, as described in the Appendix, be lifted. Permission has already been granted for the aggregation of sensitive data to the level of the employment area in which the firm is located. Indeed, since 2005, the National Institute of Statistics and Economic Studies has been authorized to collect information, through the French Labor Force Survey, on respondents' nationality at birth and country of birth as well as on the nationality at birth and country of birth of respondents' parents. Concomitantly, firms should be entitled to collect such information among their workforce to determine whether it is fairly representative of the diversity of their employment area. The integration of women, handicapped persons, and seniors can be assessed and broadcast because data collection on gender, handicap, and age is not restricted. By contrast, the difficulty for firms to collect ethnic and religious data in the workplace and to compare them with similar data collected at the level of the employment area provides a legalistic excuse for firms neglecting ethnoreligious workplace diversity policies so far.

There is a third channel through which giving up discriminatory behavior would boost firm productivity, and it operates through individual and team performance. First, nondiscrimination works to avoid the loss of potentially high-quality talent when résumés are rejected purely on the applicant's family name. Second, in what a branch of psychological research refers to as the "value in diversity" hypothesis, diversity has been shown to improve group productivity through the variety of perspectives and skills that are brought to bear on problem solving and task completion. In fact, the conflicts that are sometimes associated with diversity have been shown, when tasks are complex, to enhance the range of possibilities considered by the group (see Hoffman and Maier 1961; Nemeth 1986; O'Reilly, Williams, and Barsade 1997; Page 2007). A good theoretical foundation for this channel comes from a computer science model (Hong and Page 2001, 2004) in which agents are characterized by a "perspective-heuristic pair," where a perspective is an agent's internal representation of a problem, and a heuristic is an algorithm that the agent employs to locate solutions. Aggregated at the group level, a perspective-heuristic pair determines a group's problem-solving capabilities. Using this framework, Hong and Page showed that if problems are sufficiently difficult such that no one agent can solve the problem individually, groups with diverse perspective-heuristic pairs outperform homogeneous groups at problem solving, even when the latter are composed of individually higher-ability problem solvers.

But the evidence for this is not limited to theoretical computer models. Hoogendorn and van Praag (2012) provide corroborating empirical evidence. They followed 550 students who set up forty-five real companies as part of their curriculum in an international business program in the Netherlands. Fifty-five percent of the students were ethnically non-Dutch. Among them, roughly one-third stemmed from Muslim-majority countries. The researchers determined and assigned the degree of ethnoreligious diversity in each student team (typically composed of ten to twelve students who themselves were not alerted to the cultural mix of their groups). They then analyzed how variation in the degree of ethnoreligious diversity impacts team performance. They found that a moderate level of ethnoreligious diversity has no effect on team performance, measured as business outcomes (sales, profits, and profits per share). However, beyond a certain threshold, more ethnoreligious diversity has a positive impact on team performance (and sales, profits, and profits per share) due to a more diverse pool of relevant knowledge that facilitates mutual learning. To reap the benefits of such diversity, French firms should go beyond their commitment to eliminating discriminatory hiring practices: they should commit to utilizing a wide variety of recruitment strategies (rather than relying solely on networks from the highly elite "Grandes Écoles") in order to reach a broad range of candidates. For example, they could rely on recruitment firms such as Mozaik RH,[11] or on networks such as the one offered by the Club XXIème siècle,[12] that specialize in finding and providing technical support to talent in the largely Muslim (and once-industrial) suburbs. Moreover, in order for ethnoreligious diversity to act as a lever for the firm's economic performance, all employees and managers of the company should accord a warm welcome to new recruits from diverse backgrounds. It is doubtful that simply providing training for nondiscrimination is sufficient to achieve this goal. To be effective, such training should be accompanied by a demonstration by the top management of its commitment to policies promoting ethnoreligious diversity. As such, we can only encourage large companies to establish executive committees and director committees more representative of the ethnoreligious diversity in France. These large companies should all be incentivized to embark on this initiative given the positive economic benefits they can expect.

SPECIFICALLY ADDRESSING THE RATIONAL COMPONENT OF ANTI-MUSLIM DISCRIMINATION Fighting against anti-Muslim discrimination contributes to firms' economic performance. Yet, part of anti-Muslim discrimination is rational: firms might therefore fear that these benefits will be at least partly counterbalanced by the higher risk of problematic behavior from Muslim employees. How to re-assure them? First, trainers must emphasize during diversity training sessions that Muslims' higher religiosity and hence likelihood of ex-pressing their religious affiliation is not problematic per se. Here, the intervention would consist in making members of the workforce rec-ognize that the widely shared societal goal of laïcité ought not to imply the denial of religious affiliation. Moreover, in French law, expressions of religious affiliation within the firm are not illegal.

However, even with the proposed diversity training, enterprise managers may still worry that hiring Muslim candidates portends trouble for the firm. In this light, training sessions should empha-size that laïcité not only brings rights but also duties to employees. Laïcité, despite being an "essentially contested concept" (Gallie 1955–1956), surely implies the possibility for everybody to exert one's freedom of conscience provided that the expression of one's freedom of conscience does not impede the freedom of conscience of others. This implies that religious expressions and practices within the firm can be restricted based on two principles: the protection of individ-uals and the smooth running of the company.[13]

The protection of individuals within the firm requires first that no employee can impose her or his convictions (or worldview) on fellow workers. This means that Muslim employees should not be permitted to challenge coreligious employees for not covering their hair; nor should they be permitted to display religious paraphernalia (for example, prayer mats) prominently in public spaces. Second, the security of the workplace cannot be compromised. This means that duties requiring high concentration cannot be performed by em-ployees observing the fast if this observance undermines their vigilance and threatens themselves and/or their coworkers. Third, hygienic rules need to be observed, even if it requires the shaving of facial hair (for instance, in the food industry). Similarly, duties that require noncontaminated environments cannot be performed by employees who refuse to wear sterilized uniforms.

The second principle permitting restrictions to religious norms is that of the smooth operation of private firms. Examples abound: employees must agree to take orders from superiors no matter what their sex; Muslim waitstaff must agree to handle bottles with alcoholic beverages or serve pork to customers; employees, save for absences due to flex time (for which we present a proposal), must attend scheduled meetings during regular work hours even if they conflict with time of worship; and employees must be willing to show their faces to clients and fellow workers, as being able to read each other's faces constitutes a key element in fostering communication and coordination among people for the smooth operation of a team or enterprise.[14]

These principles—whether in the form of a corporatist pact signed onto by the government, employers, and labor or in the form of law—should have a salutary effect in yielding an equilibrium shift in the labor market. It would give employers the right to fire employees who fail to observe these rules and therefore dissuade current and future employees from violating them. As such, it should further decrease the religiously inspired behavior that disrupts firm performance, which, as noted in Chapter 6, is already quite rare.

Enforcing legal restrictions on problematic religious expressions and practices should reduce recruiters' statistical discrimination against Muslims by reducing the probability that such problematic behaviors are ever observed within the firm. However, residual statistical discrimination is likely to persist. The "freedom of conscience" rule, for instance, impels management to not reject a priori the variety of requests coming from Muslim employees facilitating their religious practices (namely, demand for days off during Muslim religious holidays, demand for an adjustment of work hours during the month of Ramadan, and demand to enable prayer at the workplace).[15]

This obligation to take into account all these requests can be considered by any manager as a constraint against recruiting Muslim candidates. Indeed, thinking about how to best respond to such requests such that they are compatible with individual rights and with the smooth functioning of the firm demands time and thus resources on the part of the manager. Furthermore, the manager may worry that accommodating to a religious request (because it is not incompatible with the safe and smooth running of firm operations) could be perceived by colleagues and coworkers as favoritism toward members of a certain religion, hence undermining cohesion within the work team.

To address these challenges, we can imagine the implementation of new firm protocols that would immediately address the most typical requests on the part of Muslim employees by anticipating them in such a way as to benefit other employees as well. As such, requests for work-hour accommodation for religious reasons could easily be met if the firm has committed itself toward initiatives that promote work-life balance. We imagine the implementation of a common core of nonnegotiable work hours with a set of modular negotiable work hours for individual needs. The implementation of a set of flexible work hours would allow Muslim employees observing Ramadan to adapt their work hours such that they can be at work at a time when they feel most productive; or to accumulate enough flexible work hours to attend Friday afternoon prayer. But such flexibility would also enable all working parents to begin work later or leave work earlier to accommodate their needs. Similarly, firms can anticipate requests for praying space by making available a private room to all employees looking for a place where they may exercise a calm and individualized activity, such as praying or reading.

With regard to employees' dietary restrictions, it is in the firm's best interest to propose—if it has its own cafeteria—a meatless meal in addition to the traditional scheduled meal and to specify the composition of each dish (alcohol, nuts, and so forth). This approach enables each employee to make his or her own choice in accordance with his or her own dietary requirements (whether this be a weight-loss diet, a vegetarian diet, restrictions due to allergies, or religious restrictions). It is worth noting that such an approach is already widespread, which explains why accommodating dietary restrictions does not show up as one of the religious requests French firms reported in the 2014 OFRE/Randstad survey. Because many firms already have cafeterias that offer a diversity of meals that accommodate various dietary constraints (not just religious ones), any potential problem related to Muslims' dietary habits is defused.[16]

Many more initiatives can be undertaken to limit statistical discrimination against Muslim candidates in the workplace. The 2014 OFRE/Randstad survey informs us that the "religious demands" that firms most often address are requests for time off to observe religious holidays. These requests are mostly made by non-Christian employees, because the dates of non-Christian holidays rarely coincide with the holidays of the Christian calendar used in France. This imbalance between Christian and non-Christian employees may explain, at least in part, the statistical discrimination we observe against non-Christians. In light of this asymmetry, the National Association of Human Resource Directors put forth a proposal in 2012 such that firms maintain only three of the six Christian holidays in place. As such, Christmas, Easter Monday, and All Saint's Day, whose societal importance has become cultural rather than merely religious, would remain. But the Pentecost, Ascension, and Assumption observances would be replaced by generic holidays that employees could take at these dates or at other dates (for instance for Eid Al-Fitr and Eid Al-Adha for Muslims and Yom Kippur and Pesach for Jews). The implementation of this proposal is a possible solution: instead of increasing the number of national holidays, which is already high in France, it offers a more flexible solution. Furthermore, it enables recruiters to perceive requests for time off due to religious observance not just as a demand from non-Christian employees but as a demand from all employees.

There is yet another source of residual anti-Muslim statistical discrimination. Although stressing the existence of legal restrictions to religious expressions and practices is likely to substantially reduce the proportion of Muslim employees who engage in behavior that compromises firm efficiency, it is doubtful that this proportion will drop to zero. Therefore, recruiting a Muslim will still be perceived by recruiters as riskier than recruiting a Christian: the probability that Muslim recruits refuse to comply with reasonable restrictions on religious expression within the firm and hence force the firm to dismiss them will indeed remain higher—even if trivially so—than the probability that a similar behavior be observed with Christian recruits. Yet, the legal outcome of dismissing an employee, especially when this dismissal potentially violates France's penal code, is risky (and potentially costly) for the firm.

The question is how best to dissuade the few Muslims who might be tempted to engage in extremist behavior with respect to religious norms (fanaticism) and to gender norms (misogyny) from doing so. We envision three interventions. First, the discriminatory equilibrium we have identified suggests that one of the reasons underlying extremist behavior is the anti-Muslim discrimination Muslims face in France. It is therefore critical that firms engage in the variety of initiatives we have recommended in this section and communicate about them.

Second, the moderating role of Islamic representatives in France must be privileged and emphasized. Islamic representatives in France largely condemn without reservation both the fanaticism and misogyny invoked in the name of Islam. Indeed, in June 2014, the French Council of the Muslim Religion (CFCM) published the French Muslim Civil Convention for Cohabitation, claiming that "In France, [Islam]'s founding principle is the respect for republican laws. [These laws] underlie cohabitation and ensure the harmonious development of men and women in this country. . . . All Muslims must take to heart a need to separate oneself from extremism. Places of worship and mosques are devoted entirely to worshipping God, and nothing else. French Muslims call for the Government to wed its efforts to those of Muslim families and religious leaders to halt those subversive and radical acts that tarnish the image of the Muslim religion. . . . French Muslims fully recognize equality between man and woman. They call for the personal and professional fulfillment of Muslim women within the legal context. . . . French Muslims, following the position of most Muslim theologians, consider the full veil not as a religious imperative."[17] And yet this message must be better transmitted throughout French society, and organizations such as the CFCM should be given a stronger policy profile.[18]

To facilitate this tolerant and moderate interpretation of Islam, the CFCM highlights the importance of training imams and Muslim religious leaders in France. Indeed, out of France's 1,800 imams, the Ministry of the Interior estimates that under 10% are trained in France.[19] We envision state funding of religious and theological training centers managed by the CFCM;[20] this training should be complemented with a compulsory layperson and generalist module (a recommendation called for by the CFCM in its Civil Convention). This additional training[21] would inculcate future imams and religious leaders with a nuanced understanding of French laïcité, of the history of religion and religious rights afforded by French law, and of the possibilities of as well as constraints against Islamic practices in non-Muslim countries. It would further train these leaders in the French language to improve their integration into French society.[22] Messages of republican integration in the context of religious adherence should bring hope to Muslims, Muslim youths especially, and therefore reduce their temptation to disassociate themselves from French cultural practices.

Third, in order to fight specifically against misogyny, we support a generalized implementation of the ABCD-Equality program launched in September 2013 in 600 primary schools and preschools. Najat Vallaud-Belkacem, then minister for women's rights, proposed this plan—to intervene among the youngest and most impressionable members of society—in order to fight against the perpetuation of gender stereotypes. Its message, which stresses gender roles as social constructs, finds support in social scientific research.[23] In a novel study, Gneezy, Leonard, and List (2009) showed that gender differences in competitive attitudes is indeed a social construct. They ran a controlled experiment in two distinct societies, one a textbook example of a patriarchal society (the Maasai in Tanzania), the other a matrilineal society (the Khasi in India). In the patriarchal society, men opted to compete at roughly twice the rate of women. In the matrilineal society, this result was reversed, with women choosing the competitive environment more often than men. These results show that even gender differences largely considered to be genetic are in fact contextual, that is, shaped by the gender stereotypes of the society in which they are observed. Generalizing the ABCD-Equality educational program to all educational and firm environments would help young Muslims, boys as well as girls, separate from the more traditional gender norms of their parents. And it would help fight against the glass ceiling that women continue to experience in French firms today.[24]

Overcoming Discrimination at Educational Institutions

Moving from the labor market to the educational establishment puts us on the border between the meso and macro levels. Although education is a state function and all aspects of curricula and programs for remedying inequalities within the schools are the preserve of the state, the schools themselves stand outside the structures of governance. We therefore address educational reform in the context of societal change.

As we have shown in Chapter 2, a résumé sent by a French Muslim does not obtain the same response as an equally impressive résumé from a matched Christian applicant and a fortiori as an equally impressive résumé from a rooted French applicant. Improved integration of Muslim immigrants and their descendants obviously requires the elimination of discriminatory behavior among recruiters. But it also necessitates ensuring that the average French Muslim can produce a résumé as impressive as that typically produced by the rooted French.

This is hardly a foregone conclusion: the French educational system today does not ensure equality of opportunity. To be fair, this problem is not unique to French educational institutions; it is characteristic of those institutions across the advanced industrial world. But the data in France are unsettling. As France's High Council of Education reported in 2007, primary education in France does not reduce the difficulties in learning faced by children of poorer backgrounds, and the rates of being held back a grade are correlated with social background. In this context, we can expect that, among the descendants of immigrants from Muslim-majority countries (who typically had lower education levels than nonmigrants), the proportion of individuals with no degree is greater than the proportion of similar individuals among descendants of people who are born in France. And indeed, a study by Aeberhardt et al. (2010) has shown that 28% of those who have at least one parent who was born in North Africa have failed to obtain at minimum a secondary school degree as compared with 19% whose parents are both French born. Yet, having a degree is the key in France to integrating successfully in the labor market: three years after completion of one's studies in France, 70% of those with a master's diploma *(maîtrise)* had stable employment (the "Contrat à Durée Indéterminée") compared with 45% of those without such a degree. Furthermore, for those without a degree, the unemployment rate is about three times greater than for those with a master's degree and ten times greater than for graduates of a commercial or engineering program.

Additionally, comparative evidence suggests that France performs particularly worse in terms of scholarly inequalities than the other thirty-two advanced industrial countries in the Organization for Economic Cooperation and Development (OECD). Since 2000, under the auspices of the OECD, the Program for International Student Assessment (PISA) has been examining secondary school students in literacy, mathematics, and science on a three-year basis. PISA results reveal that the difference between the minimum and the maximum grade in each subject is higher in France than the average PISA participating country. Furthermore, France has both a higher percentage of students who do not meet a minimum knowledge threshold and a higher percentage of students above a threshold marking superior performance. This French particularity does not vanish over time: between 2000 and 2009, the gap between the successful and unsuccessful students worsened (a pattern not observed in the average PISA participating country). Far from France's pretentions, Baudelot and Establet (2009) refer to the French educational system with the oxymoron "republican elitism."

Why is this so? It has been suggested that the French educational curriculum is so dense and specialized that only the most prepared students can take advantage of it, while the remainder drop out mentally and/or physically. Furthermore, the French system of student evaluation is particularly problematic. Indeed, the nefarious consequences of France's elitist educational programs could be halted if student evaluations actually tested whether students have assimilated the topic's knowledge, allowing all students—including those from disadvantaged backgrounds—who have understood the essential concepts in the course to obtain a good grade. In other settings, student evaluations incentivize students to master the fundamental knowledge of each course; they contribute to the equalization of opportunity in knowledge accumulation. Unfortunately, this is not what student evaluation in France accomplishes. In fact, intensive teacher interviews reveal that nearly all teachers in France give poor grades to a well-understood proportion of the students. André Antibi (2003), who conducted this research, calls these lower grades a "constant macabre"—that is, a norm instilled throughout the teacher corps that ensures a constant level of failing grades. Similarly, Cahuc et al. (2011) characterize this system, which is specific to France, as a "triage machine." It serves again to discourage students of immigrant backgrounds with weaker preparation because they know that, regardless of their efforts, they are likely to be members of this constant macabre.

The hierarchical teaching style in France adds to the inequalities of achievement. Typically in French schools, student participation in discussion is frowned upon, and this prevents less prepared students (often minorities) from digesting what they are taught. Yet the value of horizontal methods—such as activating interactions among classmates—was impressively demonstrated in an experimental approach to the teaching of physics, first at Harvard University but now spreading across American universities.[25] The basic idea was to have groups of students sitting around tables rather than in a lecture theater. The instructor then plans regular pauses in the course of a lecture in which each group is given several minutes to discuss among themselves what they just heard. The result was that students who previously excelled continued to do so; but those who fell behind in the standard programs—typically minorities and women who were equally qualified in standardized entrance exams—performed much better in the experimental program.

The French educational establishment has not been blind to the failure of the education system to remedy inequalities. In 1982, the French government designated areas as Zones of Priority Education (ZEPs), in which it increased the number of teachers in order to decrease class size in secondary school. Alas, early statistical evaluations of this program (Bénabou, Kramarz, and Prost 2009) cannot demonstrate a positive effect of this treatment.

Similarly working with the designated ZEPs, Richard Descoings, then the director of Sciences-Po, one of the prestigious institutes of higher education in France, instituted a program whereby students living in precarious economic neighborhoods were given easier access to admission, and many young people from immigrant backgrounds began to appear in Sciences-Po's classrooms in the elite seventh district of Paris. This affirmative action program focused not on race or on immigrant status but (as with a similar program in Texas) on the economic condition of the school districts. Descoings's program spread throughout many French "Grandes Ecoles" (Erlanger 2010). What do we know of the implications of these quasi–affirmative action programs on incentives for second-generation migrants to orient their ambitions toward professional success in France? The *Chronicle of Higher Education*, based on a study led by political scientist Vincent Tiberj conducted for Sciences-Po, declared this experiment a great success (Kahlenberg 2011) as the accepted students performed well in the Sciences-Po program as well as in the subsequent job market. However, this study looks only at those students accepted and enrolled at Sciences-Po. What about the set of all students given the same incentive? A preliminary statistical analysis (Diagne and Wasmer 2009; see also Oberti, Sanselme, and Voisin, 2009) concluded that the Descoings program incentivized teachers to focus their attention on the very top students in sensitive economic areas but that on average school performance declined. Here, as we have already noted with our suspicions for these affirmative action–type treatments in the job sector, the returns have not been stellar.

French law (Article 9 of the law of April 23, 2005) offers a new vision for the future of the school, one that would provide a common core *(socle commun)* for all students, an approach advocated by the U.S. secretary for education, Arne Duncan, in the Obama administration. This law is aimed at reducing the elitist bias in the French educational curriculum but also at promoting a less hierarchical teaching style.

Here the educational establishment needs to create new incentives for the teacher corps to turn to a less dense and less specialized curriculum. To counter the constant macabre, it is also worth considering the government's own efforts at addressing and changing the current system's tendency to sharpen social inequalities. A law of July 8, 2013, directed schools to evaluate students not according to what they do not know or have not learned but according to a more transparent set of criteria that emphasize progress and positive reinforcement. In June 2014, the then minister of education Benoît Hamon launched a National Conference on Student Evaluation, proposing a national dialogue and consultation with the scientific community and professional educators in an effort to give flesh to the 2013 law. This effort was ongoing in 2014 under Vallaud-Belkacem's incumbency as France's minister of education.

Finally, to further improve the educational achievement of students of immigrant background, the relationship between school and parent needs to be better cultivated (Avvisati et al., 2014). This was attempted in 2008–2009 in the context of a randomized field experiment in partnership with the Ministry of Education.[26] This experiment was conducted in French middle schools located in Créteil, an economically distressed district that comprises all suburbs located to the east of Paris. Parents in treatment groups were invited to participate in a program consisting of three parent-school meetings on how to become better involved in their children's education. The main objective of these meetings was in fact to convey to parents that they can help their children, no matter what their own school record was and how familiar they are with the institution. Parents were provided tools to help instill in their children beliefs that their parents have a good perception and knowledge of the school and that they are responsive to the demands of teachers and administration. The intervention then assessed whether these children developed healthy attitudes about schools.

Although this innovative program cost between 1,000 and 1,500 euros per school (that is, eight to twelve euros per student), the researcher who administered this randomized experiment found that at the end of the school year, treated families effectively increased their school- and home-based involvement activities. Children of families who were directly targeted by the program developed more positive behavior and attitudes in school and received better marks from their teachers, especially in French. Importantly, results also reveal large spillover effects of the program on the behavior of classmates of treated families. This randomized experiment offers clues as to how one can increase parents' awareness and involvement. Moreover, it shows that parental involvement substantially improves children's behavior and, ultimately, educational achievement. Generalizing such a cost-effective intervention to other schools in economically distressed educational districts (those where the population is mainly of non-Western immigrant background) seems an obvious policy toward greater equality of opportunity at school.

An even more radical approach to an equilibrium shift in the educational system would be to advertise the potential payoffs should French firms make hiring decisions based not on diploma received but on the candidate's actual mastery of the skills sought by the firm. This recruiting process would consist in conditioning a job interview not on a résumé and motivation letter but on the ability of the applicant to solve online problems mimicking the job environment candidates would encounter if they were recruited. (This is increasingly the practice in Silicon Valley, where venture capitalists question the value of a standard diploma and typically give job aspirants online assignments instead of a standard interview.)[27] This ability might not be closely correlated with what a diploma reveals and would therefore give a chance to young dropouts (mainly descendants of non-Western immigrants) to access high-paying jobs. To be sure, designing new online tests for each skilled position represents a cost for the enterprise. But this cost might well be more than counterbalanced by the fact that this innovative recruiting process will assure the firm that it is hiring those with the aptitudes they require.

The Macro Level (The Level of the State)

Moving from meso to macro, our focus is on the general policy frameworks of the state in addressing the fundamental problem of discrimination against Muslims both in France and in other Christian-heritage societies. At this macro level, there is a fundamental debate initially outlined in Chapter 1 as to whether it is best to hasten the day when immigrants progressively adapt to and adopt the cultural practices of the dominant cultural group in the country, in a policy framework that is basically assimilationist. Its alternative is multiculturalism (Kymlicka 2012). Multiculturalism, according to Koopmans, refers to policies that "provide minorities with recognition of cultural differences and resources to maintain them" (Koopmans 2013, 157). As such, multiculturalist policies have the potential to widen or, alternatively, reduce the cultural gap between Muslim and Christian immigrants from Muslim-majority countries that we documented in Chapter 9. Multiculturalist policies may widen this gap by encouraging Muslim immigrants to live apart from the mainstream to which Christian immigrants are closer. But multiculturalist policies may also reduce the difference in cultural norms. By showing greater tolerance toward minorities than do assimilationist policies, multiculturalist policies may induce Muslim immigrants to reciprocate and adopt the host culture's dominant norms. In support of this mechanism, Fehr, Klein, and Schmidt (2007) provide experimental evidence that fair contract design by one contracting party induces cooperation by the other parties.

Although this distinction between the two macro regimes of assimilation and multiculturalism may seem clear, it doesn't fully capture the complexities of national traditions. To be sure, we will rely on a quantitative index measuring where countries stand on this dimension.[28] But before doing so, with two examples from French institutional life, we show that even a resolute assimilationist regime sometimes accommodates to multicultural realities.

French Family Law and an Accommodation of Cultural Difference

Consider family law. An assimilationist perspective would be to demand that immigrants coming from countries with legal norms that are culturally anathema to the host society, such as unilateral divorce permitted only to men or polygyny, renounce those practices and accept the laws and norms of the host society. A multicultural perspective would accommodate as much as possible the principles and practices of the immigrant cultures.

Besides divorce and polygyny, other Muslim practices violate French marriage law on a number of dimensions (Bowen 2011, chapter 8). French law, for example, requires couples to marry at city hall before any religious consecration of the marriage, while Muslim practice requires a religious "engagement" ceremony that is (from a strict legal perspective) such a consecration to precede the legal marriage. Several imams have received fines for officiating these engagement ceremonies. More difficult for judges is handling cases of Muslim family law when the marriage took place abroad, as it is customary for states to allow marriages and divorces to be recognized if they were legally performed in the home country. Here, French judges have some discretion, as they are permitted to consider *l'ordre public* glossed by Bowen as in concordance with society's "basic values" (Bowen 2010, 173). With this doctrine, courts can deny a range of benefits accruing to those who have French personal status to Algerian couples—for example—whose marriages were consecrated in Algeria but whose practices violated the ordre public.

But judges faced a practical problem with their strict view of law and ordre public, one that incentivized assimilation in order to receive social benefits. Among a set of practical issues discussed by Bowen (2010), consider the situation where a husband marries a second wife in a country permitting polygamy and in accord with its rules and then brings her and their children to France. Those children, from a legalistic viewpoint, would be denied social welfare benefits because their presence could not be justified under the rule of family reunification (since only the first marriage and offspring from that marriage would be recognized in French law). This would, however, be inhumane treatment toward those children.

French judges have had to adjust to these practical realities. They have invented new legal concepts such as "attenuated effect of ordre public," permitting Muslim family law to operate without legal sanction in France (if the couple were married outside of France). Another invention is *ordre public de proximité* (or "distance-relative ordre public"), which turns a blind eye toward these formally illegal practices if some accommodation were made to French norms and so long as no French person were one of the parties to the marriage.

In the mid-1980s, relying on such doctrines, French court decisions basically permitted wives and children of a man legally resident in France but in a polygamous marriage consecrated in a country where such marriages are legal to join him in the name of family reunification. This accommodating tendency was partially reversed during the Chirac presidency, with Charles Pasqua as interior minister (1993–1995). In the name of public order, a ministerial directive insisted that those polygamous families that were permitted to remain in France (as they were legalized during the Mitterrand presidency) had to "de-cohabit," that is, live in separate households (Bowen 2010, 175–176). While legally clean from French notions of ordre public, most immigrant husbands did not have the resources for separate living quarters for each wife and her children. The state has turned a blind eye toward this violation. These halting but "reasonable accommodations with practical life" (Bowen 2010, 177) turn a strict assimilationist orientation into one that is more multicultural and accommodating.

No Accommodation to Multiculturalism for Descriptive Representation in the French National Assembly

On another dimension of the assimilationist–multicultural divide, France looks less accommodating. Multiculturalists have been insistent that political representation, in order to give voice to all cultures, must be descriptively representative. According to a 2004 estimation (Sabeg and Méhaignerie 2004; see also Castel, 2007, 72–73), visible minorities represent 15% of the French population.[29] Yet, a mere eight deputies out of 577 (roughly 1%) were descendants from "non-Western" countries following the 2012 French legislative elections (six with roots in North Africa or the Middle East, one with roots in sub-Saharan Africa, and one with roots in Latin America). A multicultural perspective would demand that the French National Assembly descriptively represent all French citizens.[30] France's blatant failure to take on this mission properly, from a multicultural viewpoint, can only discourage ethnic and religious minorities from integrating into France. Multiculturalists see it as critical that political parties commit to electoral lists that fairly represent France's ethnoreligious diversity. Yet, this commitment might not be credible since the host population, whose turnout is typically higher than that of descendants of non-Western immigrants,[31] typically prefer coethnic candidates. To create a clear incentive for political parties to propose electoral lists guaranteeing the ethnoreligious representativeness of those who will be elected, the state could condition its subsidies for such good practices. But unlike family law, France has been slow to recognize the gaps in descriptive representation that hinder social integration. Descriptive representation is a primary concern for multiculturalists but hardly on the radar screen in the assimilatory regime that France has long been and remains today as compared with most other Christian-heritage societies.

The dimension of multiculturalism and assimilation is surely fuzzy, and no country fits unequivocally on one or the other side. But, as we show in the next section, it is possible to get useful leverage through a multifactor index. From it, we can ask: Which of these policy frameworks has a higher yield in fostering the integration of Muslims in Christian-heritage societies?

Multicultural versus Assimilationist

To compare the returns to integration of these alternative policy frameworks, we rely on the five rounds of the European Social Survey (ESS) as described in Chapter 9. We focus on those Western European countries studied in Chapter 9 for which a measure of multiculturalism is available, but this drops only Luxembourg due to missing information on its position on the multicultural–assimilation scale. This means that we retain the following sixteen countries: Austria, Belgium, Denmark, Finland, France, Germany, Greece, Ireland, Italy, the Netherlands, Norway, Portugal, Spain, Sweden, Switzerland, and the United Kingdom.

Estimating the impact of multiculturalism on the cultural gap between Muslim and Christian immigrants from Muslim-majority countries is a tricky endeavor. First, the direction of causality in the relationship between multiculturalism and a cultural gap is difficult to assess as countries where the gap is lower can more easily afford multiculturalist policies.[32] Second, a selection bias may undermine claims of a causal effect of policy on outcomes. Multiculturalist countries may attract those Muslims who are the most traditional, because these countries offer greater tolerance toward immigrant group beliefs, norms, and practices. But the opposite may also be true. Multiculturalist countries may attract the most tolerant Muslims in search for host countries that are as tolerant as they want to be.[33] Third, we also potentially face what is called a dynamic selection bias (as described in Chapter 9) that would occur if differences in integration skills of Christians and Muslims who decide to migrate to the host country vary with their time of arrival and are different in assimilationist and multiculturalist countries.[34] Overcoming each of these biases compels us to reduce our sample allowing for comparability across countries. With the necessary restrictions, we analyze a sample of 465 Muslim and Christian immigrants from Muslim-majority countries: 346 Muslims and 119 Christians.

To determine the policy environment of our 465 immigrants, we rely on the Multiculturalism Policy Index (MPI), a scholarly research project that monitors the evolution of multiculturalist policies in twenty-two Western democracies. The MPI measures the extent to which a country has implemented the constitutional, legislative, or parliamentary affirmation of multiculturalism; the adoption of multiculturalism in the school curriculum; the inclusion of ethnic representation or sensitivity in the mandate of public media or media licensing; an exemption from dress codes; permission for dual citizenship; the funding of ethnic group organizations to support cultural activities; the provision for bilingual education or mother-tongue instruction; and affirmative action for disadvantaged immigrant groups. With a point for each of the above criteria, the MPI ranges from 0 to 8. The median value of MPI in 1980 was 0.25.[35] We therefore consider a country as assimilationist if its MPI in 1980 was lower than this median value and as multiculturalist if its MPI in 1980 was higher than this median value. Table 10.1 reports the value of the MPI in 1980 for the sixteen Western European countries in our sample. It highlights the assimilationist countries in white and the multiculturalist countries in gray. Table 10.1 also reports the MPI in 2010 for these countries. The trend toward more multiculturalist policies in Western Europe between 1980 and 2010 is striking. In 2010, only one country out of sixteen, Denmark, was assimilationist according to our definition. This trend runs against us finding any difference in the impact of multiculturalism in 1980 on the cultural gap between Muslim and Christian immigrants from Muslim-majority countries. Yet, as we are about to show, this difference does exist.

Table 10.2 reports the evolution of the difference in religious and gender norms across first- and second-generation Muslim and Christian immigrants from Muslim-majority countries, depending on whether the host country is assimilationist or multiculturalist.[36] From Figure 9.2 in Chapter 9, we know that Muslims are distinctive

Table 10.1   Multiculturalism Policy Index (MPI) in 1980 and 2010 for
sixteen Western European countries

Country	MPI in 1980	MPI in 2010
Austria	0	1.5
Belgium	1	5.5
Denmark	0	0
Finland	0	6
France	1	2
Germany	0	2.5
Greece	0.5	2.5
Ireland	1	3
Italy	0	1
Netherlands	2.5	2
Norway	0	3.5
Portugal	1	3.5
Spain	0	3.5
Sweden	3	7
Switzerland	0	1
United Kingdom	2.5	5.5

Notes: The median value of the MPI in 1980 is equal to 0.25. A country is considered
assimilationist if its MPI in 1980 was below this median value, whereas it is considered
multiculturalist if its MPI in 1980 was above this median value. Assimilationist countries
are highlighted in white, while multiculturalist countries are highlighted in gray.

with respect to their religious and gender norms as compared with
their Christian counterparts: both their mean score on secularism
and their mean support for gender equality are lower. Moreover,
from Figure 9.3 in Chapter 9, we know that this cultural gap does not
improve but even worsens (in the case of secularism) from one generation of immigrants to the other. Does the degree of multiculturalism of the host country help close that gap? Table 10.2 provides a
negative answer. With respect to secularism, it reveals a much smaller
divergence between Muslim and Christian immigrants in assimilationist countries than in multiculturalist countries. A similar pattern
emerges with respect to gender norms. While convergence is observed in assimilationist countries, divergence is at work in multiculturalist countries.

Lower divergence in religious and gender norms between Muslim
and Christian immigrants should be conducive to lower discrimination perceived by Muslims (as compared with their Christian

Table 10.2   Trends in norms for Muslim and Christian immigrants in assimilationist and multicultural countries of Western Europe

Policy framework	First-generation immigrants (a)	Second-generation immigrants (b)	Evolution (b) – (a)
Difference in nonreligiosity between Muslim and Christian immigrants			
Assimilationist country	2.71 – 3.43 = –0.72	1.78 – 3.36 = –1.58**	–0.86
Multiculturalist country	3.74 – 3.64 = +0.10	0.91 – 3.28 = –2.37***	–2.27**
Difference in gender norms between Muslim and Christian immigrants			
Assimilationist country	2.61 – 3.55 = –0.94**	3.60 – 4.37 = –0.77***	+0.17
Multiculturalist country	3.13 – 3.60 = –0.47	3.15 – 4.20 = –1.05**	–0.58

Notes: Each cell should be read as follows, using the example of the shaded cell in this table: "In assimilationist countries, the mean value of nonreligiosity for first-generation Muslim immigrants is 2.71; the mean value of nonreligiosity for first-generation Christian immigrants is 3.43. The difference in religious norms between first-generation Muslim and Christian immigrants is therefore –0.72. This difference is not statistically significant." ** and *** indicate significance at the 95% and 99% levels, respectively.

counterparts). Indeed, as stressed in Chapter 6, the fact that Muslims are distinctive with respect to their religious and gender norms constitutes a source of statistical discrimination against them. Moreover, this situation is likely to fuel the host population's perception of Muslims as an outgroup and hence its tendency to discriminate against them.

We can now ask whether the evolution of the difference in discrimination faced by Muslims and Christians is indeed more favorable in assimilationist than in multiculturalist countries. Here, following Chapter 9, we rely on the joint probability of feeling discriminated against and of being unemployed or inactive. Table 10.3 reports the evolution of the difference in this joint probability across first- and second-generation Muslim and Christian immigrants depending on whether the host country is assimilationist or multiculturalist. Although this evolution is not significant in assimilationist countries, Table 10.3 reveals a statistically significant diverging trend in multiculturalist countries. The difference in this evolution between assimilationist and multiculturalist countries is statistically significant at the 95% confidence level. Moreover, Table 10.3 shows that this pattern not only emerges for the joint probability of feeling discriminated against and of being unemployed or inactive; it also

Table 10.3   Intergenerational trends in discrimination for Muslims and Christians in assimilationist and multicultural countries

Policy framework	First-generation immigrants (a)	Second-generation immigrants (b)	Evolution (b) – (a)
Difference in the joint probability of feeling discriminated against and of being unemployed or inactive			
Assimilationist country	0.05 – 0.03 = 0.02	0.21 – 0.07 = 0.14*	+0.12
Multiculturalist country	0.01 – 0.08 = –0.07*	0.28 – 0.05 = 0.23*	+0.30***
Difference in the probability of being unemployed or inactive between Muslim and Christian immigrants			
Assimilationist country	0.31 – 0.10 = 0.21***	0.80 – 0.56 = 0.24**	+0.03
Multiculturalist country	0.20 – 0.23 = –0.03	0.89 – 0.73 = 0.16*	+0.19*
Difference in the probability of feeling discriminated against between Muslim and Christian immigrants			
Assimilationist country	0.27 – 0.08 = 0.19**	0.36 – 0.07 = 0.29***	+0.10
Multiculturalist country	0.25 – 0.40 = –0.15	0.34 – 0.11 = 0.23	+0.38**

Notes: Each cell should be read as follows, using the example of the shaded cell in this table: "In assimilationist countries, the mean probability of being unemployed for first-generation Muslim immigrants is 0.31; the mean probability of being unemployed for first-generation Christian immigrants is 0.10. The difference in the probability of being unemployed between first-generation Muslim and Christian immigrants is therefore 0.21. This difference is statistically significant at the 99% confidence level." *, **, and *** indicate significance at the 90%, 95%, and 99% levels, respectively.

concerns the probability of each of these events taken separately (that is, the probability of being unemployed or inactive and the probability of feeling discriminated against).

To be sure, our results rely on a small sample of Muslim and Christian immigrants from Muslim-majority countries because of bias concerns that restrict the full use of the sample. However, they provide consistent results on the impact of multiculturalism on Muslims' prospect for integration in Western European countries. They reveal that, compared with multiculturalism, assimilationist policies reduce divergence in cultural norms between Muslim and Christian immigrants. Concomitantly, assimilationist policies reduce the divergence in the discrimination these immigrants face in their host countries. Multiculturalism seems to have fallen from grace in Western Europe, even in pioneer countries like the United Kingdom.

According to British Prime Minister David Cameron, "under the doctrine of state multiculturalism we have encouraged different cultures to live separate lives, apart from each other and apart from the mainstream" (speech at the Munich Security Conference, February 2011). Our results lend support to this skepticism.

Citizenship Contracts

Given the relative success of assimilationist policies, more attention should be directed at a recent innovation instituted mostly in countries that show lower MPI as compared with other Western European countries. As minister of interior in 2003, Nicolas Sarkozy implemented a creative policy tool called the Contrat d'Accueil et d'Intégration (Contract of welcoming and integration) which was implemented nationally in 2007 and has been widely copied mostly by center-right parties throughout the continent that have long been wary of multiculturalism. In it, all immigrants have to sign a contract committing them to learn the national language and understand (through course work) national values. These courses (including up to 500 hours of language instruction) are provided without cost to the immigrant; but without fulfillment of the contract, renewal of residence permits could be challenged. We do not yet have a proper assessment of these programs. The only evaluation of this program so far, conducted by researchers at Radboud University in the Netherlands and sponsored by the French government, offers a positive assessment based solely on interviews with those who were required to sign the contract and attended the relevant classes.[37] That does not allow us to infer very much about the counterfactual, that is, their integration success without signing the contract. However, these results confirm an analysis by Goodman (2010), who showed that providing immigrants with the tools to integrate into the labor market (for example, free language training) is correlated with better economic performance. These contracts do not require deep changes in values or full cultural assimilation—what they require is that immigrants understand the core values of their host country and have access to the necessary tools to become full productive citizens. For instance, free language training associated with the integration contract is likely to reduce the gap in mastery of the host country's language between Muslim and Christian immigrants that we documented in Chapter 6 and hence dampen statistical discrimination against Muslims. Moreover, stressing the importance of not engaging in behaviors perceived by the host population as challenging laïcité and gender equality should also limit the public display of these behaviors and, as a result, anti-Muslim statistical discrimination. State policies that promote such citizenship contracts are promising, in conjunction with the changes at the micro and meso levels, for an equilibrium shift in the relationship between host nationals and Muslim migrants in Christian-heritage societies. They reduce the burden placed solely on the indigenous society to reform and shift this burden toward both immigrant and native communities in the name of a discrimination-free society. Equal burdens, we contend, are more likely to induce consent from both the indigenous and immigrant communities, a key to successful equilibrium shift.

Conclusion

France's current integration policies are more resolutely assimilationist today than the modal policies in Western Europe. Our data on the macro level suggest that assimilationism is not the culprit for the discriminatory equilibrium in which France is locked; rather, the problems in France are influenced more by factors at the micro and meso levels. It is our belief that resolute action at all three levels would best ensure an equilibrium shift, in France as well as in other Christian-heritage societies. This shift would occur because host populations would be incentivized, by becoming aware of it, to domesticate the nonrational component of their Islamophobia; meanwhile, expecting less nonrational hostility from the host population, Muslims would be incentivized to adapt away from the few cultural traits the host populations legitimately perceive as a threat; this would in turn dampen the rational component of the host population's Islamophobia. This equilibrium shift is not wishful thinking. Our concrete policy recommendations show the way toward achieving it.

APPENDIX

NOTES

GLOSSARY

REFERENCES

INDEX

Appendix

GERMANY'S CHANCELLOR Otto von Bismarck (1815–1898) is said to have observed that "There are two things you don't want to see being made—sausage and legislation."[1] We might add a third: field-work. As is well known in psychology, although experiments should have strict protocols, it is nearly impossible to standardize every step of the process (think of the tone of the voice of the person giving the subjects their instructions; and if done by computerized voice, think of how subjects from slightly different backgrounds interpret tone to infer the expectations of the researcher). In most cases, the small differences in the protocols in different settings (or in the same setting but with different groups at different times of day) are ignored by psychometricians and are thought of as "white noise," that is, effects that are not systematic and therefore present no bias in the establishment of a causal relationship between treatment and observed outcome.

If laboratories in cleansed environments present problems for standardized protocols, laboratories "in the field," whether conducting surveys or administering experiments, are rife with everyday small adjustments to the original plan. In many cases where one would want to do field experiments because of the importance of the problem to be addressed (for example, to address issues of poverty, of autocratic rule, or of violence), researchers need to make major adjustments to their original research design due to unexpected circumstances. And because of the cost of implementing field experiments in difficult or dangerous places, future replication of the protocols is not assured. It is therefore compelling to those in the field to take advantage of unforeseen opportunities that stand outside the original protocol. Sometimes those opportunities de-mand protocol shifts that run against experimental norms set by those who conduct experiments in laboratories with near-professional subjects.

Our field experiments had an element of sausage making. What we put into our final protocols was not fully envisioned when the protocols were laid out in the form of a proposal to the National Science Foundation.[2] Recent methodological debates about these adjustments have led a consortium of social scientists to advocate preanalysis plans—where all protocols and tests are registered be-fore implementation (Miguel et al. 2014). This is seen as a remedy to what is referred to as "fishing" for significant results when those re-sults were not initially hypothesized (Humphreys, Sánchez de la Sierra, and Van der Windt 2013). Although preanalysis plans are an appro-priate tool for a range of experimental treatments, fieldwork often demands that we do not tie our hands too tightly in keeping with our original plans (Laitin 2013). So field work, alas, has an inevitable ele-ment of sausage making.

In this Appendix, we reveal some of our sausage's ingredients, not because any stomach-churning stories invalidate our results. They do not, or if we thought they did, we would not have written this book. Rather, we hope that those reading this Appendix and wishing to make further progress in understanding the sources of religious discrimination and other social issues will learn from real (as opposed to cleansed) experiences in the field.

Choosing a Field Site

This book in many respects is a case study of Muslim integration into France. Typical in such studies, there is a justification for that case in terms of what it teaches us about the problem at hand in gen-eral. Often there is language telling readers that Country X is a "hard case" for Theory Y, so if Theory Y is confirmed here, it is likely to be generally true. One ought to be skeptical of such justifications, as the literature lacks examples of hard cases that fail (Fearon and Laitin 2008). We begin our sausage recipe with a more candid justi-fication of case selection, followed by an assessment of the biases to generality that choosing France entails.

In truth, we were drawn to France to address the question of Muslim immigrant integration into Christian-heritage societies because it is home to the largest Muslim community among all Christian-heritage societies. Muslims (those above eighteen who declare themselves as Muslims and those below eighteen who have at least one parent who declares himself or herself as Muslim) constituted an estimated 4.7 million in 2010, hence 7.2% of the French population.[3] Moreover, the riots in poor outer cities near Paris, Lyon, and elsewhere in 2005 and 2007 along with a visible political challenge by the Front National, which has been, from the 1980s, blaming the Muslim presence in France for many of the country's social problems, made the issue of Muslim integration for the French a vital public concern. A rusting economy and the challenge of the Front National pushed the center parties into a confrontational stance with the immigrant Muslim population, as demonstrated in rather scurrilous anti-immigrant remarks by Mayor Jacques Chirac, quoted in Chapter 7. Once published, these remarks set off a storm of controversy, a controversy that motivated our interest in studying the Muslim presence in France.

But there is a cost to a focus on a single country, even if such a study allows for an understanding of texture and context, often missed from large cross-national surveys. Can we really learn something in general about Muslims in Christian-heritage societies through a careful study of France? To answer that question, we first need to see in what ways France is an outlier compared with other Christian-heritage societies and then explain how we nonetheless use our findings from France to paint a broader picture.

Here we focus on two historical factors having to do with religion and politics that make France distinctive and weigh heavily on contemporary society: the relationship of church and state in French history; and the imperial wars fought in a Muslim-majority country. By no means do we seek to provide a full history of these historical factors; rather, we point to them in order to underline the challenges of comparative analysis that we must face as we seek to broaden the implications of our findings. Once done, we indicate in what ways we can speak to the larger issue of Islam in other Christian-heritage societies.

Laïcité: Its Historical Sources and Implications
for French Distinctiveness

France is a state that is both Christian-heritage and resolutely secular. The tension between a secular state and a powerful church goes back centuries, often traced to the thirteenth century when King Philippe le Bel asserted state control over the church.[4] The church, however, controlled education and enormous tracts of property and through the Reformation maintained its domination over religious practice. It was not until 1598, with the Edict of Nantes, that Catholics lost their monopoly of state recognition. The next major assault on church power came with the Revolution, in which Article 10 of its Declaration of Rights of Man and the Citizen declared that "No one may be persecuted for his opinions, even religious ones, provided that their manifestation does not disturb the public order." This concept of *ordre public*, as we emphasized in Chapter 10, plays a considerable role in French legal interpretation of foreign religious practices imported into France. Once again, the monopoly of the church over French religious practices was threatened by state action.

But postrevolution, France experienced a series of pendulum swings from the state seeing the church as the key to public order (and thereby recognizing the church as an arm of its power) to articulating support for the full liberty of conscience. Consider Napoleon. In his Concordat of 1801 with the pope, the state recognized the church. But there was to be no monopoly, as the state recognized additional religions as well. Moreover, in his Civil Code of 1804, Napoleon took family law and secondary schools out of the hands of religious authorities. Napoleon's ambivalence, supporting official recognition of the church by the state, along with severe limits to its spheres of influence, persisted through much of the nineteenth century. Post-Napoleon, the pendulum swung toward the church during the July Monarchy, the Second Republic, and the Second Empire (1830–1871), as new laws permitted church responsibility in regulating family and schools.

The year 1871 marked a swing in the other direction. After France's military defeat at the hands of Prussia, and the subsequent violent Commune, in which priests were murdered as the decaying government sought to protect the church, the Radical Republicans became the dominant political party, and their manifestos demanded the emasculation of the political authority of the church. It was at this time that a new term was coined—*laïcité*—which signified the Republican goal to delimit the role of the church in French public life. The first minister of public instruction, Jules Ferry, pushed a set of laws from 1882 to 1886 requiring all teachers in public schools to be lay and made it illegal for priests to enter classrooms. These were only the first steps in what the Republicans called the "grande laïcisation de l'État," involving repealing the mandatory Sunday closings of businesses, the end of church control over hospitals, and the secularization of cemeteries (Zuber 2008).

A law formally separating church and state was passed in 1905. This law guarantees state neutrality, meaning that the state should not favor any religion. At minimum, this requires that there can be no religious signs on state buildings and that civil servants must not express their religious beliefs while on duty. In this sense, the French state became radically secular. The Republican victory was so complete that appeals to laïcité were virtually nonexistent in Fourth and early Fifth Republic. However, the emergence of a politicized Muslim identity (discussed shortly) brought the notion of laïcité to the forefront of French political discourse. And when a principal in a small town north of Paris expelled a few Muslim girls who had refused to remove their foulards (headscarves suggesting an Islamic identity), it became an *affaire* of the state. Debates about the meaning of laïcité abounded and are well chronicled by Bowen (2007).

What was at stake in this *affaire* was never quite clear. Despite some consensus on the meaning of laïcité, it is, as Bowen points out (relying on Gallie 1955–1956), an "essentially contested concept." A claim to laïcité, Bowen argues, carries the illusion that everyone agrees as to what it means and that it is associated with French republicanism. But this is a myth, as there has "never been agreement on the role religion should play in public life . . . there is no historical actor called '*laïcité*': only a series of debates, laws, and multiple efforts to assert claims over public space" (Bowen 2007, 33). But perhaps there is one bedrock. The law also grants freedom of conscience to all, with restrictions that could be justified only by the need for public order. This notion of liberty of conscience has become the standard interpretation of the republican laws today, as a majority of French respondents (56%) defines laïcité as "the possibility for each citizen to practice his/her religion."[5]

There are two implications for our study of the infusion of laïcité in French public discourse. First, it gives historical ballast to today's regulations about public spaces. When "public officials find themselves in the awkward . . . position of saying that girls must attend class bareheaded so that all citizens will learn to live together," according to Bowen (2007, 13), they typically justify this through appeals to history. In other words, the vicious battles of the Radical Republican era are distinctive to France and were reinvigorated with the mass immigration of Muslims in the 1970s. In no other European country are the historical battles over secularization to this degree a core element of contemporary debates over immigration.

Second, laïcité has served as a justification for the state to remain resolutely ignorant of the demographics of ethnic and religious communities in France. Republicans insisted that the only identity that was relevant for public affairs was that of "citizen." To be sure, the French had an expansive notion of who qualifies for that status. French citizens were those who spoke French and adopted republican values. Thus, through assimilation, one could become "French." However, outside of what is required of citizenship, republican values demanded that the state should be blind to the religious, provincial, or ethnic identities of the population, as these were private matters of no concern to the state. Laws in France forbade the collection of ethnic data by the state, as we describe later on in this Appendix. The implication of these laws for comparative analysis is that we cannot in our analyses of minority groups in France know for sure their head count. Although the state has begun to relax those restrictions, still France's resolute blindness to the religious and ethnic demography of its citizens has made it quite difficult for social scientists to see where France fits across Europe in its treatment of minorities. An ideology of laïcité, then—both embedded in French self-understandings and yet deeply contested as to its meaning—has long deprived France and its citizens from understanding the scope of their problems in incorporating religious minorities, and this ignorance also makes the French case if not unique in Europe, at least quite distinctive.

War and Imperialism in Algeria

The history of France in Algeria also makes France distinctive in its contemporary relations with a Muslim-minority population. It is the only imperial power that fought not only imperial wars of conquest but also an anticolonial war among a population that was overwhelmingly Muslim.

The issue of Muslims and their status in France is deeply linked to France's fractious relationship with Algeria, a French possession from 1830 to 1962.[6] Many French (along with other Europeans), collectively known as *pieds noirs*,[7] settled on the Mediterranean coast starting from the mid-1850s. These settlers were labeled as colonials. However, as Nobelist Albert Camus (1994) described evocatively, more than a few were impoverished and shared the same standards of living as did the Arabs, the self-proclaimed natives who were predominantly Muslims. Despite socioeconomic equality among native Algerians and some of the pieds noirs, France legally distinguished these natives from other communities in Algeria and denied full citizenship rights even to those native Algerians who converted to Christianity. Although conversion improved their social and economic status,[8] it did not grant them complete equality of rights. Thus, origin- as well as religion-based discrimination in granting citizenship rights were part and parcel of French colonial rule, and the two were inextricably intertwined.

Complementing the settlement of French into Algeria was a significant migration of Algerians into France. By 1912, 4,000 Algerians were working in France. After a substantial recruitment effort for factory work during and after World War I, tens of thousands of Algerians settled near French factories between 1920 and 1939, mostly in areas around Paris. Although their identity cards categorized them as "Muslim French of Algeria," by 1947 Algerian Muslims qualified for full citizenship rights and unrestricted passage to France (Weil 2002; Shepard 2013; Cooper 2014). By 1958, the number of Algerians in France reached 250,000, well before the massive postindependence migrations to the metropole. Given constraints on data collection, we have no clear information on the population in France of those non–pieds noirs with historical links to Algeria. Our best estimate is that as of 1999, some five to six million residents in France had Maghrebi roots.[9] This statistic is consistent with Muslims in France being primarily of North African origin.[10]

Algerian–French relations have been fraught with violence that remains in popular memory. The bloody battles to conquer Algeria are a core element of both national histories. After World War II, while France was holding out the promise of full incorporation of Algeria into an entity called "Algérie Française," a National Liberation Front in Algeria initiated an insurgency that helped dismantle France's ineffective Fourth Republic. French counterinsurgency involved horrific episodes of gratuitous torture of supposed insurgents. In the course of that war for independence, the Algerian government proclaimed that nearly a million Algerians died, and French sources reported 27,000 casualties to their forces. President de Gaulle, ushering in the Fifth Republic, in which he promised victory in Algeria, decided to cut France's losses and to grant Algeria independence. This provoked an attempted military coup that nearly toppled the Fifth Republic.

The brutality of the counterinsurgency against the Algerian nationalists is deeply part of contemporary French memory; it has had, according to Sa'adah (2003, 78), "enduring and intertwined effects on French politics, society and culture," though without clear acknowledgment of French guilt. But after decades of official silence, the horrors of French rule in Algeria were alluded to by French president François Hollande shortly after his 2012 electoral victory. He then officially acknowledged that Algerian protesters peacefully demanding independence were killed by police in a Parisian rally in 1961. Months later, in his state visit to Algeria, he spoke of the "profoundly unjust and brutal" nature of France's rule. He explicitly made reference to the massacre in Sétif, where Algerian civilians— predominantly autochthonous—were attacked by French soldiers in 1945 when campaigning for freedom.

After the war about one million residents of Algeria descended on the French hexagon. These included the *harkis* (those Algerians who fought with the French); the pieds noirs, who were devastated at being abandoned by France; and many other Algerian autochthones, often French speaking and technically trained. These refugees carried with them the historical tensions between the pieds noirs and the autochthonous population, thereby driving the conflict zone from Algeria onto the European mainland. This cleavage was not initially categorized as one opposing France to Islam; rather, it was interpreted as a cleavage between French society (along with the newly arrived pieds noirs) and France's former colonized populations in North Africa (but mostly Algeria) and their descendants living in France.

Indeed, Kepel (1987, 9) reported that as recently as the 1970s in the Muslim-dominated ghettoes in urban France, there were almost no mosques or symbols of Islamic identity. The young Algerians referred to themselves as "beurs," a slang form of "arabe," and some worked with the organization SOS Racisme to address their discrimination in France as a result of race. It was not until what Kepel calls "the Iranian Moment" in 1979 (1987, pp. 225–312) that the Algerian population in France began to self-identify as Muslims.[11]

This new identity construction played well into the hands of the radical right, which found in Islam the perfect target for its anti-immigration campaigns. Furthermore, the continued appearance of Islamic movements in North Africa and the Middle East changed the frame of reference for the rooted French population in regard to the descendants of the mass Algerian migrations. In 1992, the Islamic Salvation Front (FIS) in Algeria was on the verge of a parliamentary majority before the military government canceled the runoff election. Three years later, a rump group of the FIS Islamists (the Groupe Islamique Armé, or GIA) began an insurgency in Algeria against the secular military government. This war spilled into France, as the GIA implicated the French government for support of its allied regime in Algiers. By now, these Algerian insurgents were viewed in France as Muslim radicals.

The September 2001 jihadist attacks in the United States again brought the religious component of Algerian identities to the fore, as became apparent one month later in the aftermath of the first French-Algerian football match since Algeria had gained independence. Organizers had high expectations for political reconciliation between former metropole and colony. The Algerian players were hailed as "messengers of peace" in a presentation just before kickoff. But comity soon ended. Hisses were heard during the ritual singing of "La Marseillaise" before the match. Later on, supporters of the visiting team trespassed onto the field of play. The popular press was quick to express indignation. At first, however, only the national origin of these trespassers seemed relevant. *France Info* and *France Inter,* for example, spoke of "Algerians" who invaded the pitch. *Le Figaro* in its first articles covering the event was bothered only by the fact that "the children of immigrants prefer to fly the flag of their parents." But the tone quickly changed. A later edition of *Le Figaro* denounced "the surge by those more or less manipulated young French Muslims [emboldened by] an ideology, one that since the mid-seventies, has consistently denied [France's] values and institutions."[12]

We observe the same phenomenon in the November 2005 riots in the suburbs of Paris. An initial reaction by the then minister of interior Nicolas Sarkozy was to call the rioters *racaille* (rabble), with no suggestion of their cultural or religious identities. Although the commentator in the radio interview sought to provoke him into making claims about the social identities of the rioters, Sarkozy refused to do so, saying that the responsible youth should not be labeled as members of any social group; rather, and true to his republican spirit, they were in the eyes of the law simply lawbreakers. Notably, he did not raise the specter of religion.[13] Indeed, objective analysts such as the International Crisis Group reported no direct connection between the riots and Islam. Nonetheless, a subsequent article in *Le Monde* reported that it was not lost on the general French population that "most of the rioters were of Muslim origin" (Ternisien 2006; see also Laurence and Vaisse 2006, 39).

Our point here is that the deeply troubling history of France in Algeria has provided a frame of reference for many French and the media outlets to interpret expressions of urban rebellion today as a sequel to the Algerian wars. Algerian, Arab, and Muslim get conflated throughout the history of relations between France and its citizens of Algerian origin. Yet movements with origins in the Middle East and North Africa have brought increasing prominence to the Islamic aspects of Algerian identities, reframing the tortuous history of France in Algeria as one centered on religious difference. The association of current Muslim integration problems with this colonial history makes host country–Muslim relations in France distinctive among Christian-heritage societies.

France is distinctive; but every Christian-heritage society is distinctive in its own way. France's republicanism and its Algerian legacy do not allow us to judge whether France was more or less likely to integrate a new Muslim population in the late twentieth century. But readers should have learned, as we show in Chapter 9, that our conclusions about France hold for other Christian-heritage societies.

France as a Difficult Environment: Ethnic and Religious Data Collection

Beyond distinctive historical legacies, France's republican ideology presented practical challenges to the measurement of the effects of religious difference on economic success. For one, French republican ideology emphasizes that the state has no interest in knowing the ethnic past of any of its citizens, as from the state's point of view, all citizens are equally French. In the reckoning of the distinguished French sociologist Dominique Schnapper (1998, 16–17), who later became an important voice on these issues as a member of the Constitutional Council, the nation is a "community of citizens" and is to be distinguished from "ethnies, or whatever the name given by contemporaries and historians to ethnies: nations before the Revolution; nationalities of the nineteenth century, protonationalisms." According to republican thinking, these ethnic attachments are not only irrelevant to national membership; any official recognition of them undermines the solidarity crucial for the fulfillment of national goals.

Because of this resolute republican foundation in French political thinking, the collection of ethnic data by the state has long been an anathema. Going back to the flow of migrants from Algeria, we can see one implication. In an important study seeking to measure intergenerational inequalities linked to immigration, a team from the state-affiliated research group Institut national de la statistique et des études économiques (INSEE, a branch of the Ministry of the Economy and Finance) alerted readers that the North Africa data on which it relied from a public survey was ambiguous, as it could not distinguish between descendants of French nationals born abroad and descendants of immigrants from the same country. By some estimates, INSEE noted, descendants of French returnees made up 55.8% of the second generation of Algerian-origin population. An inserted box accompanying this article noted that "the fact that they cannot be distinguished in our data leads to an underestimation of the negative effects of inadequate social capital among immigrants" (Meurs, Pailhé, and Simon 2006, 676).

The issue of ethnic data and its collection has become embroiled in philosophical debates stemming from ideologies of laïcité and republicanism. The flavor of this debate has been nicely captured in a special issue of *French Politics, Culture, and Society* entitled "French Color Blindness in Perspective: The Controversy over 'Statistiques Ethniques.'"[14] This controversy is a long-standing one, with many twists and turns.[15] From 1891, official statistics recognized only those who were "French," those who were "French by acquisition" (though with no legal status differentiating them from the first category), and those who were "foreigners." But there were two deviations from this. During the Vichy government under Nazi oversight, Jews were officially categorized and counted, a stain on French history that republicans do not let their nation forget. And the project of "Algérie Française" had its own contradictions, as official records distinguish, through use of names, "Muslim natives of Algeria" from "French-born natives of Algeria." After the war, in the French census report of 1968, there remained one table for natives from Algeria that distinguished "French Muslims" from "Algerians" and both from "Algerian repatriates."

French law remains resolutely republican. A 1978 law (amended in 2004, though with the possibility for exceptions, quite often granted) prohibited the collection or processing of data that reveal the racial or ethnic origins (or political, philosophical, or religious opinions, or union membership, or health, or sexual life) of persons. The French Data Protection Authority was established at that time to ensure more assiduous implementation of the law and after some time took responsibility for making recommendations on the "measurement of diversity." In 1984, a committee on secret statistics (Comité du Secret Statistique), an organ of the National Council of Statistical Information, was created. Meeting quarterly, it determines whether proposed research by members of the scientific community has safeguards to ensure privacy and has important ends to justify any risks to individual privacy. In 2005, the High Authority for Antidiscrimination and Equality (HALDE) was created and funded by the state, but it was unable, due to lack of data, to establish general trends in discrimination based on ethnicity. As a result (but also because French torts law does not recognize class action suits), HALDE lawyers immersed themselves in particular cases of discrimination by the thousands, without collecting data themselves on the scope of discrimination.

But with the obvious facts of discrimination (supplemented by a number of sociological investigations that skirted legal constraints) in the public realm, researchers at the Institut national d'etudes démographiques (INED) began to collect sociocultural information on the French population. Their survey in 1992, called "Mobilité Géographique et Insertion Sociale," asked respondents about native language, which served as a proxy for what they called "ethnic belonging" (Simon 2008). Over time, this approach toward ethnic data created a storm of protest within INED. Opponents of these surveys argued that the survey instrument reified incoherent categories: it distinguished Kurds from Turks but not Catalans from Spaniards; and a category "of French extraction" gave a quasi-ethnic implication of a legal category (Blum and Guérin-Pace 2008). Researchers in INED, as well as INSEE, were split between those who felt that republican ideals could best be met by addressing discrimination through the analysis of ethnic data and those who felt republican ideals would best be met with a state that did not recognize its citizens through an ethnic lens.[16]

The storm continued for nearly two decades of controversy. On the one hand, there was slow adjustment toward a clearer understanding of the diverse nature of the population and its implications for social mobility and integration. A new law passed in 2006 ("loi pour l'égalité des chances") included a provision that opened the possibility for tests of discrimination (such as the correspondence test we presented in Chapter 2), which would allow researchers to indicate through subtle signals the ethnicity of job or housing applicants. Then came the 2007 law on immigration that opened the possibility for the collection of data on the ethnic and racial backgrounds of the population, allowing for a better understanding of its diversity.

On the other hand, there were public outcries against any such possibility. An inflammatory petition published in the leftist newspaper *Libération* (February 23, 2007, cited in Simon 2008, 12–13), entitled "Engagement républicain contre les discriminations," defended the idea that it was possible to fight against discrimination without any more statistical data, which would only foster interethnic confrontations ("affrontements communautaires"). A response published in *Le Monde* (cited in Simon 2008, 12–13) pushed for a wider (but not predefined) set of statistical categories for data collection. One of the authors of that response, Patrick Simon, an INED scholar, has been a leading correspondent on a blog justifying a mode of ethnic data collection consistent with republican principles. In the special issue of *French Politics, Culture, and Society*, Simon (2008, 8) summarizes the opposition's radical republican strategy as "equality through invisibility." Simon calls this the "choice of ignorance," and he finds this objectionable when "No one would contest the fact that the absence of the official use of ethnic or racial categories fails to curb the spread of prejudice and stereotypes." The provision in the 2007 law allowing for a census of the ethnic–racial backgrounds of the French population was subsequently declared unconstitutional by the Constitutional Council.

As president of France (2007–2012), Nicolas Sarkozy sought to give France the "statistical tools permitting it to measure its diversity." He demanded that these tools be "objective and uncontestable," without giving a privileged "ethnic" reading of French society, and be fashioned by the scientific community. Yazid Sabeg—an Arab born in Algeria, educated by the Jesuits, with a doctorate from the Sorbonne, and subsequently a successful businessman—was appointed commissioner of diversity and equality of opportunity (Smith 2005). Rather than drafting a new law, President Sarkozy appointed François Héran, at that time director of INED and president of the European Association of Population Studies, to draft a report addressing the president's charge (Van Eeckhout 2009). The final product was a model of scientific hedging, and it reported on the consensus of the committee that there is no absolute answer— neither "tout ethnique" nor "l'ethnicité zero"—but rather the entire question, they advised, is to define the circumstances and the guarantees that can make the collection of any such data useful and legitimate. Oddly, given the circumstances of the time, with the Muslim question dominant in public debate, this report analyzed data collection for six types of ethnic discrimination but not that of religion. Religion, apparently, is a cleavage too politically hot to handle.

As the debate on ethnic data rages to this day, a near invisible path has been forged pointing toward greater access by social scientists to ethnic data. Underneath the public radar, sensitive data were already available to authorized personnel as early as 2002. The French Housing survey of 2002 (Enquête Logement, INSEE) provided detailed information on the intensity and quality of social interactions within each housing block. But it also collected information about the ethnic, economic, and social backgrounds of surveyed households. Subsequently, the French Labor Force survey (Enquête Emploi, INSEE) has been providing relevant information about ethnic background, economic characteristics, and geographic location of individuals since 2005. Then in 2008–2009, a collaboration of INED and INSEE constructed a supersample of immigrants from diverse backgrounds in order to measure their trajectories of integration into French society (Beauchemin, Hamel, and Simon 2010). Second-generation migrants were identified (even though 95% of them were French citizens and by republican standards should not be distinguished from those French with deeper roots). Furthermore, the previously forbidden "religion question" was asked. Although the data are heavily guarded and released only to members of the scientific community, this is a big step forward for data collection on minorities in France. Access to sensitive data that is considered potentially threatening to individual privacy is now facilitated through a simple bureaucratic process by the French Data Archives for Social Sciences (Réseau Quetelet). Sensitive variables can through this process be merged into the larger data sets from which they were expunged once project approval is granted.[17]

There is yet another force pushing France down this same path—European data institutions. To be sure, Eurostat has not played a role demanding the collection of ethnic data for member censuses. However, the European Convention on Human Rights demands fulfillment of antidiscrimination regulations that will likely require France to produce data on its record in combating racial and religious discrimination. Also, European Union scientific bureaus provide substantial research funds to academics who collect cross-national data, with ethnic issues receiving increasing attention. Being part of Europe, in other words, has slowly pushed France toward a European norm of sociological investigations and surveys on ethnicity. Even Dominique Schnapper, who had for a long time taken the "republican" position on these data and voted with the Constitutional Council in 2007 limiting such data collection, is now more open to data collection on ethnicity, because, in her words, it is "impossible, politically and morally, for researchers to renounce their role in the creation of the self-awareness of a democratic society by establishing knowledge that is as objective as possible" (Simon 2008, 26).

France's difficult path in authorizing the collection of sensitive ethnic data posed several thorny issues for the research project described in this book. For identification purposes, we needed to compare immigrants who were the same in all respects save for the world religions to which their ancestors in the nineteenth century converted. These, as discussed at length in the text, were the Serers and Joolas of Senegal. We knew about the antecedent (to immigration) conditions of these groups from Senegalese census data, but once in France data problems arose. Given the lack of ethnic data collected in France, we could not estimate the precise numbers of these two communities living in France (or even the precise number of Muslims in France). Nor could we specify quotas or stratified samples without data on the population as a whole. French census data will tell us the country from which immigrants came, but their children are identified only as French. Therefore, state-collected data did not permit us to isolate Serers and Joolas from all Senegalese immigrants; and until the recent Trajectoires et Origines survey, they did not even permit the recognition of second- and third-generation immigrants.

To address these issues, for our survey and corresponding ethnographies, we relied on the chain-referral sampling techniques developed by Douglas Heckathorn (2002) to get as diverse a set of Joolas and Serers as possible. Furthermore, our reliance on a survey firm's proprietary Internet sources to get a preliminary list of over 6,000 surnames of people living in France was a second-best solution for finding a true representative sample. Another problem was that well-established survey firms were reluctant to allow direct questions about respondent religion for fear of facing legal challenge. Here we negotiated a set of indirect questions, such as the mosque or church attendance of parents and grandparents, that would easily pass legal muster. In the experimental games, this problem did not arise. We ran the experimental games by ourselves and did not receive funding from the French government (ours was funded by the National Science Foundation in the United States) and could therefore ask our subjects directly their religion. Still, we were discrete about this question for methodological reasons and because we did not want to arouse republican resentment among our subjects. We therefore did not inform our subjects that we were focusing on their religion; we justified our treatment based on our interest in how people from Île-de-France reasoned about money. Even so, as we report shortly, several of our subjects were appalled that we would raise questions of religion in a public space among people who were not intimates. Nonetheless, we believe that we ensured privacy, kept within French law, and elucidated an important policy issue for France; but readers should be aware of the sensitive issues involved.

From Identification to Implementation

The route from proper identification—for example, selecting the Senegalese Serer and Joola migrant communities in France—to a well-designed experiment is rarely straightforward. In this section, we consider how reality intervened with our attempts to design the perfect correspondence test and sample a representative population of Parisians in the Nineteenth District while recruiting enough French with no recent immigrant background.

The Correspondence Test

Let us first consider the travails in implementing the correspondence test, which is one of the more standardized protocols in the discrimination literature. The choices we needed to make were complex, especially given the fact that our experiment was to be conducted in 2009, at the height of the Great Recession, when few jobs anywhere in Europe were in the offering. The fewer the job opportunities, the fewer the variations we could make in our experimental protocol— to give but one example, if we wanted to know if discrimination against Muslims was higher or lower depending on gender, we would need to send out résumés for twice as many jobs. To help us work through these difficult issues, we contracted with the ISM-CORUM, a nongovernmental organization specializing in the study of discrimination.[18] Its research director Eric Cédiey consulted with us at every stage. With the help of Daniel Sabbagh, co-leader of the research group "Anti-discrimination policies" at Sciences-Po (the Institute of Policy Studies in Paris), Cédiey organized a seminar and invited a wide range of experienced social researchers and practitioners to examine every step of our protocol.

To begin with, we needed to design a treatment—that is, a signal to those receiving the résumés—that would differentiate Muslim from Christian applicants while at the same time keeping all other things equal. We recognized that we could not signal directly the applicants' religion, as that would violate French republican law. Thus, we had only to signal "presumed religion," which would have nothing to do with degrees of belief or of commitment by the job applicants. The standard signal, as with the standard experiments in the field, is the name of the applicant. We therefore assigned both the Muslim and Christian applicant the surname "Diouf," which is a common Senegalese surname and certainly recognized by rooted French as African. With this surname, we assured ourselves that we were controlling for race, colonial experience, and region of origin. Meanwhile, the first names would reflect differential religious communities, though even that presented problems. Our first choice for the Muslim female name was "Fatima" until we learned from our consultants that Fatima was a common name for

Portuguese (Catholic) migrants to France a generation ago. We then settled on Khadija.

For our Senegalese Christian woman, we began with Anne-Marie, a first name that had the strong signal "Marie" of Christianity but which had somewhat fallen out of fashion for those in their late twenties, the generation of our applicants. Furthermore, Laitin recalled from his own work in Africa that "Maryanne" is a common Muslim first name but that the simple "Marie" was a signal of Christian baptism; we settled on Marie. In sum, our treatment was a noisy signal delivered to the employer implying the applicant's religion rather than an explicit statement of the religion itself.

We further decided to strengthen the signal so that there would be less ambiguity about the presumed religion of the applicants. Because the jobs on which we focused—accountant, accounting assistant, and accounting secretary—required experience, we included a period of work for Marie as "Aide Comptable au Secours Catholique" (accounting assistant for Catholic Relief) and for Khadija as "Aide Comptable au Secours Islamique" (accounting assistant for Islamic Relief). Although researchers at Sciences-Po voiced no objections about this signal, we received a great deal of push-back once we reported our results. Critics were contending that "Secours Islamique" was a signal of religious radicalism that would make any human resources manager nervous. We presented a double defense of our choice. First, we argued that Secours Islamique is the same type of organization as Secours Catholique. For example, during the Ramadan breakfast celebration organized by the mayor of Paris in the year of our experiment, in a celebration descriptively covered by Kepel (2012), members of Secours Islamique were in attendance. It was described as one of the four top humanitarian nongovernmental organizations in France, which in 2009 had raised 19.4 million euros. Much of its monies went to rebuild Gaza, and it is a popular charity for the new Muslim middle classes. It has given donations to the children of Haiti and the Romani people of St. Denis. In the celebration covered by Kepel, the table for Secours Islamique was administered by two young girls, not veiled, with a sign on the table: "La souffrance n'a ni origine, ni religion, ni genre. La solidarité non plus. Oeuvrons ensemble pour un monde solidaire" [Suffering has no origin or religion, or gender. Nor does solidarity. Let us work together for a just world]. The first point here is that Secours Islamique is the same type of organization as Secours Catholique. This leads to our second point. It is probably the case that rooted French assume that Secours Islamique is radically religious while Secours Catholique is absolutely secular. If this is true, the same activity by a Muslim and a Christian in France would be differentially interpreted, one negatively and one positively. This is the very sort of prejudice our correspondence test was designed to tap.

A final signal of religious identification on the résumés was that of leisure activity. Marie was active in "Scouts et Guides de France" (French Scouts and Guides) while Khadija was active in "Scouts Musulmans de France" (French Muslim Scouts). Interestingly, this signal did not raise many eyebrows, as "Muslim" is less incendiary in French public debate than "Islamic."

Note that we have not discussed male names. Given the low number of job openings, we decided not to vary gender. Our original idea was to indicate religion through an accessory—for Muslims, men wearing a kaffiyeh (cap) and women a foulard (shawl); for Christians, a visible cross on a necklace. But our consultants were adamant that a picture of a male wearing a kaffiyeh on a job application was a provocation in France and would be immediately recognized as an experimental test. So we decided to limit ourselves to female applicants. But we ran into trouble again, as social scientists at Sciences-Po insisted that the foulard had double meaning to the French: it could be a sign of religion but also of gender submission. With the foulard we would not be able to distinguish whether employers were discriminating on religion or on indications of submissiveness. Furthermore, legal scholars pointed out to us that Article 9 of the European Convention on Human Rights permits restrictions on religious accessories under certain health or hygiene issues and even due to certain commercial imperatives. Therefore, using an accessory as a signal of religious adherence might confound legal and religious motivations for discrimination. We therefore had to drop the foulard and the photo as well. But we stayed with women, about which we were asked time and again. Our answer has been, would you ask the same question if we reverted to men? Perhaps more cogent are the data, released in 2010, that since the 1990s there has been in France a marked flux of feminization in the immigrant pool. From sub-Saharan Africa, the data from an INSEE and INED collaboration reveals that 60% of the post-1990 immigrants are women (Lhommeau and Simon 2010). We were therefore choosing the gender of the larger immigrant pool.

Our focus on jobs such as accounting assistant was also the result of many discussions and compromises. Outside of pure distaste by the human resource officials evaluating the résumés, there are two possible mechanisms that would deter companies from giving a Muslim applicant a job position. First, directors may be unprejudiced but assume the worst of their suppliers, their other employees, and their customers. If this is the case, we should see greater discrimination to the extent that the job involves mixing with other divisions in the firm and the public. Here the mechanism is a matter of assumed taste. Second, directors may have strong priors about the probable job performance of certain minorities, and these expectations of competence could determine the probability that among equally qualified candidates, the applicant who is Muslim would be evaluated as less promising. Here the mechanism is that of statistical discrimination. Thus, we inferred, it would be best to vary the job types into four categories: contact with public/no specific skills required; contact with public/need for specific skills; no contact with public/no specific skills; and no contact with public/need for specific skills. Doing this would require four times as many applications to assure ourselves of sufficient statistical leverage, at a time when very few jobs were being announced. Further counting against this differentiation was the recognition that these two routes to discrimination were not as clear-cut as originally thought. Following the reasoning of Arrow (1998), if employers do not hire Muslims in fear that their customers won't return to their shops if Muslims are visible (the taste mechanism), then Muslims have no incentive to develop skills for future advancement, and if they do not develop those skills, it is reasonable for employers to associate Muslim names with poorer performance. We elaborated on this outcome as an equilibrium in Chapter 8. Here we note that we focused on a single set of jobs—ones with moderate demands on skills (requiring two years of postsecondary school education and three years of job experience) and with at least some contact with either fellow employees or the wider public. If discrimination were found in this experiment, separating out the "taste" from the "expectations of competence" demanded separate investigation, which we conducted in the course of our experimental games.

Specifying the precise set of relevant jobs required a new set of choices. We had to drop jobs in sales, as these jobs generally require in-person applications to a local office. We also had to drop those jobs, mostly in construction, for which we thought applications from women would be seen as curious and possibly a test of adherence to laws about gender discrimination. We thus settled on a group of administrative and clerical jobs that were "feminized" in popular understanding. We could then list the set of advertisements that met this standard: *secrétaire polyvalent(e)* (general secretary), *agent administratif* (administrative agent), *aide comptable* (accounting assistant), *administration des ventes* (sales representative), and *gestion des approvisionnements* (supply management). Although these are diverse categories of employment, by randomizing which résumé got sent to which job category, we did not foresee problems of systematic bias.

To avoid detection with two applicants named Diouf applying for the same job, with nearly identical qualifications, we implemented a "difference-in-difference" design. To do this, we created a third fictional applicant—one who would have the exact same qualifications, the exact same citizenship, the exact same work experience, and the exact same neighborhood of residence—who would be seen clearly as a rooted French applicant. This applicant needed to bear a name that would imply being French and having origins in a Christian-heritage family but one not associated in France with high Catholicism. We chose "Aurélie." This is a name that is not perfectly secular—there was once a saint by that name in the Christian tradition, one of two legendary sisters, virgin pilgrims from Asia Minor who wound up in Palestine and then in Rome in their escape from the Sarrazins—yet it does not connote in the French context high Catholicism. Her ascribed family name "Ménard" is common among the rooted French population. In our research design, we randomly matched Aurélie with either Khadija or Marie for every qualifying job opening. Our results therefore do not compare the number of callbacks between Khadija and Marie. Rather, we compare the relative success of Khadija versus Aurélie with the relative success of Marie versus Aurélie. Aurélie's success provides a baseline of opportunity for someone of her qualifications; and we can then see the difference between Marie and Khadija against the same baseline. This is what statisticians mean by difference-in-difference.

About halfway into the administration of our experiment, Cédiey phoned to tell us that the results of bias against Khadija were too strong, and perhaps employees did not realize that "Diouf" was a Senegalese name and that we were therefore confounding religious and national differences. He recommended that for the two Diouf applications we insert the same photo of a Senegalese woman in an utterly secular guise. We implemented this suggestion immediately but found no difference in the results after this change in protocol.

The choice of a single gender, the withdrawal of the foulard as a signal, the choice of job categories, the introduction of a baseline candidate (Aurélie), and the attachment of a photograph of the Senegalese applicants for the final set of applications—all in the context of a Great Recession, where few positions were open—required a series of adjustments from the initial protocols while in the field.

Obtaining a Sample for Our Experimental Games

Our experiments in the Nineteenth District required that we obtain a sample of participants that would allow us to observe and analyze interactions between rooted French (the French born, French parents, French grandparents, or FFFs) and Senegalese Muslims (SMs) and Senegalese Christians (SXs). But we also needed other participants to ensure the smooth progress of our experiments with a large enough sample size. In this section, we describe the methods we used to recruit these players and how we were able to obtain a large enough sample of FFFs.

In our search for game participants, we moved from the idea of distributing flyers for people to come to register, to one of doing a random recruitment walk during the weekends through the many apartment complexes. However, we realized during a planning meeting that you need a code to get into apartment buildings, and entering those buildings without authorization would be trespassing. We needed an alternative. On a freezing Sunday in January, Laitin walked the neighborhood to explore alternatives. He hardly saw anyone outside, other than a few homeless people. The only action was in and out of Metro stations. This led to the procedure of randomly recruiting through Nineteenth District Metro stations, stratified by population size in the surrounding subdistrict. Little did he know that once the weather warmed up, the Nineteenth became a lively district with a great amount of foot traffic. In fact, instead of setting up tables in the warm Metro station, our recruiters stood at the top of the station exits and approached passersby based on a protocol that was updated and refined in the field.

A major goal (inspired by comments from Macartan Humphreys at an early stage of planning) was to get the set of players at each session to look like typical neighbors, such that players would not suspect some ethnic or religious targeting as our experimental purpose. The random recruitment from the diverse Nineteenth District worked well for that purpose, but we realized that for making inferences about FFF behavior toward our target group, we had too few FFFs in our initial registration list. Although the percentage of FFF recruits was a reasonable approximation of their proportion in the Nineteenth District, we needed to oversample them. We therefore, in our later recruitment days by the Metro stations, ethnically profiled potential subjects. We did not only solicit every nth person (as required in our recruitment algorithm), but we also approached every person who might qualify as FFF. We even did some extra recruiting on the beautiful Quai de la Seine. The yield of FFFs (given that it is a place for leisure, dog walking, and bocce ball) was greater in this more upscale setting. We therefore sacrificed a degree of randomness in our sample of players in order to obtain statistical leverage through the overrepresentation of FFF. This was not pre-planned but rather an adjustment performed in the field.

Before final implementation of our experimental sessions, and at a presentation of our experimental protocols at the Toulouse School of Economics, we were asked how we would handle intra- versus intergender dyads in our group sessions, which led to a plan for having three all-male and three all-female sessions as well as two sessions that were mixed gender. This is something that we did not think to address (and was not in our original protocol) until it was forced upon us in a seminar only weeks before implementation. In any case, all the experimental results reported in this book and in our research papers that involve dyads of players are based on statistical models that control for the gender of each game partner as well as for each game session. This is one more example where adjustments in the field trumped the original setup protocol for our experimental games.

One of us raised at nearly the last moment the potentially embarrassing issue that some will wonder why we are assuming no Joola/Serer effect, and if we controlled for tribe, the quality of our econometric analysis would weaken given the low number of observations at our disposal in the experimental games. We therefore separated sessions for Joolas and Serers as best we could, given our other constraints in forming groups. Because our econometric analysis controls for session fixed effects, meaning that we compare individuals' behavior with coreligionists and with non-coreligionists within each session, nearly all of the interactions we report among the Senegalese are intra- rather than intertribal, and this allows us to identify clearly the religious difference across our Senegalese players.

Glitches

Field experiments are not laboratories in the traditional sense. They are, as we have already mentioned, sites of ad hoc improvisation and unexpected crises.[19] We had our share of them.

At Registration

The biggest shock to our protocol—already adjusted to adapt to local conditions—occurred on the first day of registration at the language school we rented at Quai de la Seine. Our night watchman cum recruiter for our Serer/Joola subjects was true to his word that he would not tell potential subjects anything about religion as a criterion of eligibility. Rather, he told them—unbeknownst to us—that we were movie directors wanting to cast Serer and Joola actors for a new film. Our office was subsequently bombarded with exquisitely dressed applicants, angry that they had come to the Nineteenth District only to play small games for money. One of us (Adida) had the diplomatic task of calming them down. And then we worried that the Serer and Joola communities in the Île-de-France region would all meet and coordinate. However, Etienne Smith (one of our ethnographers, who was fluent in Wolof, the lingua franca of Senegal) brought us into contact with notables in the French Senegalese community to help us unwind the social networks of the applicants such that we separated players who were socially connected across game sessions. We nonetheless added in our exit questionnaire and controlled in our statistical models for a variable as to whether the player knew anyone playing in his or her session or knew anyone who played in a previous session.

Many less worrisome biases arose at the registration stage: when recruiting heavily on Saturdays, religious Jews (who are plentiful in the Nineteenth) would not sign up, as writing on the day of the Sabbath is proscribed. At least this is what one Orthodox Jew we solicited told us, after saying he otherwise would have been happy to register. We thus had no Orthodox Jews in our sample, nor did we recruit subjects of Asian origin, though we approached many of them as part of our protocol; also, we found men less willing to be recruited than women and have no explanation for why we were more attractive to women in the Nineteenth District than to men. Nevertheless, as explained in Chapter 4, we are able to identify the direction of the bias coming from the fact that FFFs who participated in our games and who constitute the players of interest among those recruited in the Nineteenth District are those who accepted to participate in it and hence not a random sample of FFFs. This bias in fact runs against us finding any discriminatory behavior of FFFs toward Senegalese Muslims (relative to Senegalese Christians) as we show that our FFF participants are more open to diversity than a true representative (random) sample of FFFs would be.

Our recruits surely had outliers among them. One of our registered players (neither FFF, SM, nor SX), as reported to us by one of our research assistants from her field notes, refused on principle to take any of the money that she had earned in a practice game. Our research assistant asked her why she allocated so much money to herself in a practice altruism game if she did not want the money for herself but got no clear answer. Although this woman was surely not of the type that has participated in experimental games in university settings and is probably nontypical of the population among whom we were recruiting, we retained her for the full experiment as we wanted to include in our games as broad a range of sensibilities that our near-random selection of players allowed. In a protocol with only eighty players, we always risk that effects can be due to outliers, and we paid particular attention to this in our data analysis to ensure that results were never determined by only a few of our players.

Play

Our games required us to include at least one Senegalese of each religion and two FFFs in each session. During the first weekend of play, two of the sessions were missing a crucial Senegalese. Each time, one of our research assistants had to intervene directly, calling the player to find out that she was stuck on the Metro or that he had not properly understood that our start times were fixed. Getting these players to the game session, while all other participants were patiently sitting and waiting for the games to start, required quite a bit of logistical juggling and diplomacy; but eventually, we were able to get the games going. Again, this unforeseen circumstance runs against us finding a discriminatory behavior of FFFs toward SMs (relative to SXs). Indeed, the players whose tardiness may have infuriated their FFF game partners, hence making them more hostile toward them, were SXs, not SMs. To our benefit, any bias on this score would have worked against our finding a penalty for being an SM.

By the eighth session, we were desperate for extra Senegalese, especially Christians. We contacted former players for help in recruitment. We then found out that those they had recommended to us performed too well on the speed chatting quiz, arousing our suspicions that they had been briefed on the questions that would be asked of them. This gave us further reason to control in our analysis for whether players knew someone who had played in an earlier session.

In one session, a player (neither FFF, SM, nor SX) had a severe hearing problem. He wound up earning far less than any of the players who had already participated in the games. One of the other players in the session appealed to Adida, telling her that the others did not know about this disability, and interpreted his behavior during the speed chatting as diffidence. Consequently, he was less appreciated than he should have been. We considered giving him a bonus. But we looked at his playing of the altruism game and noticed that he was very generous to others. Additionally, he wrote in his exit survey that he participated not for the money but for the experience. We decided that it would undermine the spirit of the game if we financially rewarded folks who had consciously ceded their funds to others. He left happy with his meager rewards and thanked the entire team, individually, for the experience.

For the trust game administration, we knew from the literature (Eckel and Wilson's 2004 and 2006 work on the beauty of the players affecting strategy selection) that small differences in the context of the game can have big implications. We therefore asked our game monitors to tell us of such differences. Karine observed that she and Matthieu, at their tables administering the trust game, tried to make the players relax with light humor and this might have made them more trusting than at Josselin's table, where he was strict about no talking. Severine, another research assistant, noted that several of the players, once they had played more than once, began to chat up their co-player, perhaps in the hope of instilling in them a sense of their trustworthiness, and this deviation from the rules was not monitored at the same level by all the game monitors. Yet each of our trust dyads was randomly assigned to tables and their monitors, meaning that differences in our game monitors' behavior was ultimately inconsequential to our results. Nonetheless, we report these observations in the name of full disclosure.

Our Religious Coding

Two subjects were offended by the questions we asked about other people's religion. One older lady thought that it was wrong to expect in a first meeting between people (during the speed chatting game) to learn anything about one's religion. (This was Agathe, who stuck to her principles at some personal cost, leaving a missing value on Question 2—what is the religion of the person you met?—in speed chatting for all her interlocutors.) Another was offended by the question on the inscription survey wanting to know his religion. He felt our research was a threat to the laïcité of France.

Disturbing some of our subjects in unexpected ways gave us new insight about what the religion question means in the French context. One of the players answered on the exit form that she did not know the religion of one of her partners in the speed chatting game and gave up the chance even to guess for a one-euro gain. Yet when given an opportunity to add anything else she had learned about her partner, she responded that he was a Moroccan Jew. Asking the religious question for her, and we infer for other FFFs, implied asking about belief, not heritage. This helped us clarify in our own minds that our targeted subjects were considered by FFFs, as defined by Bowen (2010, 11), as "sociological Muslims," that is, "people whose background and traditions form part of the long history of Muslim civilization" regardless of present practice or beliefs. The point here is that a rigid preanalysis plan would have constrained us from reinterpreting our "religion" question from how we understood it at the National Science Foundation proposal stage.

It Wasn't All Crisis Management

Lest aspiring field researchers get too distressed hearing about the deviations from our original protocols and the small fires we put out, let us underline that we not only were seeking to answer immensely important questions, but we created an experimental environment that was pleasant for our subjects. When our players finished and checked out of the sessions with their game earnings in an envelope, we noticed that no one looked inside to check whether the funds for which they had signed a receipt were there; they simply trusted us. And there were invariably smiles and thanks offered for participation, rather than any frustration about misadvertising or misleading these people into these games.

In general, our subjects left the sessions not only with money but with pleasant experiences. Mathieu, a research assistant, wrote us subsequently: "I hope that all goes well and that all of us have returned to a normal life after an intense month of March! I'm contacting you with some news, but also to tell you that I had a telephone call from one of our players. He contacted me to learn of any news from our team, but also to thank us for the games and especially for the gains. At the time of the games he found himself broke, and the gains were a great benefit."

Postplay, there were more kudos to be enjoyed. To pay the recipients in the dictator game (those who posed for the pictures), we made regular text message and phone calls to those who won more than the fifteen-euro deposit we had given in advance. This was to invite them to come to the language school we were renting, right in front of Quai de la Seine, where their pictures were taken, for payment. Nine of the twelve recipients showed up (although one sent a friend). Two had given unreachable numbers, and one never picked up the phone. The recipients were totally delighted to get this unexpected payday. The man we identified to our subjects as either Georges or Mohammed in the dictator game left our office, incredulous about the size of his "winnings," and we saw him fifteen minutes later with some buddies and with a bottle of wine dancing on the Quai de la Seine.

Fishing

After completing the treatments and coldly examining our results, there were two significant interpretive moves we made that were post hoc. This means that they were not tests of our theoretical suppositions (which are usually referred to as "confirmatory" findings) but rather correlations we saw in the data that we could not ignore (usually referred to as "exploratory" findings and not having the same scientific status as confirmatory). A strict rule demanding only analysis of tests that were preplanned would have required us to either ignore these results or to put them to further test with new data, for purposes of confirmation. A less strict rule (to which we abide) is to report what we find at the exploratory level and to alert readers that these findings should be put under more careful scrutiny.

Speed Chatting and the Socialization Phase

The original purpose of the speed chatting experiment (as described in Chapter 5) was to test the so-called technology mechanism of coethnic cooperation (Habyarimana et al. 2009). Could it be, we asked, that Senegalese Christians, once in France, would spend their Sundays in French churches and thereby interact with FFFs in a way not possible for Senegalese Muslims, who would spend their Fridays at mosques, mostly interacting with people whose roots were in North Africa? If so, the SXs would better be able to "read" their FFF coreligionists—that is, understand subtle messages and have acquired the technology of conversation with FFFs to make a good impression. The speed chatting protocol, in asking SXs and SMs to meet with FFFs and learn about each other in a short amount of time was a fascinating test of this conjecture. To the extent that SXs and FFFs learned about each other more successfully than SMs and FFFs, we could infer that a communication technology was helping the SXs succeed in the French labor market. It turned out that there was no improvement in how much SXs either learned about FFFs or were able to infer about FFFs compared with their SM counterparts. In our ethnographic interviews, we asked one of our informants if she had interactions with FFFs in church. She responded with a mocking smile that she never saw any FFFs at church, only coreligionists from the Antilles.

However, in examining the panoply of games, we noted a subtle change in FFF behavior after the speed chatting game, in which levels of distaste for SMs seemed to abate. This suggested to us the interpretation that the speed chatting game served a purpose in socializing FFFs with SMs, and maybe for the first times in their lives the FFFs were having a relaxed informal meeting with Muslims and seeing them as individuals. We consequently (in Chapter 7) interpreted the FFF–SM interactions post–speed chatting as demonstrating a limited (but noticeable) effect of socialization. But socialization was not a preplanned treatment.

The Hortefeux Effect

Serendipitously, our experimental sessions had a varying mix of SMs and SXs. As we observed the administration of the dictator game, it dawned on us that the religious composition of the group might be affecting FFF behavior: sessions with more Muslims might affect FFF behavior relative to sessions with fewer Muslims. We called this the Hortefeux effect, giving prominence to a leading advisor to the president (and minister of the interior) who openly told a provincial gathering—not aware that he was being recorded—that interactions with Muslims are unproblematic, just so long as there is no more than one. Postulating this Hortefeux effect was a surmise that came from casual observation of the treatment designed for other purposes. We ran tests (in Chapter 7) of this observation, and the findings held up as we suspected even after a barrage of robustness tests. Still, these results must be reported as post hoc analysis of the data.

Conclusion

Unlike sausages, the findings that this book has reported are not appetizing. They reveal a self-sustaining process of religious discrimination in France, despite a resolutely secular ideology that pervades French society. We have shown the reality of this discrimination and the mechanisms that sustain it through surveys, experiments, and ethnographic interviews. But with results as important as they are for public policy, it is incumbent on us to reveal the potential sources of bias through (1) case selection based on political importance of the topic in France rather than its inferential power, (2) improvisation with unexpected occurrences, (3) glitches in the administration of our protocols, and (4) the exploratory nature of post hoc conjectures. Although we are convinced that our results are, if anything, biased against finding religious discrimination, this Appendix provides a realistic portrayal of the actual conduct of the research that should be part of the scientific record.

Notes

CHAPTER ONE *The Challenge of Muslim Migrants into Christian-Heritage Societies*

1. De Gaulle quoted in Fetzer and Soper (2006, 62).

2. On the scope of "Christian-heritage societies," see Bartlett (1993, p. 5). His historically based definition of Europe includes "that area of Christendom [in the High Middle Ages] that recognized papal authority and celebrated the Latin liturgy." It is these countries and their settler offshoots that we consider as "Christian-heritage societies."

3. See Laurence (2012, 147) for a chart on failed and successful attempts in "Islam-related terrorism in Europe."

4. The term "Islamophobia" was coined in the 1980s. See Runnymede Trust Commission on British Muslims and Islamophobia (1997, 1).

5. But see Pfaff and Gill (2006) and Olivier Roy's foreword in Laurence and Vaisse (2006). Both present evidence that Muslims in Europe, because of their diverse backgrounds, are not well positioned to provide a political threat.

6. Sponsored by the Bertelsmann Foundation, the Religion Monitor is a data collection instrument that surveys traditional and new forms of religiosity and examines the changing face of religion in the context of pluralism.

7. Religion Monitor 2013 (see http://www.gatestoneinstitute.org/3696 /germany-islam-threat for a summary of the findings).

8. See http://www.comres.co.uk/polls/BBC_Radio_1_Newsbeat_Discri mination_Poll_September_2013.pdf.

9. The first correspondence test investigated labor market discrimination against immigrant applicants in the United Kingdom (Jowell and Prescott-Clarke 1970).

10. L'Association SOS Racisme, Cass. crim., June 11, 2002, Bull. Crim., No. 131 at 482. See also L'Association SOS Racisme, Bull. Crim. June 3, 2003, No. 02:86158.

11. Commission Nationale Consultative des Droits de l'Homme (2014). It is summarized in Vincent (2014).

12. Copé (2012). In the original, the statement refers to "college," which can be rendered as either junior or senior high school in American classification; here we render it as "school."

13. According to Judd and Park (1993), a group stereotype is "the set of attributes that subjects agree on as typical of the group."

14. The fundamental model was originally proposed by Phelps (1972); in subsequent references, as in the literature, we credit this approach to Arrow (1973).

15. Allport (1954, 6–7), in his classic study, defines prejudice as an "avertive or hostile attitude toward a person who belongs to a group, simply because he belongs to that group."

16. On the fears, see Huntington (2004); on the exaggeration, see the review of Huntington's book by Gary Segura, in *Perspectives on Politics* (2005), 3:640–642.

CHAPTER TWO *Anti-Muslim Discrimination in the French Labor Market and Its Consequences*

1. The findings presented in this chapter diverge from the far more optimistic results based on data collected by M. Tribalat. As analyzed in Laurence and Vaisse (2006, 43–44), it points to the near universal reliance on the French language by Muslims, their high rates of exogamy, and their fertility rates trending toward the French mean.

2. According to a survey conducted by IFOP (2010), only 4.5% of the French population goes to church every Sunday (http://www.ifop.com/media /pressdocument/238-1-document_file.pdf).

3. On standards for natural experiments, see Dunning (2012).

4. On the progress of Islam in West Africa, see Trimingham (1964). On the zone where the two religions meet, and using this for identification purposes, see Laitin (1986).

5. Chapters 3–5 provide full details on the procedures and protocols generating the results presented here.

6. Studies of French voters support this view, namely, that their relationship with the church was an excellent predictor of their vote, at least through the 1980s. See Berger (1974).

7. We did have a few extra subjects in several sessions to ensure against dropouts.

8. Subjects were told that because they would be interacting with strangers for the next few hours, interactions would be more personal if they revealed their given names to fellow players.

9. For full technical details, see Adida, Laitin, and Valfort (2015b).

10. For full technical details, see Adida, Laitin, and Valfort (2010).

11. Difficult choices in the implementation of this design for the French environment will be discussed in the Appendix.

12. ISM-CORUM stands for "Inter Service Migrants—Centre d'Observation et de Recherche sur l'Urbain et ses Mutations."

13. For full technical details, see Adida, Laitin, and Valfort (2010).

14. We present full protocols for this survey in Chapter 4.

15. As expected, our results without controls do not change when we control for the educational level of the respondent's ancestor who was the first to migrate to France (because SM and SX first-generation migrants are similar

in terms of education). Our results are also unaffected by controlling for the respondent's gender and age.

16. Institut national de la statistique et des études économiques (2010). In 2009, this average net monthly household income was equal to 2,984 euros. See http://www.insee.fr/fr/themes/tableau.asp?reg_id=0&id=45.

CHAPTER THREE *Solving the Problem of Causal Identification*

1. Thanks to Chris Beauchemin of Institut national d'études démographiques for giving us access to the raw data for the 2002 Senegalese census (Troisième Recensement Général de la Population et de l'Habitat [RGPH-III] 2002). A World Bank survey of randomly selected internal migrants to cities in Senegal revealed a breakdown of 23% Catholic and 77% Muslim in combining the Serer and Joola respondents. See World Bank (2009). The Joshua Project (http://joshuaproject.net/) estimates the Catholic population for the Joola at 7% and that of the Serer at 22%; nearly all of the remaining are counted as Muslim. In all these data sources, we observe an overrepresentation of Christians compared with Senegal as a whole.

2. These results stem from the survey we conducted in 2009. We present this survey in greater detail in Chapters 4 and 5.

3. This section relies on Crowder (1962) and Cruise O'Brien (1975).

4. Unique to Senegal, the four communes of Senegal (Saint-Louis, Dakar, Gorée, and Rufisque), the oldest colonial towns in French West Africa, had special status in the colonial empire. In 1848, the Second Republic extended the rights of full French citizenship (for those who were *évolués*, that is, assimilated to French culture) to the inhabitants of these communes. In 1916, these rights were granted to all indigenous residents (called *originaires*) of the communes.

5. We present this survey for our estimate of family income in Chapter 2 and describe the protocol in Chapter 4.

CHAPTER FOUR *Procuring a Sample*

1. As emphasized in Chapter 2, we did have a few extra subjects in several sessions to ensure against dropouts.

2. We deviated from our randomized rule for approaching passersby at the assigned Metro stations due to our goal of recruiting enough FFFs to observe in an experimental setting the behaviors of FFFs toward SMs and SXs. Indeed, the Nineteenth District, even though it has immense advantages for us as a field site, has one disadvantage, namely, that there are not an abundance of FFFs to be recruited. We therefore instructed recruiters to deviate from the protocol if a passerby had the appearance of an FFF, a form of ethnic profiling.

3. Research to date confirms that right-wing ideology is associated with more hostile attitudes toward immigrants. Hoskin (1985), Meertens and Pettigrew (1997), and Pettigrew (1998), for example, all found that those who are

more prejudiced against immigrants in Europe tend to be more conservative politically, while Lahav (1997) discovered that party affiliations and traditional ideological orientations are the most important determinants of immigration attitudes. Relying on the Thirtieth Eurobarometer on Immigrants and Out-groups, Saxton and Benson (2003) confirmed that political ideology is the most compelling explanation of hostility toward immigrants. More recently, Albertson and Gadarian (2012) have used a video experiment conducted in an online, opt-in panel to show that anti-immigrant threatening advertisements lead to more punitive attitudes among white Republicans in the United States.

4. We discuss this issue in greater detail in Chapter 6.

5. Nonetheless, on the side of caution, we control for level of religiosity in all our analyses to neutralize this difference.

CHAPTER FIVE *Research Protocols*

1. The accounts were real, as demanded by Stanford University's institutional review board (IRB) overseeing the ethical standards of our research. IRBs also monitor mistreatment of subjects. Only minor deceptions are permitted, as long as they are necessary for experimental success and do not threaten player self-esteem.

2. The novelty of our simultaneous trust game with respect to the original trust game introduced by Berg, Dickhaut, and McCabe (1995) is in the simultaneity of the decisions made by the sender and by the receiver. (In the original trust game, the receiver learns the amount sent by the sender before making his or her decision of how much to send back.) We preferred the simultaneous trust game over the original trust game for several reasons. Our objective was to treat each trust game played by our subjects as a one-shot game in order to mimic everyday random encounters between strangers. It was therefore critical to avoid any reputation effect that would have occurred if receivers learned how much particular senders had sent in previous games. This procedure also brings a touch of realism as most interactions in real life happen under incomplete information. In this respect, removing sequentiality in the decision process looks less artificial. Furthermore, because our protocol introduced a socialization phase after the simultaneous trust game, in which players would get to know each other, we did not want their conversations to be biased by knowledge of their partners' actions during the simultaneous trust game.

3. Our illustrations of game materials in this chapter are exact reproductions from the experiments, and consequently they are in French.

4. So as not to prime players to the ethnicity of the FFF model, we did not advertise that this model would specifically be FFF. The choice appeared to the players as random because we picked the player identification number out of a hat, not telling the players that all the player identification numbers in the hat were the same, all referring to a player we knew to be an FFF. This strategy involved deception toward the players; however, because it was minor and could not affect players' self-esteem, it was approved by the IRB overseeing the ethics of our experimental treatments.

5. It is a convention among economists in the experimental tradition never to lie to subjects. Although we violated this convention once in regard to the choice of a model (and for this we received special IRB approval), in all other cases we told the truth, but not all of it, in order that our games better approximate everyday expectations and behaviors.

6. In the speed chatting game, the religion of each SM and SX was reported by a maximum of three FFFs, which is too small a sample of respondents for statistical estimation. We therefore cannot rely on this game to analyze FFF beliefs about SM and SX players' religious affiliation.

7. Only two of the eleven SMs with first names of Arabic origin were not characterized as "Muslim" by a majority of FFFs (these first names were Ibou and Sidy). Similarly, only one of the seven SMs with first names not of Arabic origin was characterized as "Muslim" by a majority of FFFs (this first name was Ndeye).

8. For expediency, a random half of the 2010 FFF players were shown half of our 2009 Senegalese and FFF players; the other random half were shown the other half of our 2009 Senegalese and FFF players.

CHAPTER SIX *Muslim Characteristics That Feed Rational Islamophobia*

1. Institut français d'opinion publique (2010).

2. This gap holds when one compares, as Brouard and Tiberj (2011) did, "new French" Muslim immigrants of North African, sub-Saharan African, and Turkish origin, as well as their children and grandchildren born in France, with a sample of the French general population. Whereas 28% of the former saw religion as extremely important, only 4% of the latter reported that religion was extremely important in their lives.

3. Addressing why Muslims are in today's world more religious than Christians is beyond the scope of this book, but the question has attracted much attention in popular commentary. A typical answer (and here a summary of Maalouf 2001) focuses on globalization, which is accompanied by cultural domination of the West, with its Christian tradition that portrays itself as the incarnation of modernity. This domination creates a will to resist on the part of Islam, the second world religion behind Christianity. And this translates into a reemergence of traditional values among which piety is one element.

4. See http://www.eurel.info/IMG/pdf/randstad_fait_religieux.pdf.

5. See http://www.ifop.com/media/poll/benoit16.pdf. We elaborate on the multiple meanings of laïcité in the Appendix.

6. http://www.grouperandstad.fr/wp-content/uploads/sites/3/2014/05/SLIDES_%C3%A9tude_fait_religieux_OFRE_InstitutRandstad_2014.pdf.

7. Zuber (2008, 88) reported that the interpretation of laïcité as promoting secularism arose largely to justify the prohibition of the veil (in the foulard affair, 1989) for school children in French public schools. Thomas (2012, chapter 8) pointed out that this interpretation was promoted by the Stasi Commission, charged with recommending rules for religious expression in public schools.

8. The literature on the headscarf, from the political repercussions of a ban on wearing the headscarf in France's public schools to state laws banning the veil in public places, is extensive. Excellent sources on the headscarf include Bowen (2007) and Thomas (2012, chapter 7).

9. In 1 Corinthians: "every woman who prays or prophesies with her head uncovered dishonors her head."

10. See http://www.eglise.catholique.fr/foi-et-vie-chretienne/la-celebration -de-la-foi/les-grandes-fetes-chretiennes/paques-et-la-semaine-sainte/quest -ce-que-le-careme/370712-le-jeune-en-questions/.

11. This conflict between the rooted French population and Muslim norms can have countervailing implications. Because the republican tradition in France provides equal opportunity to girls, French public schools enable Muslim girls to escape from the gendered hierarchy of their home lives. In reference to one of her female informants, Kakpo (2007) in her ethnography of Muslim youths in France writes, "Nassima does not break with the religion of the fathers, but seeks [through conservative behavior tied to educational achievement] to transform it into an instrument of self-reliance" (103–104).

12. For full technical details, see Adida, Laitin, and Valfort (2014a).

13. One may wonder whether our results could be driven by the fact that SMs give less to female than to male recipients simply because they expect other donors around them to give more to female than to male recipients. In this case, SMs may decide to give less to female recipients not because they are less supportive but because they are more supportive of gender equality (they wish male and female recipients to receive overall a similar amount of money). However, results from our 2009 strategic dictator game, although they inform us only about SM beliefs about FFF generosity toward the various recipients, are not supportive of this interpretation. They show that SMs expect FFFs to give similar amounts to male and female recipients. Another alternative explanation for our results would be that SMs expect female recipients to be less needy than male recipients, thereby justifying that they give more to the latter than to the former. But this interpretation is inconsistent with French reality. In 2001, the employment rate of women between the ages of twenty and sixty-four is 67%, nine percentage points below the employment rate of men of similar age (http://www.insee.fr/fr/themes/document.asp?ref_id =ip1462). Moreover, in 2010, the average wage of women employed in the private sector was 28% lower than the average wage of their male counterparts (http://www.insee.fr/fr/themes/document.asp?ref_id=ip1436). Put differently, women are not only more likely to be unemployed than men; they also have lower wages than men when they are employed. It would therefore be a stretch to interpret our results as SM men sustaining equality by donating more to SM men.

14. This was recognized in the Contrat d'Accueil et d'Intégration of 2003, introduced by then minister of the interior Nicolas Sarkozy and brought to national implementation in 2007. Here all immigrants are required to take courses promoting French values. The most intensive aspect of these courses is the 400 hours of free language instruction, part of the first pillar of the

program. See Office français de l'immigration et de l'intégration (n.d.) for full details.

15. Consult Rounds 2, 3, and 4 of the Afrobarometer (http://www .afrobarometer.org/) in Senegal, isolating responses from Serers and Joolas. The dependent variable is a question asked to the interviewer: "What is the language of interview?" The probability that the language of interview is French is significantly greater when the interviewee is SX than when the interviewee is SM.

16. Put differently, we do not find strong evidence for the "technology" mechanism introduced by Habyarimana et al. (2009), according to which a common religion would provide a technology for successful communication.

17. See http://www.ifop.com/media/poll/benoit16.pdf.

18. See http://www.lemonde.fr/societe/article/2014/08/12/le-reglement -controverse-de-wissous-plage-a-nouveau-suspendu-par-la-justice_4470635 _3224.html.

CHAPTER SEVEN *Evidence of Nonrational Islamophobia*

1. This remark was uttered in French during a photo op on September 5, 2009, at the Summer School in Seignosse, organized by the Union for a Popular Movement (the center-right political party in France led at the time by Nicolas Sarkozy). The video of this interaction, procured by *Le Monde*, is available at http://www.dailymotion.com/video/xafz5w_le-derapage-de-brice -hortefeux-la-h. Translated from the French by the authors.

2. For full technical details, see Adida, Laitin, and Valfort 2014b.

3. This result persists when we neutralize the influence of SM and SX facial traits on FFF behavior toward SMs and SXs. We do so based on the measure of FFF perception of those traits (in terms of beauty, friendliness, and trustworthiness) provided by the beauty game (see Chapter 5 for the protocol).

4. One of the reasons why FFF receivers send back less to SM senders than to SX senders could be that they hold different second-order beliefs about SMs and SXs, that is, FFFs expect SM beliefs about FFF pure altruism toward SMs to be more pessimistic than SX beliefs about FFF pure altruism toward SXs. Such beliefs would make FFFs expect that SM senders send less money to them than do SXs because FFFs expect that SMs consider FFFs as less trustworthy than do SXs. Consequently, FFFs send back less money to SM senders than to SX senders, out of belief-based reciprocal altruism. The analysis of the double strategic dictator game (see Chapter 5 for the protocol) rules out this possibility. It reveals that FFFs believe that SMs and SXs hold FFFs to be equally trustworthy. This provides further support to the fact that differences in taste toward SMs and SXs, not differences in beliefs about SM and SX behavior, accounts for FFF discriminatory behavior toward SMs in the simultaneous trust game.

5. Given names are socially revealing, as we saw in the correspondence test discussed in Chapter 2. A particularly poignant example of this reported in *Le*

Monde (April 16, 2008) concerned a children's television program and a prese-lected nine-year-old contestant named Islam Alaouchiche. When the casting agent heard the name, she exclaimed, "Calling a boy Islam is like wearing a veil for a girl. . . . We need you to understand [she told the boy's mother] that your child's name is reference to a religion that the French do not like." Her col-league added, "This might shock" (Duwat 2008).

6. For full technical details, see Adida, Laitin, and Valfort (2015a). By "sa-lience" of Muslims, we refer to Muslims' increasing percentage in the popula-tion, not to the fact that Muslims may become more visible (through the wearing of Islamic headscarves, for instance) irrespective of their number. Hence, the meaning of "salience" here is purely quantitative, not qualitative.

7. The fact that the number of SMs varies from one to three while the number of SXs varies from one to two introduces a concern: Could our results derive from the fact that FFF exposure to SM outgroup salience means an exposure to three SMs, while FFF exposure to SX outgroup salience means an exposure to two SXs? In Adida, Laitin, and Valfort (2015a), we show that this asymmetry does not drive our results.

8. See Adida, Laitin, and Valfort (2015a) for more sophisticated econo-metric tests that yield the same patterns.

9. The popular image of Sarkozy as minister of the interior and as presi-dent was one that was hostile to the Muslim presence in France. As minister of the interior, Sarkozy was active in protecting the French Jewish commu-nity from any restrictions on the preparations of kosher foods but refused to give assurances to the French Muslim community about the protection for their preparations of halal. This difference in treatment was interpreted as a prejudice signifying that Muslim but not Jewish practices are a threat to France's culture (Kepel 2011, 458). When Claude Gueant served as Sar-kozy's minister of the interior after Hortefeux, he justified to the press his intensive deportation campaign of illegals by commenting that Muslims praying in the street lead the French to "no longer [feeling] at home." See Khetani (2012).

10. In our technical analysis of donations in Adida, Laitin, and Valfort (2015a), with a range of controls and what statisticians call fixed effects for faces, we find that FFFs believe that other FFFs increase their donations to SX guises by about 2.78 euros with an additional SX in the room. Meanwhile, they decrease the amount they believe other FFFs donate to the SM guises by about twenty-nine cents with each additional SM in the room. The latter is not itself significant, but the comparison of the effect of increasing SXs and increasing SMs is highly significant.

11. Harris Interactive (2013): "Le regard des Français sur la religion musul-mane," http://www.harrisinteractive.fr/news/2013/Results_HIFR_PAI_1604 2013.pdf.

12. Quoted in "Le maire de Paris: 'Il y a overdose,'" *Le Monde*, June 21, 1991, 40.

13. Respondents were provided with the French credentialing system. Answer 7 corresponds to "B.A.C. + 2 ans ou niveau B.A.C. + 2 ans (D.U.T., B.T.S.,

instituteurs, D.E.U.G., diplômes paramédicaux ou sociaux)"; for the United States, this is comparable to completion of community college, postsecondary technical training, or college. Answer 8 corresponds to "Diplôme de l'enseignement supérieur (2ème, 3ème cycles, grandes écoles)" and is comparable to postgraduate work in the United States.

14. As of this writing (February 2015), it is too early to assess the impact on FFF thinking about Islam in light of the attacks of January 2015. There were reports of a spate of mosque burnings in France, suggesting a guilt by association by some elements in France. But polls taken shortly thereafter indicated a significant but declining set of negative associations for Islam and its compatibility with French values. See Montvalon and Chambraud (2015).

CHAPTER EIGHT *A Discriminatory Equilibrium*

1. Although we find that statistical discrimination is not at stake in the context of our games, we do not exclude the possibility that it may be relevant outside our laboratory. In our simultaneous trust game, one might expect FFF female senders to send less to SM male receivers than to SX male receivers because of a (correct) belief that male SM donors in the dictator game send less to FFF female recipients than to FFF male recipients, relative to male SX donors. But in our experiments, with a very low number of mixed-gender sessions, we do not have the power to detect this effect in a statistically significant manner. Still, outside our games and specifically in the context of the labor market, statistical discrimination on the part of FFF recruiters may be a relevant part of the story. In Chapter 6, we emphasized three Muslim traits that could provide a basis for statistical discrimination on the part of FFF recruiters: higher levels of religiosity, more conservative views toward women, and poorer grasp of the French language.

2. For full technical details, see Adida, Laitin, and Valfort (2014b).

3. Spire (2008) reported on the clear realm for bureaucratic discretion and revealed taste in the administration of work permits and more generally in French institutional culture. Thomas (2012, 84) made a similar point in regard to citizenship, noting that the "non-automatic . . . process was notoriously inscrutable, partly because the administration was not obliged to offer those rejected any explanation of the reasons for its adverse decisions."

4. Combined with the fact that SMs are also less trusting of the French environment, SM lower altruism led SMs to be consistently less cooperative in all our experimental games. Besides giving less in the dictator game, SM sent less as senders and sent back less as receivers in the simultaneous trust game. They also allocated less as leaders in the voting game.

5. Both of these surveys rely on nationally representative samples.

6. Bowen (2010), though optimistic about practical solutions, provides a litany of issues that prevent full integration of Islam into France.

7. By "time" we technically mean the length of time since the first migrant in the respondent's family (that is, parent or grandparent) arrived in France.

CHAPTER NINE *Beyond France: Muslim Immigrants in Western Europe and in the United States*

1. These countries are Austria, Belgium, Denmark, Finland, France, Germany, Greece, Ireland, Italy, Luxembourg, the Netherlands, Norway, Portugal, Spain, Sweden, Switzerland, and the United Kingdom. All countries belonging to the United Nations Western European and Others Group that are typically considered as Western European are therefore included in our analysis, with the exception of Andorra, Iceland, Liechtenstein, Malta, Monaco, and San Marino.

2. Note that our results hold if we exclude individuals enrolled in an education program.

3. Again, this variable is not a perfect operationalization of discrimination. Indeed, certain types of respondents may be more likely to be unemployed and to report experiencing discrimination, even if they are not, in fact, discriminated against. Due to data limitations, however, this is the best measure we could find. Data limitations of this sort were instrumental in our choice to conduct well-identified experiments at the micro level.

4. These mean values are computed when the respondent's gender, age, education level, household income, number of household members, year of interview, and host country characteristics are held constant. It is important to emphasize that controlling for the respondent's household income runs against us finding any religion effect. Indeed, as shown in Chapter 2, if Muslim immigrants are discriminated against in the labor market, they are likely to have a lower income as compared with their Christian counterparts. Analysis of the ESS data confirms this premise. Ours is therefore a conservative approach in isolating the religious effect, which if anything would be an underestimate of the true effect.

5. Again, these results are computed when the respondent's gender, age, education level, household income, number of household members, year of interview, and host country's characteristics are held constant.

6. In Adida, Laitin, and Valfort (2014c), we go a step further. We demonstrate that Muslims from Muslim-majority countries are discriminated against in Western Europe only because of their religion. Their region of origin (that is, the fact that the bulk of Muslim-majority countries are located outside Europe) plays no role in accounting for such discrimination. More precisely, Muslim immigrants from Muslim-majority countries face the same level of discrimination should their country of origin be located in Europe (Albania), Middle East North Africa, Asia-Pacific, or sub-Saharan Africa.

7. Focusing on different generations of immigrants also avoids any confound between the "time spent in the host country" and the "age" effects. Indeed, first- and second-generation immigrants are already, on average, the same age. By contrast, the time elapsed since arrival of first-generation immigrants in the host country is strongly correlated with their age. This is problematic if age has a differential impact on immigrants' integration skills for Muslims and Christians. For instance, it may be the case that Muslim immigrants become more attached to their country of origin as they age, irrespec-

tive of the host country's context, while the reverse may occur among Christian immigrants. If so, we run the risk of wrongly interpreting these different age effects as evidence that the time Muslim and Christian immigrants spend in the host country generates a divergence in their integration patterns.

8. It is also the only study with sufficient sample size to allow for the kind of statistical analysis we provide. As presented by Howell and Jamal (2009, 69–71), and relying on surveys of Arab Americans conducted in 2000 and 2002 by Zogby International (http://www.aaiusa.org/demographics), Detroit was chosen not because it was typical, but rather because it is exceptional. In their words, Detroit has long been "the golden city of assimilationist desires." Furthermore, its "Arab communities, by virtue of their visibility, accessibility, and concentrated otherness, were in fact exceptional to national patterns" (69, 71).

9. See Fishman (1966), whose research shows the rapid acquisition of English (and equally rapid disappearance of the home country language) intergenerationally in the United States, more or less at the same pace across different ethnic groups.

10. Three of the questions reveal intergenerational shift. For one question—second- and third-generation Muslim immigrants are less likely than first-generation Muslim immigrants to read newspapers in Arabic—we see a decreasing gap between the religious groups across generations. But for two questions, the later generations report lower degrees of assimilation: they are more likely than the earlier generations to self-identify as Arab rather than white or any other race and are more likely to consider it important to speak Arabic.

CHAPTER TEN *What Is to Be Done?*

1. Faiola and Mekhennet (2014, 1); Belefsky (2014, A9).

2. The association Coexister in France specializes in such in-school interventions: http://www.coexister.fr/.

3. This strategy was employed by Bengalis living in the United States and the United Kingdom, as a cultural backdrop in Jhumpa Lahiri's (2003) novel.

4. In the French context, the anonymous résumé is one in which the "civil status" of the applicant (including the surname, the given name, the address, and the date of birth of the applicant) is suppressed.

5. This approach, despite failures in inducing employment of the handicapped, is gaining wider application. The law of January 27, 2011, calls for the gradual implementation of gender quotas on boards of directors and supervisory boards of companies listed on the stock exchanges and public companies. Two thresholds are scheduled: (1) a 20% female quota must be reached within three years of the law's promulgation; and (2) a 40% female quota must be reached within six years of the law's promulgation. There would be added complexity for quotas applying to ethnoreligious minorities, as it would demand the elimination of all restrictions on ethnoreligious data collection in France (see the Appendix).

6. Aeberhardt et al. (2010) indeed show that discrimination against immigrants from Muslim-majority countries (relative to French without recent

immigrant history) is salient primarily at the hiring stage but much less for promotion within a firm (as measured by salaries). Hence, diversity training at the recruitment stage is necessary for all hiring agents on the labor market, including HR intermediaries: recruiting firms, temp agencies, but also Pôle Emploi and the Association for Executive Hiring (APEC). For these intermediaries, diversity training must be complemented with workshops that train HR personnel to better resist the discriminatory demands of their clients. On APEC, see http://fr.wikipedia.org/wiki/Association_pour_l%27emploi _des_cadres.

7. Targeting managers can ensure that (1) they do not discriminate when they recruit; (2) if they delegate or outsource recruitment activities, they do not pressure those agents responsible for recruitment; and (3) they do not discriminate in the choice of their collaborators or subcontractors.

8. See http://defenseurdesdroits.fr.

9. A diversity-compliant label has been awarded by the Association Française de Normalisation since 2009. We urge that this be expanded to address religious diversity.

10. Simultaneously, and jumping to the macro level, the state could condition tax and other advantages (for example, special advantages in garnering government tenders) on firms that meet the "diversity-compliant" standard.

11. See http://www.mozaikrh.com/.

12. See http://www.21eme-siecle.org/.

13. This formulation was articulated by the Haute Autorité Contre les Discriminations et pour l'Égalité, which since 2011 has been embedded in the state organ, previously mentioned, Défenseur des Droits. In its present administrative role, its rulings are now part of French organic law.

14. See Chwe (2001) for an extensive discussion on mutually reading faces to enhance social coordination.

15. According to the OFRE/Randstad 2014 study, expressions of religious conviction are as follows: requesting a leave of absence for religious holidays (16%); requesting the accommodation of work hours (12%); praying (12%); ostentatiously displaying a religious symbol (10%); and adopting unacceptable behaviors in the name of religious conviction, such as refusing to work with a woman (7%). See Observatoire du fait religieux en entreprise (2014).

16. We are aware that putting in place initiatives that anticipate Muslim employees' requests while ensuring that all employees benefit is more easily feasible for larger firms. These firms' incentive to appear socially responsible has already guided their investments in initiatives that improve their employees' well-being. For smaller firms, the adoption of a "diversity-compliant" certification, as previously mentioned, could incentivize them to contribute to this effort.

17. Conseil Français du Culte Musulman (2014).

18. Laurence (2012) deems the CFCM as merely symbolic, with inadequate tools to advance its moderate agenda.

19. See Le Bars (2014).

20. France has only three training centers: the first is part of the Paris Grande Mosquée; the second is in the Nièvre Department, belonging to the

Union of French Islamic Organizations (a member organization of the CFCM); and the third is with the University of Strasbourg.

21. For now, this complementary training is optional. It is offered in only four French cities: in Paris by the Catholic Institute of Paris; in Strasbourg through the law faculty; in Lyon through a partnership of the University of Lyon-III, the Catholic University of Lyon, and the Central Mosque of Lyon; and in Aix-en-Provence through the city's branch of Sciences-Po.

22. These suggestions are clearly consistent with those that were leaked from a 2013 report on the training of imams in France that then interior minister Manuel Valls confided to Francis Messner, an expert on religious rights. This report was released in the spring of 2014. See http://abonnes.lemonde.fr /societe/article/2014/04/23/former-les-imams-une-priorite-contrariee_440 5681_3224.html.

23. See http://www.cndp.fr/ABCD-de-l-egalite/accueil.html.

24. In 2013, for example, only 8% of board directors in large French firms were female. See http://www.lexpress.fr/actualite/societe/femmes-en-entreprise -la-parite-reste-a-la-porte-des-comites-de-direction_1278014.html.

25. For a self-congratulatory summary of this innovation led by Professor Eric Mazur, see Lambert (2012). On the relationship of teaching styles and performance, see Algan, Cahuc, and Shleifer (2013).

26. http://www.education.gouv.fr/cid53083/le-dispositif-mallette-des -parents.html.

27. Online vocational training as a substitute for an elite bachelor's degree is being promoted as earning a "nanodegree." Web sites now advertise the returns to wealth from dropping out of degree-granting programs. See http://en.wikipedia.org/wiki/List_of_college_dropout_billionaires.

28. The index on multiculturalism among sixteen Western European countries, to be introduced shortly, shows France in 1980 to be more multicultural than the median country. By the 2010 accounting, two-thirds of the countries had a higher value on this multicultural index than France. This reveals, we believe due to its strong republican values, a resistance in France to accommodation to the cultural practices of those who might identify themselves principally in terms of their ethnicity (Schnapper 1998).

29. According to the Institut national d'études démographiques (2010), members of a visible minority include non-European immigrants, individuals born outside metropolitan France, and their children.

30. The idea of descriptive representation goes back to the formulations of Edmund Burke. It encompasses the idea that elected representatives in democracies should represent not only their constituents' preferences but also their ascriptive identities, such as ethnicity, religion, and gender. Multiculturalists see descriptive representation as an important democratic value; but as Pitkin (1967) points out in her classic work on representation, there are several other criteria for representation that are consistent with democracy. All voting rules in a democracy have biases, and there is no unbiased system that a democracy can install (Arrow 1951). For example, decreasing religious inequality of representation might increase geographic inequality by favoring urban areas.

31. See Liégey, Muller, and Pons (2013) for an explanation of why ethnic minorities vote less than other citizens.

32. We seek to rule out this reverse causality by measuring the impact of multiculturalism in 1980 on the difference in cultural norms between Muslim and Christian immigrants whose exposure to the host country (whether by birth or migration) came after 1980.

33. In this setting, simply comparing the cultural gap between first-generation Muslim and Christian immigrants in multiculturalist and assimilationist countries does not solve this selection bias. For example, observing that this gap is lower in multiculturalist countries than in assimilationist countries may simply reflect the fact that Muslims who decide to migrate to multiculturalist countries are initially less radical than Muslims who decide to migrate in assimilationist countries. To solve this selection bias, we therefore compare the evolution of the cultural gap between first- and second-generation Muslim and Christian immigrants in multiculturalist and assimilationist countries.

34. In this case, in order to mitigate dynamic selection bias, we focus on first-generation immigrants who belong to the same wave of immigration as second-generation immigrants. This means that we restrict our attention to first-generation immigrants who arrived after 1980 and who could be the parents of second-generation immigrants born after 1980. More precisely, they are those among the first-generation immigrants settled after 1980 who were of parental age (between eighteen and forty-five) for each year of birth of second-generation migrants born after 1980.

35. There are limitations to indices that conjoin a wide range of policies onto a single dimension. The MPI research team does provide scores for each element of its index for each country, permitting finer distinctions across countries than the full index itself. For our purposes, we are interested in the relative standing across countries based on all dimensions, and the full index is a reasonably reliable guide to those relative standings.

36. Recall from Chapter 9 that religious norms are measured based on a question that asks the respondent how religious he or she is. The answer to this question is coded from 0 (very religious) to 10 (not at all religious). Gender norms are based on a question that asks the respondent whether she or he agrees or disagrees with the following statement: "When jobs are scarce, men should have more right to a job than women," a probe widely used to assess gender norms, as shown in Chapter 6. The answer to this question is coded from 1 (agree strongly) to 5 (disagree strongly).

37. See Strik et al. (2010) for the project Integration and Naturalisation Tests, conducted at the Centre for Migration Law (Radboud University, the Netherlands).

APPENDIX

1. Alas, there is no direct evidence that the chancellor ever made this comparison. A similarly piquant remark has been attributed to John Godfrey Saxe. *University Chronicle*, University of Michigan (March 27, 1869).

2. Readers interested in examining the relationship of the original research plan and what is actually described in this book can access the abstract at National Science Foundation, Division of Social and Behavioral Sciences, Grant 0819625, "Muslim Integration into EU Societies: Comparative Perspectives." The project description is available at http://politics.as.nyu.edu/docs/IO/6903 /Laitin_paper.pdf.

3. Pew Research Center Forum on Religion and Public Life (2011). Relying on the Trajectoire et Origines (TeO) survey conducted by INED and INSEE in 2008, Simon and Tiberj (2013) provide a slightly lower estimate. They find that Muslims (those of all ages who self-declare as "Muslims") encompass 4.15 million individuals, hence 6.3% of the 2010 French population. However, these estimates are based on extrapolations on the proportion of Muslims for those below eighteen and those above sixty (TeO covers a population whose age is between eighteen and sixty).

4. See Bowen's (2007, 21–25) sensitive gloss on the historical background to the emergence of laïcité, on which this short summary relies.

5. In French, "la possibilité laissée à chaque citoyen de pratiquer sa religion." See IFOP (2008). There is a broad consensus in France on the positive value of laïcité. In one poll reported by *Paris Match* (2011), 81% of the respondents reported a positive view of laïcité.

6. Alain Boyer (1998), the doyen of Islamic studies in France, emphasizes the historical tensions that persist in France between the French and their Muslim subjects and citizens.

7. For a social and national portrait of the pieds noirs population in one French Algerian port city, see Prochaska (1990, chapter 5).

8. The Algiers Court of Appeal ruled in 1903 that the term "Muslim" was not "purely confessional, but that it [designated] on the contrary the entire body of individuals of Muslim origin who, not having been granted full nationality rights, necessarily retained their Muslim personal status, without there being any need to distinguish whether they [belonged] to the Mohometan cult or not." Quoted in Weil (2002). This translation is from the Duke University Press edition, 2008, 217.

9. This figure is from a study by l'Institut Montaigne (2004) and based on data from the 1999 census provided by the state statistical bureau (INSEE). For a discussion of these data, see Sabeg and Méhaignerie (2004).

10. According to Tribalat (2004), more than 80% of the population in France likely to be Muslim are from the Maghreb (43.2% from Algeria; 27.5% from Morocco; and 11.4% from Tunisia), all former French colonies. The others are from former French colonies in sub-Saharan Africa (9.3%) and Turkey (8.6%).

11. See also Alba and Silberman (2002). In their study of the parallel immigration of pieds noirs and autochthonous Algerians into France, they point out (p. 1171, fn. 2) that although the Algerians were often called "Muslims" in the French literature about them, they were "stereotyped in popular consciousness as 'Arabs.'" Brouard and Tiberj (2005, 38–40) similarly report that the first generation of Muslim migrants did not have sharp Muslim identities.

12. On this incident and the press reactions, see Gastaut (2008); see also Harzoune (2003).

13. The minister's remarks are quoted in *Le Monde*, November 11, 2005. http://www.lemonde.fr/societe/article/2005/11/11/nicolas-sarkozy-persiste-et -signe-contre-les-racailles_709112_3224.html. President Chirac similarly categorized the lawbreakers not by their religious identities but rather by their economic challenges. In his speech during the final days of the riots, he declared that "There are some areas where unemployment is massive and development inhuman . . . Some territories where children are out of school, where too many young struggle to find a job, even when they have succeeded in their studies. At the roots of the events we have just lived through there is obviously this situation." See http://www.jacqueschirac-asso.fr/fr/wp-content/uploads/2010/04 /Les-%C3%A9v%C3%A8nements-des-banlieues.pdf.

14. Vol. 26, no. 1, Spring 2008.

15. For a comprehensive discussion of that history, as the state statistical bureaus navigated between a desire for objectivity of categories and one that could accurately depict the legal and the historical aspects of the French population, see Simon (1998).

16. See Elaine Thomas (2012), who delineates the strands of republicanism across France's political spectrum and how Chirac's Nationality Commission (1988) and the subsequent loi Méhaignerie that changed nationality law were able to create an uneasy compromise among those strands.

17. See Algan, Hémet, and Laitin (2016) for a publication relying on the ethnic data from the Labor Force and Housing Surveys. The authors were required by INSEE to perform all data analysis within its headquarters and not permitted to download the raw data.

18. See http://www.ismcorum.org/.

19. Glitches are reduced when sites become institutionalized for continuing experiments, as has developed under the tutelage of the Poverty Action Lab at MIT (Cambridge, MA) (http://www.povertyactionlab.org/). However, research in institutionalized sites cannot address relationships—as we have sought to do in this project—particular to a political context, such as religious discrimination in France.

Glossary

THIS BOOK WAS WRITTEN in order to be read and understood by a large public. We therefore took care to avoid statistical jargon as much as we could. However, four standard expressions in statistics remain. We explain their straightforward meaning below.

For illustrative purposes, we consider two variables: X and Y. X captures the probability for an individual to be a Muslim immigrant rather than a Christian immigrant in Christian-heritage societies (X is equal to 1 when the individual is a Muslim immigrant, and X is equal to 0 when the individual is a Christian immigrant). Y captures the probability for this individual to integrate well.

Correlation

The correlation between X and Y refers to how X and Y relate to one another. If this correlation is positive, this means that Muslim immigrants in Christian-heritage societies are more likely to integrate well as compared with Christian immigrants. Conversely, if this correlation is negative, this means that Muslim immigrants in Christian-heritage societies are less likely to integrate well as compared with Christian immigrants.

Difference-of-Means Analysis

A difference-of-means analysis consists of comparing the average value of a variable within two subpopulations. In our example, a difference-of-means analysis would consist in comparing the average value of Y when X = 1 (that is, within the subpopulation of Muslim immigrants) and when X = 0 (that is, within the subpopulation of Christian immigrants).

Clearly, a difference-of-means analysis is another way of showing correlations. Assume that Muslim immigrants in Christian-heritage societies are more likely to integrate well as compared with Christian immigrants (X and Y are positively correlated). In this case, the difference-of-means analysis should reveal a higher mean value of Y when one focuses on Muslim rather than on Christian immigrants. By contrast, if Muslim immigrants in Christian-heritage societies are less likely to integrate well as compared with Christian immigrants (X and Y are negatively correlated), then the difference-of-means analysis should reveal a lower mean value of Y when one focuses on Muslim rather than on Christian immigrants.

Statistical Significance

Finding a correlation between X and Y or a difference between the mean value of Y when $X = 1$ and $X = 0$ is not enough to claim that a substantial result was found. One must also ensure that this correlation or difference-of-means is large and systematic enough (that is, it concerns a sufficiently large number of individuals in the population) in order to rule out the possibility that this correlation or difference-of-means was uncovered by chance. A statistical procedure available in any statistical software package allows for computing a "confidence level." This confidence level represents the probability that we would discover such a correlation or a difference-of-means in our sample if and only if that relationship truly exists in the wider population. In other words, it represents the probability that a correlation or a difference-of-means was not uncovered by chance. In this context, a correlation or a difference-of-means is deemed by social science convention as statistically significant if its confidence level is greater or equal to 90% (that is, the probability that they were uncovered by chance is lower than 10%).

Regression Analysis

As we have emphasized in our focus on Serer and Joola populations in France, a correlation between X and Y does not ensure that X has a causal impact on Y. It may also capture the fact that X is correlated to a third variable, say Z, which itself determines Y. In this case, the correlation between X and Y not only measures the possible causal impact of X on Y; it also captures the possible causal impact of Z on Y. In fact, it may only capture the latter, showing that the correlation of X and Y is not at all causal.

Let us illustrate this claim. Assume that X and Y are negatively correlated: Muslim immigrants in Christian-heritage societies are less likely to integrate well as compared with Christian immigrants. And assume that Muslim immigrants migrate to Christian-heritage societies with an education level, denoted by Z, that is lower than the education level of Christian immigrants. Put differently, Z is negatively correlated with X. And yet we also know that Z is positively correlated with Y: immigrants with higher education levels upon arrival to Christian-heritage societies are obviously more likely to integrate successfully. In this context, how can one be sure that the integration deficit of Muslim immigrants in Christian-heritage societies is due to their religion rather than to their lower education?

To address this question, one must ensure that the negative correlation between X and Y persists (statisticians would say "is robust") when one compares a subgroup of Muslim and Christian immigrants with similar education levels. Put differently, one must analyze the correlation between X and Y, holding the education level of immigrants constant. By so doing, this approach allows for neutralizing the impact of different education levels across Muslim and Christian immigrants. Such logic is precisely the one behind a regression analysis. A regression analysis allows one to analyze the relationship between X and Y by holding constant (statisticians would say "by controlling for") other variables that are correlated with both X and Y. Note that all the correlations or difference-of-means that are reported in this book hold up to regression analysis and rigorous robustness tests.

References

Actis, W., M. Angel de Prada, C. Pereda, and R. P. Molina. 1996. "Labor market discrimination against migrant workers in Spain." International Migration Papers 9. Geneva: International Labor Office.

Adida, C. L., D. D. Laitin, and M. A. Valfort. 2010. "Identifying barriers to Muslim integration in France." *Proceedings of the National Academy of Sciences* 107: 22384–22390.

———. 2014a. "Gender norms, Muslim immigrants, and economic integration in France." *Economics and Politics* 26: 79–95.

———. 2014b. "Muslims in France: Identifying a discriminatory equilibrium." *Journal of Population Economics* 27: 1039–1086.

———. 2014c. "Region of origin or religion? Understanding why immigrants from Muslim-majority countries are discriminated against in Western Europe." Sorbonne University. https://sites.google.com/site/mavalfortwebpage/home/research.

———. 2015a. "One Muslim is enough! Evidence from a field experiment in France." *Annals of Economics and Statistics.*

———. 2015b. "Religious homophily in a secular country: Evidence from a voting game in France." *Economic Inquiry* 53: 1187–1206.

Aeberhardt, R., D. Fougère, J. Pouget, and R. Rathelot. 2010. "L'emploi et les salaires des enfants d'immigrés." *Economie et Statistique* 433–434: 31–46.

Afrobarometer Survey. 2008. http://www.afrobarometer.org/.

Ahmed, A. M., L. Andersson, and M. Hammarstedt. 2010. "Can discrimination in the housing market be reduced by increasing the information about the applicants?" *Land Economics* 86: 79–90.

Alba, R., and R. Silberman. 2002. "Decolonization immigrations and the social origins of the second generation: The case of North

Africans in France." *International Migration Review* 36: 1169–1193.

Albertson, B., and S. K. Gadarian. 2012. "Who's afraid of immigration? The effects of pro- and anti-immigrant threatening ads among Latinos, African Americans and whites." In *Immigration and public opinion in liberal democracies*, edited by G. Freeman, R. Hansen, and D. L. Leal, 286–304. New York: Routledge.

Alesina, A., R. Baqir, and W. Easterly. 1999. "Public goods and ethnic divisions." *Quarterly Journal of Economics* 114: 1243–1284.

Alexander, A. C., and C. Welzel. 2011. How robust is Muslim support for patriarchal values? A cross-national multi-level study. Irvine, CA: Center for the Study of Democracy.

Algan, Y., and P. Cahuc. 2007. *La société de défiance: Comment le modèle social français s'autodétruit.* Paris: Centre pour la recherche économique et ses applications.

Algan, Y., P. Cahuc, and A. Shleifer. 2013. "Teaching practices and social capital." *American Economic Journal: Applied Economics* 5: 189–210.

Algan, Y., P. Cahuc, and A. Zylberberg. 2012. *La fabrique de la défiance . . . et comment s'en sortir.* Paris: Albin Michel.

Algan, Y., C. Dustmann, A. Glitz, and A. Manning. 2010. "The economic situation of first- and second-generation immigrants in France, Germany, and the UK." *Economic Journal* 120(542): F4–F30.

Algan, Y., C. Hémet, and D. Laitin. 2016. "Diversity and local public goods: A natural experiment with exogenous residential allocation." *Journal of Political Economy.*

Algan, Y., T. Mayer, and M. Thoenig. 2013. "The economic incentives of cultural transmission: Spatial evidence from naming patterns across France." Discussion Paper 9416, Center for Economic Policy Research. http://econ.sciences-po.fr/sites/default/files/file/yann%20algan/AMT.pdf.

Allport, G. 1954. *The nature of prejudice.* New York: Doubleday.

Amadieu, J. 2004. "Enquête 'testing' sur CV." Paris: L'Université Paris I Panthéon Sorbonne, l'Observatoire des Discriminations, Centre d'Etude et de Recherche sur les Organisations et les Relations Sociales. http://cergors.univ-paris1.fr/docsatelecharger/pr%E9sentation%20du%20testing%20mai%202004.pdf.

Antibi, A. 2003. *La constante macabre, ou, Comment a-t-on découragé des générations d'élèves?* Toulouse, France: Math'Adore.

Arrow, K. J. 1951. *Social choice and individual values.* New York: Wiley.

———. 1973. "The theory of discrimination." In *Discrimination in labor markets*, edited by O. Ashenfelter and A. Rees, 3–33. Princeton, NJ: Princeton University Press.

———. 1998. "What has economics to say about racial discrimination?" *Journal of Economic Perspectives* 12: 91–100.

Asante, M. K. 2009. "Serer." In *Encyclopedia of African religion*, edited by M. K. Asante and A. Mazama. Thousand Oaks, CA: Sage.

Attias-Donfut, C. 2006. *L'enracinement: Enquête sur le vieillissement des immigrés en France.* Paris: Armand Colin.

Avvisati, F., M. Gurgand, N. Guyon, and E. Maurin. 2014. "Getting parents involved: A field experiment in deprived schools." *Review of Economic Studies* 81: 57–83.

Baker, W., R. Stockton, S. Howell, A. Jamal, A. C. Lin, A. Shryock, and M. Tessler. 2003. *Detroit Arab American Study.* Ann Arbor, MI: Inter-University Consortium for Political and Social Research. doi:10.3886/ICPSR04413.v2.

Bartlett, R. 1993. *The making of Europe: Conquest, colonization, and cultural change, 950–1350.* London: Penguin Books.

Baudelot, C., and R. Establet. 2009. *L'élitisme républicain: L'école française à l'épreuve des comparaisons internationales.* Paris: Seuil.

Beauchemin, C., C. Hamel, and P. Simon. 2010. *Trajectoires et origines: Enquête sur la diversité des populations en France.* Paris: Institut national d'études démographiques and Institut national de la statistique et des études économiques.

Becker, G. 1957. *The economics of discrimination.* Chicago: University of Chicago Press.

Bénabou, R., F. Kramarz, and C. Prost. 2009. "The French zones d'éducation prioritaire: Much ado about nothing?" *Economics of Education Review* 28: 345–356.

Berg, J., J. Dickhaut, and K. McCabe. 1995. "Trust, reciprocity and social history." *Games and Economic Behavior* 10: 122–142.

Berger, S. 1974. *The French political system.* New York: Random House.

Bilefsky, D. 2006. "Cartoon dispute prompts identity crisis for liberal Denmark." *International Herald Tribune*, February 12.

———. 2014. "France moves to clarify restrictions on full veil." *New York Times*, October 21.

Bisin, A., E. Patacchini, T. Verdier, and Y. Zenou. 2008. "Are Muslim immigrants different in terms of cultural integration?" *Journal of the European Economic Association* 6: 445–456.

Blalock, H. M. 1967. *Toward a theory of minority-group relations.* New York: Capricorn Books.

Bloemraad, I. 2011. "'We the people' in an age of migration: Multi-culturalism and immigrants' political integration in comparative perspective." In *Citizenship, borders and human needs*, edited by R. Smith, 250–272. Philadelphia: University of Pennsylvania Press.

Blommaert, L., M. Coenders, and F. van Tubergen. 2013. "Discrimination of Arabic-named applicants in the Netherlands: An Internet-based field experiment examining different phases in online recruitment procedures." *Social Forces* 92: 957–982.

Blum, A., and F. Guérin-Pace. 2008. "From measuring integration to fighting discrimination: The illusion of 'ethnic statistics.'" *French Politics, Culture, and Society* 26: 45–61.

Booth, A. L., A. Leigh, and E. Varganova. 2012. "Does ethnic discrimination vary across minority groups? Evidence from a field experiment." *Oxford Bulletin of Economics and Statistics* 74: 547–573.

Bouzar, D., and L. Bouzar. 2009. *Allah a-t-il sa place dans l'entreprise?* Paris: Albin Michel.

Bovenkerk, F., M. J. I. Gras, and D. Ramsoedh. 1995. "Discrimination against migrant workers and ethnic minorities in access to employment in the Netherlands." International Migration Papers 4. Geneva: International Labor Organization.

Bowen, J. 2007. *Why the French don't like headscarves: Islam, the state, and public space.* Princeton, NJ: Princeton University Press.

———. 2010. *Can Islam be French? Pluralism and pragmatism in a secularist state.* Princeton, NJ: Princeton University Press.

Boyer, A. 1998. *L'Islam en France.* Paris: Presses Universitaires de France.

Brouard, S., and V. Tiberj. 2005. *Français comme les autres? Enquête sur les citoyens d'origine maghrébine, africaine, et turque.* Paris: Presses de Sciences Po.

———. 2011. *As French as everyone else? A survey of French citizens of Maghrebin, African, and Turkish origin.* Philadelphia: Temple University Press.

Cahuc, P., S. Carcillo, O. Galland, and A. Zylberberg. 2011. *La machine à trier: Comment la France divise sa jeunesse.* Paris: Eyrolles.

Caldwell, C. 2009. *Reflections on the revolution in Europe: Immigration, Islam, and the West.* New York: Doubleday.

Cameron, D. 2011. Speech at Munich Security Conference. Munich, February 5.

Camus, A. 1994. *Le premier homme.* Paris: Gallimard.

Cannot-Brown, W. 2009. "Jola." In *Encyclopedia of African religion,* edited by M. K. Asante and A. Mazama, 355–356. Thousand Oaks, CA: Sage.

Carlsson, M. 2010. "Experimental evidence of discrimination in the hiring of first- and second-generation immigrants." *Review of Labor Economics and Industrial Relations* 24: 263–278.

Carlsson, M., and D.-O. Rooth. 2007. "Evidence of ethnic discrimination in the Swedish labor market using experimental data." *Labor Economics* 14: 716–729.

Castel, R. 2007. *La discrimination négative: Citoyens ou indigènes?* Paris: Seuil.

Cédiey, E., and F. Foroni. 2007. "Les discriminations à raison de 'l'origine' dans les embauches en France: Une enquête nationale par tests de discrimination selon la méthode du Bureau International du Travail." *Cahiers des migrations internationales* no. 85F. Geneva: Bureau International du Travail. http://www.ismcorum.org/stock_images/actus/361/embauche-bit-ism-corum.pdf.

Cédiey, E., F. Foroni, and H. Garner. 2008. "Discrimination à l'embauche fondée sur l'origine à l'encontre des jeunes français(e)s peu qualifié(e)s." *Premières Informations Premières Synthèses* 6. Paris: Direction de l'animation de la recherche, des études et des statistiques.

Chirac, J. 2005. Speech, translated by the authors. Paris, November 14. http://www.jacqueschirac-asso.fr/fr/wp-content

/uploads/2010/04/Les-%C3%A9v%C3%A8nements-des
-banlieues.pdf.

Chwe, M. 2001. *Rational ritual: Culture, coordination, and common knowledge.* Princeton, NJ: Princeton University Press.

Coly, J. M. 2002. *Situation migratoire et ethnicité: Essai d'analyse fonctionnelle des stratégies d'intégration des migrants Diolas à Bordeaux.* Thesis, Université Victor Segalen Bordeaux 2. Atelier national de reproduction des thèses.

Commission Nationale Consultative des Droits de l'Homme. 2014. "Rapport racisme, antisémitisme et xénophobie 2013: Banalisation de la parole raciste et poursuite de la montée de l'intolérance." Paris: La Documentation Française. http://www .ladocumentationfrancaise.fr/var/storage/rapports-publics /144000199.pdf.

Conseil Français du Culte Musulman. 2014. "Convention Citoyenne des Musulmans de France pour le vivre-ensemble." http://www .lecfcm.fr/wp-content/uploads/2014/06/cfcm_texte_convention __version_finalisee2.pdf.

Constant, A. F., L. Gataullina, and K. F. Zimmermann. 2009. "Ethnosizing immigrants." *Journal of Economic Behavior and Organization* 69: 274–287.

Cooper, F. 2014. *Citizenship between empire and nation.* Princeton, NJ: Princeton University Press.

Copé, J.-F. 2012. Speech, translated by the authors. Draguignan, France, October 5. https://www.youtube.com/watch?v =VmzoPK94k08.

Crowder, M. 1962. *Senegal: A study in French assimilation policy.* London: Oxford University Press.

Cruise O'Brien, D. B. 1975. *Saints and politicians: Essays in the organization of a Senegalese peasant society.* Cambridge: Cambridge University Press.

Destelle, N. 2010. "Marine Le Pen dénonce les hamburgers halal de Quick." *Libération*, February 15.

Diagne, M.-F., and E. Wasner. 2009. "Addressing premarket discrimination through geographically-targeted affirmative action: The 'Conventions Education Prioritare' of Sciences Po." Brussels: European Center for Advanced Research in Economics and Statistics.

Duguet, E., N. Leandri, Y. L'Horty, and P. Petit. 2010. "Are young French jobseekers of ethnic immigrant origin discriminated against? A controlled experiment in the Paris area." *Annals of Economics and Statistics* 99–100: 187–215.

Dunning, T. 2012. *Natural experiments in the social sciences: A design-based approach.* Cambridge: Cambridge University Press.

Duwat, M. 2008. "Islam, 9 ans, recalé d'un jeu télé pour enfants à cause de son prénom." *Le Monde*, April 16.

Eckel, C. C., and R. K. Wilson. 2004. "Is trust a risky decision?" *Journal of Economic Behavior and Organization* 55: 447–465.

———. 2006. "Judging a book by its cover: Beauty and expectations in the trust game." *Political Research Quarterly* 59: 189–202.

Erlanger, S. 2010. "Top French schools, asked to diversify, fear for standards." *New York Times*, June 30.

European Social Survey. "About the European Social Survey European research infrastructure." http://www.europeansocialsurvey.org/about/index.html.

Faiola, A., and S. Mekhennet. 2014. "Denmark's welcome mat for Islamists." *Washington Post*, October 20.

Fearon, J., and D. Laitin. 2008. "Integrating qualitative and quantitative methods." In *The Oxford handbook of political methodology*, edited by J. Box-Steffensmeier, H. Brady, and D. Collier, 756–776. Oxford: Oxford University Press.

Fehr, E., A. Klein, and K. M. Schmidt. 2007. "Fairness and contract design." *Econometrica* 75: 121–154.

Fetzer, J. S., and J. C. Soper. 2005. *Muslims and the state in Britain, France, and Germany.* Cambridge: Cambridge University Press.

Fish, M. S. 2011. *Are Muslims distinctive? A look at the evidence.* Oxford: Oxford University Press.

Fishman, J. 1966. *Language loyalty in the United States: The maintenance and perpetuation of non-English mother tongues by American ethnic and religious groups.* The Hague, the Netherlands: Mouton.

Ford, R. 2012a. "Europe's young cosmopolitans: Explaining generational differences in immigration attitudes." Working Paper. http://www.sociology.ox.ac.uk/documents/events/slides/anthony_heath_conference/europes%20young%20cosmo politans.docx.pdf.

———. 2012b. "Parochial and cosmopolitan Britain: Examining the social divide in reactions to immigration." http://www.gmfus .org/wp-content/blogs.dir/1/files_mf/1337623670Ford _BritishImmigrationAttitudes_Apr12_web.pdf.

Foroni, F. 2008. "Résultats du Testing Sollicité par le Groupe Casino: Un diagnostic partagé sur les discriminations liées à 'l'origine.'" Lyon, France: ISM-CORUM.

Fouka, V. 2014. "Backlash: The unintended effects of language prohibition in U.S. schools after World War I." Unpublished manuscript, Barcelona, Universitat Pompeu Fabra. http://www.econ.upf.edu /gpefm/jm/pdf/paper/JMP%20Fouka.pdf.

Gallie, W. B. 1955–1956. "Essentially contested concepts." *Proceedings of the Aristotelian Society*, New Series 56: 167–198.

Gastaut, Y. 2008. "Le sport comme révélateur des ambiguïtés du processus d'intégration des populations immigrées: Le cas du match de football France-Algérie." *Société contemporaines* 69: 49–71.

Gastellu, J.-M. 1981. *L'égalitarisme économique des Serer du Sénégal*. Paris: ORSTOM.

Ghosh, B. 2010. "Islamophobia: Does America have a Muslim problem?" *Time*, August 30.

Giavazzi, F., I. Petkov, and F. Schiantarelli. 2014. "Culture: Persistence and evolution." Working Paper 20174. Cambridge, MA: National Bureau of Economic Research.

Gneezy, U., K. L. Leonard, and J. A. List. 2009. "Gender differences in competition: Evidence from a matrilineal and a patriarchal society." *Econometrica* 77: 1637–1664.

Goldberg, A., U. Kulke, and D. Mourinho. 1995. "Labor market discrimination against foreign workers in Germany." International Migration Papers 7. Geneva: International Labor Organization.

Goodman, S. W. 2010. "Integration requirements for integration's sake? Identifying, categorising and comparing civic integration policies." *Journal of Ethnic and Migration Studies* 36: 753–772.

Habyarimana, J., M. Humphreys, D. N. Posner, and J. M. Weinstein. 2009. "Coethnicity: Diversity and the dilemmas of collective action." New York: Russell Sage Foundation.

Hanks, A. S., D. R. Just, and B. Wansink. 2013. "Smarter lunchrooms can address new school lunchroom guidelines and childhood obesity." *Journal of Pediatrics* 162: 867–869.

Harzoune, M. 2003. "Psychodrame autour d'un ballon rond." *Hommes & Migrations* 1244: 54–64. http://www.hommes-et-migrations.fr /docannexe/file/1244/1244_07.pdf.

Heckathorn, D. D. 1997. "Respondent-driven sampling: A new approach to the study of hidden populations." *Social Problems* 44: 174–199.

———. 2002. "Respondent-driven sampling II: Deriving valid population estimates from chain-referral samples of hidden populations." *Social Problems* 49: 11–34.

Henrich, J., J. Ensminger, R. McElreath, A. Barr, C. Barrett, A. Bolyanatz, J. C. Cardenas, M. Gurven, E. Gwako, N. Henrich, C. Lesorogol, F. Marlowe, D. Tracer, and J. Ziker. 2010. "Markets, religion, community size, and the evolution of fairness and punishment." *Science* 327: 1480–1484.

Hoffman, L. R., and N. R. F. Maier. 1961. "Quality and acceptance of problem solutions by members of homogeneous and heterogeneous groups." *Abnormal and Social Psychology* 62: 401–407.

Hong, L., and S. E. Page. 2001. "Problem solving by heterogeneous agents." *Economic Theory* 97: 123–163.

———. 2004. "Groups of diverse problem solvers can outperform groups of high-ability problem solvers." *Proceedings of the National Academy of Sciences* 101: 16385–16389.

Hoogendoorn, S., and M. van Praag. 2012. "Ethnic diversity and team performance: A field experiment." Discussion Paper 6731, Bonn, Germany: Institute for the Study of Labor. http://ftp.iza.org /dp6731.pdf.

Hortefeux, B. 2009. Speech, translated by the authors. Seignosse, France, September 5. http://www.dailymotion.com/video/xafz5w _le-derapage-de-brice-hortefeux-la-h.

Hoskin, M. 1985. "Public opinion and the foreign worker: Traditional and nontraditional bases in West Germany." *Comparative Politics* 17: 193–210.

Howell, S., and A. Jamal. 2009. "The aftermath of the 9/11 attacks," in *Citizenship and crisis: Arab Detroit after 9/11*, by W. Baker et al., 69–100. Russell Sage Foundation: New York. 69–100.

Humphreys, M., R. Sánchez de la Sierra, and P. Van der Windt. 2013. "Fishing, commitment, and communication: A proposal for comprehensive nonbinding research registration." *Political Analysis* 21: 1–20.

Huntington, S. P. 1997. *The clash of civilizations*. New York: Simon & Schuster.

———. 2004. *Who are we?* New York: Simon & Schuster.

Institut français d'opinion publique. 2008. "Les Français, la religion et la laïcité après la visite du Pape Benoît XVI." http://www.ifop .com/media/poll/benoit16.pdf.

———. 2010. "Le catholicisme en France en 2010." http://www.ifop.fr /media/pressdocument/238-1-document_file.pdf.

———. 2011. "Analyse 1989–2011: Enquête sur l'implantation et l'évolution de l'Islam de France." http://www.ifop.fr/media /pressdocument/343–1-document_file.pdf.

———. 2012. "L'image de l'Islam en France." http://www.ifop.com/ ?option=com_publication&type=poll&id=2028.

———. 2013. "Les Français et le port du voile ou du foulard islamique par des employées de lieux privés accueillant du public." http://www.ifop.fr/media/poll/2195–1-study_file.pdf.

Institute Montaigne. 2004. "Les oubliés de l'égalité des chances." http://www.institutmontaigne.org/fr/publications/les-oublies-de -legalite-des-chances.

———. 2014a. *Dix ans de politiques de diversité: Quel bilan?* http://www .institutmontaigne.org/res/files/publications/rapport _politique%20de_diversit%C3%A9_institut_montaigne.pdf.

———. 2014b. *Et la confiance, bordel? Faire le pari de la confiance en entreprise*. http://www.institutmontaigne.org/fr/publications/dix -ans-de-politiques-de-diversite-quel-bilan.

Institut national d'études démographiques. 2010. "Les discriminations: Une question de minorités visibles." *Populations et Sociétés*, no. 466.

Institut national de la statistique et des études économiques. 1999. "Résultats du recensement de la population." http://www .recensement-1999.insee.fr/.

———. 2010. "Revenu disponible par ménage (moyenne et médiane)." http://www.insee.fr/fr/themes/tableau.asp?reg_id=0&ref_id =natsos04202.

Ireland, P. R. 1994. *The policy challenge of ethnic diversity: Immigrant politics in France and Switzerland.* Cambridge, MA: Harvard University Press.

Jowell, R., and P. Prescott-Clark. 1970. "Racial discrimination and white-collar workers in Britain." *Race and Class* 11: 397–417.

Judd, C. M., and B. Park. 1993. "Definition and assessment of accuracy in social stereotypes." *Psychological Review* 100: 109–128.

Kaas, L., and C. Manger. 2012. "Ethnic discrimination in Germany's labor market: A field experiment." *German Economic Review* 13: 1–20.

Kahlenberg, R. D. 2011. "An affirmative-action success." *Chronicle of Higher Education,* September 13.

Kahneman, D., J. L. Knetsch, and R. H. Thaler. 1986. "Fairness and the assumption of economics." *Journal of Business* 59: S285–S300.

Kakpo, N. 2007. *L'islam, un recours pour les jeunes.* Paris: Presses de la fondation nationale des sciences politiques.

Kepel, G. 1987. *Les banlieues de l'Islam.* Paris: Seuil.

———. 2011. *Banlieue de la république.* Paris: Gallimard.

———. 2012. *Quatre-vingt-treize.* Paris: Gallimard.

Khetani, S. 2012. "Sarkozy deported a record number of illegal immigrants last year." *Business Insider,* January 11. http://www.businessinsider.com/sarkozy-immigration-2012-1.

Koopmans, R. 2013. "Multiculturalism and immigration: A contested field in cross-national comparison." *Annual Review of Sociology* 39: 147–169.

Kotecha, S. 2013. "Quarter of young British people do not trust Muslims." *BBC Newsbeat,* September 25.

Kymlicka, W. 2012. "Multiculturalism: Success, failure, and the future." In *Rethinking national identity in the age of migration,* edited by Migration Policy Institute, 33–78. Berlin: Verlag Bertelsmann Stiftung.

Lahav, G. 1997. "Ideological and party constraints on immigration attitudes in Europe." *Journal of Common Market Studies* 35: 377–407.

Lahiri, J. 2003. *The namesake.* Boston: Houghton Mifflin.

Laitin, D. D. 1986. *Hegemony and culture: The politics of religious change among the Yoruba.* Chicago: University of Chicago Press.

———. 2010. "Rational Islamophobia in Europe." *European Journal of Sociology* 51: 429–447.

———. 2013. "Fisheries management." *Political Analysis* 21: 42–47.

Lambert, C. 2012. "Twilight of the lecture." *Harvard Magazine*, March–April. http://harvardmagazine.com/2012/03/twilight-of -the-lecture.

Lambert, M. 2002. *Longing for exile: Migration and the making of a translocal community in Senegal, West Africa*. London: Heinemann.

Laurence, J. 2012. *The emancipation of Europe's Muslims*. Princeton, NJ: Princeton University Press.

Laurence, J., and J. Vaisse. 2006. *Integrating Islam: Political and religious challenges in contemporary France*. Washington, DC: Brookings Institution Press.

Le Bars, S. 2014. "Former les imams, une 'priorité' contrariée." *Le Monde*, April 23. http://abonnes.lemonde.fr/societe/article/2014 /04/23/former-les-imams-une-priorite-contrariee_4405681 _3224.html.

Lebovics, H. 1992. *True France: The wars over cultural identity, 1900– 1945*. Ithaca, NY: Cornell University Press.

Leveau, R., C. Wihtol de Wenden, and G. Kepel, eds. 1988. *Les Musulmans dans la société française*. Paris: Presses de la Fondation Nationale des Sciences-Politiques.

Lhommeau, B., and P. Simon. 2010. "Les populations enquêtées." In *Trajectoires et Origines, Documents de Travail*, by C. Beauchemin, C. Hamel, and P. Simon. Working Paper 168. Paris: INED and INSEE. http://www.ined.fr/fichier/s_rubrique /19558/working_paper_2010_168_population.diversity.france.en .pdf.

Liégey, G., A. Muller, and V. Pons. 2013. *Porte à porte: Reconquérir la démocratie sur le terrain*. Paris: Calmann-Lévy.

Linares, O. H. 1992. *Power, prayer, and production: The Jola of Casamance, Senegal*. Cambridge: Cambridge University Press.

Maalouf, A. 2001. *In the name of identity: Violence and the need to belong*. New York: Arcade.

Meertens, R. W., and T. F. Pettigrew. 1997. "Is subtle prejudice really prejudice?" *Public Opinion Quarterly* 61: 54–71.

Meurs, D., A. Pailhé, and P. Simon. 2006. "The persistence of intergenerational inequalities linked to immigration: Labour market
outcomes for immigrants and their descendants in France."
Population 61: 645–682.

Miguel, E., C. Camerer, K. Casey, J. Cohen, K. M. Esterling, A.
Gerber, R. Glennerster, D. P. Green, M. Humphreys, G.
Imbens, D. Laitin, T. Madon, L. Nelson, B. A. Nosek, M.
Petersen, R. Sedlmayr, J. P. Simmons, U. Simonsohn, and M.
Van der Laan. 2014. "Promoting transparency in social science
research." *Science* 343: 30–31.

Montvalon, J.-B. de, and C. Chambraud. 2015. "Sécurité, politique,
Islam: Comment réagissent les Français après les attentats ?"
Le Monde, January 28. http://www.lemonde.fr/societe/article
/2015/01/28/securite-politique-islam-comment-reagissent-les
-francais-apres-les-attentats_4564681_3224.html#meter
_toaster.

Nayer, A., and B. Smeesters. 1998. "La discrimination à l'accès à
l'emploi en raison de l'origine étrangère: Le cas de la Belgique."
International Migration Papers 23. Geneva: International Labor
Organization.

Nemeth, C. J. 1986. "Differential contribution of majority and
minority influence." *Psychological Review* 93: 23–32.

"Nicolas Sarkozy continue de vilipender 'racailles et voyous.'" 2005.
Le Monde, November 11.

Norris, P., and R. Inglehart. 2003. "Islamic culture and democracy:
Testing the 'clash of civilization' thesis." In *Human values and
social change*, edited by R. Inglehart, 5–34. Leiden, the Netherlands: Brill.

Nunn, N., and L. Wantchekon. 2011. "The slave trade and the origins
of mistrust in Africa." *American Economic Review* 101: 3221–3252.

Nyborg, K. 2014. "Do responsible employers attract responsible
employees?" *IZA World of Labor* 17. http://wol.iza.org/articles/do
-responsible-employers-attract-responsible-employees-1.pdf.

Oberti, M., F. Sanselme, and A. Voisin. 2009. "Ce que Sciences Po fait
aux lycéens et à leurs parents: Entre méritocratie et perception
d'inégalité." *Actes de la Recherche en Sciences Sociales* 180: 102–124.

Observatoire du fait religieux en entreprise. 2014. "Synthèse des
résultats de l'étude 2014." http://www.grouperandstad.fr/wp

-content/uploads/sites/3/2014/05/SLIDES_%C3%A9tude_fait _religieux_OFRE_InstitutRandstad_2014.pdf.

Office français de l'immigration et de l'intégration. n.d. "La formation CAI." http://www.ofii.fr/s_integrer_en_france_47/la _formation_cai_21.html.

O'Reilly, C. A., K. Y. Williams, and S. Barsade. 1997. *Demography and group performance: Does diversity help?* Stanford, CA: Stanford University Graduate School of Business.

Page, S. E. 2007. "Making the difference: Applying a logic of diversity." *Academy of Management Perspectives* 21(4): 6–20.

Parekh, B. C. 2002. *Rethinking multiculturalism: Cultural diversity and political theory.* Cambridge, MA: Harvard University Press.

Paris Match. 2011. "Les valeurs des Français à six mois de l'élection présidentielle." December 1.

Petit, P. 2007. "The effects of age and family constraints on gender hiring discrimination: A field experiment in the French financial sector." *Labour Economics* 14: 371–391.

Pettigrew, T. F. 1998. "Reactions toward the new minorities of Western Europe." *Annual Review of Sociology* 24: 77–103.

Pew Research Center Forum on Religion and Public Life. 2011. "The future of the global Muslim population: Projections for 2010–2030." http://www.pewforum.org/files/2011/01 /FutureGlobalMuslimPopulation-WebPDF-Feb10.pdf.

Pfaff, S., and A. J. Gill. 2006. "Will a million Muslims march? Muslim interest organizations and political integration in Europe." *Comparative Political Studies* 39: 803–828.

Phelps, N. 1972. "The statistical theory of racism and sexism." *American Economic Review* 62: 659–661.

Pincus, Steve. 2009. *1688.* New Haven, CT: Yale University Press.

Pitkin, H. 1967. *The concept of representation.* Berkeley: University of California Press.

Pope, D. G., J. Price, and J. Wolfers. 2014. "Awareness reduces racial bias." Brookings Economic Studies Working Paper Series, February. http://www.brookings.edu/~/media/research/files /papers/2014/02/awareness%20reduces%20racial%20bias /awareness_reduces_racial_bias_wolfers.pdf.

Prochaska, D. 1990. *Making Algeria French: Colonialism in Bône, 1870–1920.* Cambridge: Cambridge University Press.

Religions Monitor. 2013. "Religiousness and cohesion in Germany." http://religionsmonitor.de/pdf/Religionsmonitor_Deutschland .pdf.

Rooth, D.-O. 2010. "Automatic associations and discrimination in hiring: Real world evidence." *Labor Economics* 17: 523–534.

Runnymede Trust Commission on British Muslims and Islamophobia. 1997. *Islamophobia: A challenge for us all.* London: Runnymede Trust.

Sa'adah, A. 2003. *Contemporary France.* Lanham, MD: Rowman & Littlefield.

Sabeg, Y., and L. Méhaignerie. 2004. "Les oubliés de l'égalité des chances." Paris: Institut Montaigne.

Saxton, G. D., and M. A. Benson. 2003. "The origins of socially and politically hostile attitudes toward immigrants and outgroups: Economics, ideology, or national context?" *Journal of Political Science* 31: 101–137.

Schnapper, D. 1998. *Community of citizens: On the modern idea of nationality.* Piscataway, NJ: Transaction Publishers.

Shepard, T. 2013. "Algerian nationalism, Zionism, and French laïcité: A history of ethnoreligious nationalisms and decolonization." *International Journal of Middle East Studies* 45: 445–467.

Simon, P. 1998. "Nationality and origins in French statistics: Ambiguous categories." *Population* 53: 541–567.

———. 2008. "The choice of ignorance: The debate on ethnic and racial statistics in France." *French Politics, Culture, and Society* 26: 7–31.

Simon, P., and V. Tiberj. 2013. "Sécularisation ou regain religieux: La religiosité des immigrés et de leurs descendants." Paris: Institut national d'études démographiques.

Smith, C. S. 2005. "What makes someone French?" *New York Times,* November 11.

Spire, A. 2008. *Accueillir ou reconduire: Enquête sur les guichets de l'immigration.* Paris: Raisons d'Agir.

Stigler, G. J., and G. S. Becker. 1977. "De gustibus non est disputandum." *American Economic Review* 67: 76–90.

Strik, T., A. Böcker, M. Luiten, and R. van Oers. 2010. "The INTEC project: Synthesis report." Nijmegen, the Netherlands: Radboud University, Center for Migration Law. http://www.ru.nl/law/cmr /projects/intec/.

Tajfel, H. 1970. "Experiments in intergroup discrimination." *Scientific American* 223(5): 96–102.

Taylor, C. 1994. *Multiculturalism: Examining the politics of recognition.* Princeton, NJ: Princeton University Press.

Ternisien, X. 2006. "Les 'barbus' dans le 9–3." *Le Monde*, November 17.

Thaler, R. H., and C. R. Sunstein. 2008. *Nudge: Improving decisions about health, wealth, and happiness.* New Haven, CT: Yale University Press.

Thomas, E. R. 2012. *Immigration, Islam, and the politics of belonging in France: A comparative framework.* Philadelphia: University of Pennsylvania Press.

Tribalat, M. 1996. "L'enquête mobilité géographique et insertion sociale: Remise en cause des habitudes statistiques françaises." *Espace, Populations, Sociétés* 14(2–3): 215–225. http://www.persee .fr/web/revues/home/prescript/article/espos_0755-7809_1996 _num_14_2_1746.

———. 2004. "Une estimation des populations d'origine étrangère en France en 1999." *INED* 59: 51–81.

———. 2008. "Le nombre de musulmans in France: Qu'en sait-on?" In *L'islam en France*, edited by Y. C. Zarka, S. Taussig, and C. Fleury, 21–31. Paris: Presses Universitaires de France.

Trimingham, J. S. 1964. *A history of Islam in West Africa.* London: Oxford University Press.

"Troisième Recensement Général de la Population et de l'Habitat (RGPH-III)." 2002. Dakar, Senegal: Ministère de l'Economie et des Finances, Agence Nationale de la Statistique et de la Démographie.

Tversky, A., and D. Kahneman. 1982. "Judgment under uncertainty: Heuristics and biases." In *Judgment under uncertainty: Heuristics and biases*, edited by D. Kahneman, P. Slovic, and A. Tversky, 3–20. Cambridge: Cambridge University Press.

Van Eeckhout, L. 2009. "Mesure de la diversité." *Le Monde*, May 8.

Vincent, E. 2014. "Les Français sont de moins en moins tolérants." *Le Monde*, April 1.

Voors, M. J., E. E. M. Nillesen, P. Verwimp, E. H. Bulte, R. Lensink, and D. P. Van Soest. 2012. "Violent conflict and behavior: A field experiment in Burundi." *American Economic Review* 102: 941–964.

Weber, M. 1946. "India: The Brahman and the castes." In *From Max Weber: Essays in sociology*, translated by H. H. Gerth and C. W. Mills, 396–416. New York: Oxford University Press. First published 1916.

Weil, P. 2002. *Qu'est-ce qu'un français? Histoire de la nationalité française depuis la révolution.* Paris: Grasset. [Translated by Catherine Porter in 2008, as *How to be French*, Duke University Press.]

World Bank. 2009. "Senegal—Migration and remittances household survey." http://microdata.worldbank.org/index.php/catalog/534 .page.

World Values Survey. 2006. http://www.worldvaluessurvey.org/.

Wright, M., and I. Bloemraad. 2012. "Is there a trade-off between multiculturalism and socio-political integration? Policy regimes and immigrant incorporation in comparative perspective." *Perspectives on Politics* 10: 77–95.

Wylie, L. 1957. *Village in the Vaucluse.* Cambridge, MA: Harvard University Press.

Zuber, V. 2008. "La séparation des églises et de l'état en France et à Genève (1905–1907): Une solution pour deux histoires." *French Politics, Culture, and Society* 26: 71–91.

Index

The letter *t* following a page number denotes a table. The letter *f* following a page number denotes a figure.